Color, Environment, and

Human Response

Color, Environment, and Human Response

An Interdisciplinary Understanding of Color

and its Use as a Beneficial Element

in the Design of the Architectural Environment

Frank H. Mahnke

Van Nostrand Reinhold

I(T)P® A Division of International Thomson Publishing Inc.

New York • Albany • Bonn • Boston • Detroit • Madrid • Melbourne
Mexico City • Paris • San Francisco • Singapore • Tokyo • Toronto

Cover design: Paul Costello
Van Nostrand Reinhold Staff
Editor: Jane Degenhardt
Production Editor: Carla Nessler
Production Manager: Mary McCartney
Designer: Mike Suh

I⟨T⟩P® A division of International Thomson Publishing Inc.
The ITP logo is a registered trademark under license

Printed in the United States of America

For more information, contact:

Van Nostrand Reinhold
115 Fifth Avenue
New York, NY 10003

Chapman & Hall GmbH
Pappelallee 3
69469 Weinheim
Germany

Chapman & Hall
2-6 Boundary Row
London
SE1 8HN
United Kingdom

International Thomson Publishing Asia
221 Henderson Road #05-10
Henderson Building
Singapore 0315

Thomas Nelson Australia
102 Dodds Street
South Melbourne, 3205
Victoria, Australia

International Thomson Publishing Japan
Hirakawacho Kyowa Building, 3F
2-2-1 Hirakawacho
Chiyoda-ku, 103 Tokyo
Japan

Nelson Canada
1120 Birchmount Road
Scarborough, Ontario
Canada M1K 5G4

International Thomson Editores
Campos Eliseos 385, Piso 7
Col. Polanco
11560 Mexico D.F. Mexico

2 3 4 5 6 7 8 9 10 HAM 02 01 00 99 98 97

Library of Congress Cataloging-in-Publication Data

Mahnke, Frank H., 1947-
    Color, environment, and human response: an interdisciplinary understanding
of color and its use as a beneficial element in the design of the architectural
environment / Frank H. Mahnke.
        p.   cm.
Includes bibliographical references and index.
ISBN 0-442-01935-1
    1. Color in architecture.   2. Architecture—Environmental aspects.
    3. Architecture—Human factors.   I. Title.
NA2795.M35   1996   95-38572
729—dc20   CIP

Contents

Epigraph

On the grounds of the knowledge and the scientific findings regarding the effects of color, its influence on the human organism, on psychosomatic well-being, and color's significance for the "quality of an appearance" and the acceptance thereof, it cannot be disregarded that color, as an essential element in design, is often thoughtlessly misused.

——Dr. Bettina Rodeck, Certified Interior Architect and Pedagogue
    and
——Professor Gerhard Meerwein, Certified Architect and Interior
    Architect—Dean of Interior Architecture, College of Mainz,
    Germany

Colors as an Element of Quality in Environmental Design

Preface

For well over two decades I have collected and kept abreast of research concerning the interaction between man and his environment—specifically, how human beings react to color and light on a psychological and a physiological basis. An interdisciplinary approach must be adopted for the design of our man-made environment to keep to its true goal: the creation of optimum conditions that correspond to the function of an architectural space and safeguard the mental and physical well-being of the user. The condition of the ultimate man-made environment; the identity of our cities; and the interiors where we work, learn, live, and have our welfare regarded are the most important factors in the integration of man and his "built" environment.

This book is based upon research pertaining to the relationship between human beings and their environment, where color has proved to be a key element. I have combined hard scientific evidence with empirical studies and my own experience and observations of human behavior. This book has been written in a style that keeps the needs of the designer in mind, thereby making it not just a theoretical exposition, but one that also serves as a practical and useful guide.

There are many professionals in various fields to whom I owe thanks for work that in some way influenced this book. A formal acknowledgment, listing all their names, would be too voluminous. However, a special thank you goes posthumously to the American color consultant Faber Birren, often called the father of applied color psychology, for having led me many years ago to the understanding of the significance of color's effect on human beings. It was his encouragement that prompted me to pursue the subject further. Little did he know that I would devote my professional life totally to this endeavor. The more immersed I became in it, the less it would let go of me.

I express my deepest gratitude to Dr. Heinrich Frieling, Institute of Color Psychology, Marquartstein, Germany, for his monumental lifetime work in this field, his advice, and his clarification of many questions that only he, with his vast interdisciplinary knowledge, could answer.

My thanks also go to my colleagues Dr. Bettina Rodeck, Professor Gerhard Meerwein, and Professor Edda Mally for many hours of stimulating discussion in Salzburg, talks that influenced the scope of this book.

Final acknowledgment must go to the participants in the educational program of the International Association of Color Consultants/ Designers (IACC), and the IACC seminars in Europe and the United States, for their enthusiasm in adopting the philosophy that the human being must be the first consideration in the creation of our architectural environment.

Introduction

Color, or the concept of color, can be approached from different perspectives and different disciplines, such as the natural sciences, color theory, technology, philosophy, biology, medicine, psychology, human factors engineering, and art. This book discusses color from the standpoint of designing the man-made environment, and the human response to this environment, which to some extent includes all of these perspectives and disciplines.

Color is not the property of objects, spaces, or surfaces; it is the sensation caused by certain qualities of light that the eye recognizes and the brain interprets. Therefore, light and color are inseparable, and, in the design of the human habitat, equal attention must be devoted to their psychological, physiological, visual, aesthetic, and technical aspects.

Many books and studies are available that discuss color, its aesthetic aspects, color systems, color therapy, color in marketing, color psychology, color's effects on physiology, and so forth. But books on how all these different aspects of color, in addition to the perspectives and disciplines I mentioned before, tie into the design of the architectural environment are, indeed, few. For the architect, interior designer, and color consultant it has been extremely difficult to find a comprehensive reference of such expanded base as we hope this book now provides.

What complicates a complex subject even further is that most professions that are responsible for the creation of our architectural environment, especially when it comes to color, do not realize how much information relevant to the use of color can be found in disciplines that seem unrelated to architecture and interior design. Such information should be evaluated and considered as to its relevance in creating optimum environmental conditions.

This book is a step toward understanding all relationships having to do with color and its important role in the design process. It presents crucial information for anyone in the business of creating architectural environments. It is also my aim to suggest that architects and designers need to adopt a new philosophy and perspective in their work with light and color. Architects, designers, city planners, lighting engineers, and color consultants today are confronted with problems and faced with questions that they are often ill-equipped to answer. The design community must adopt a new attitude toward scientific research conducted in many fields and covering many disciplines. The first consideration in the creation of interior and exterior architectural spaces must be the evidence that has been accumulated concerning human response to the environment. Embracing this information will aid designers in understanding the psychological and physiological factors that must be considered in creating beneficial and healthy surroundings.

Color and light are major factors in our architectural environment. They have great impact on our psychological reactions and physiological well-being. Research has proven that light and color affect the human organism on both a visual and nonvisual basis. It is no longer valid to assume that the "only" significant role of light and color is to provide adequate illumination and a pleasant visual environment.

It has become evident in my work, which has been both investigative and practical, that an interdisciplinary approach is the most effective one in dealing with and recognizing environmental problems and design solutions to them. These problems also include potential psychological and physiological risks induced by man-made environmental factors. Nervousness, headaches, lack of concentration, inefficiency, bad moods, visual disturbances, anxiety, and stress usually are blamed on everything except a "guilty" environment, which may often be the root cause.

For all practical purposes, this book has two parts. The first discusses the factors, some of which are often overlooked in environmental design, that make up and influence human response to our indoor and outdoor surroundings. The importance of environmental color and light and their effects on the human organism are not only relevant to the design professions. The information presented here should also be of concern to urban developers, school officials, administrators, medical practitioners, and psychologists. The fact is, we are all affected by our artificial surroundings.

The second part of this book gives practical advice in the use of color and light for a variety of environments. Besides answering the basic questions of "why" and "how," I've included a useful short review of color fundamentals. Even though an abundance of published information is available on such topics as color systems, aesthetic color schemes, and contrast relationships, since this book offers practical advice, I think that the inclusion of some basics is warranted.

It is not possible to include everything known about color, light, and the human response to it, including practical advice, in one single work. However, I have tried to make this book a fairly broad-based reference work that is detailed in regard to the philosophy that must be adopted in order to understand the significance of creating beneficial environments. This book will be a useful tool for any profession responsible for creating our architectural environment, and I hope that it will inspire further interest and investigation into man–environment relationships.

What Is Color?
An Introduction
from the Psychological
Viewpoint

Since color is a part of many sciences—for example, physics, color theory, and art—it can be introduced in various ways. The physicist's approach to color is different from the psychologist's or the artist's—although the artist is closer to the psychologist than he thinks. I would like to introduce color to you from the viewpoint of psychology. The psychologist Ulrich Beer wrote:

> *Seldom, surely, is the psychological part of an appearance in nature so great as it is in the case of color. No one can encounter it and stay neutral. We are immediately, instinctively, and emotionally moved. We have sympathy or antipathy, pleasure or disapproval within us as soon as we perceive colors. (Beer 1992, p. 11)*

Beer has summed up the primary psychological reaction we humans have toward color. However, we will delve a little deeper into psychology to investigate how this primary reaction develops.

First we must answer the question: What is psychology? Psychology is the science that deals with the mind, with mental and emotional processes, with special reference to behavior, provided it is understood that behavior includes thoughts, feelings, and dreams—anything a person experiences. These experiences have their roots in conscious, subconscious, and unconscious processes. Conscious experience implies that we are aware of what we are thinking and feeling. Subconscious refers to mental processes occurring without conscious perception or with only slight perception. The unconscious is the sum of all thoughts, memories, impulses, desires, and feelings of which we are not conscious, but which influence our emotions and behavior.

Color is also a part of the conscious, subconscious, and unconscious, and an experience that is integral to human behavior. The human reaction to a color, a color combination, and to the environment is always initially a psychological one, but it can also result in a physiological reaction—a point that I will expand later.

Although the emphasis here is on psychology, we cannot do without the *physicist's* viewpoint of color, and it must be explained in the language of the physicist if we are to understand what color is, scientifically, and where its origins lie.

All life on earth is determined by the radiation of the sun. A section of this electromagnetic energy is visible light, which is measured by light waves of certain frequencies called a nanometer; a nanometer is a billionth of a meter. We perceive visible light in the wavelength region from approximately 380 nanometers, which is comparable to the color violet, to 780 nanometers, which is perceived as red. This means that light is color, because if we pass white light through a prism and break it down into the individual wavelengths that visible light consists of, we have violet (380–436 nm); blue (436–495 nm); green

(495–566 nm); yellow (566–589 nm); orange (589–627 nm); and red (627–780 nm).

For the physicist, therefore, color is a wavelength of light that an object either generates or reflects. This means we use the language of the physicist to describe the sensory stimuli we perceive as color. But it is the language of the psychologist that describes what effects these stimuli have upon us. For the physicist, red, for example, equals an external stimulus of a light wave that has a frequency of 627–780 nanometers. For a psychologist, red suggests an internal process that may or may not be associated with a physical event.

For example, close your eyes momentarily, and picture in your mind a ripe tomato. Was the tomato red? Probably so. But the input that caused you to see red was not a light wave between 627–780 nanometers. In other words, no external object, either generating or reflecting color, was the stimulus causing you to see the tomato as being red. This testifies to the fact that color is in the brain; it is within us.

All of the color stimuli that we receive from the external world are connected with our internal world: our psyche. At the same time we may consider that color is not just dependent on the external world, but may also originate through the power of imagination of our inner world.

Now we have arrived at color and the psyche. A color impression is not only a mechanism of seeing, but also a sensation or feeling that simultaneously activates our thoughts and our cognitive mechanism. For example, if I say *green grass,* obviously *grass* is immediately associated with the color *green* or vice versa. From the standpoint of the physicist, this green of the grass is nothing other than the pigment chlorophyll, which in its molecular structure is so devised as to absorb all the wavelengths of sunlight, with the exception of green, which it reflects. However, in the perception of green, whether real or imagined, do most people think about chlorophyll? I doubt it. They might think about a walk in a green meadow, or a certain event in their life which is triggered by the association with green or green meadow. A whole range of thoughts and emotions may be set in motion that interact automatically, so that at the end, the green may have nothing more to do with it. But it was the impulse *green* that triggered the whole process. In short, colors have cognitive and emotional content.

It may be difficult for the pure scientist to pinpoint or explain emotional processes. However, they are a fact. The Swiss psychologist Carl Jung wrote:

> *I know enough of the scientific point of view to understand that it is most annoying to have to deal with facts that cannot be completely or adequately grasped. The trouble with these phenomena is that the facts are undeniable and yet cannot be formulated in intellectual terms. For this one*

would have to be able to comprehend life itself, for it is life that produces emotions and symbolic ideas. (Jung 1968, p. 80.)

I would like to place emphasis on the words *emotion* and *symbolism,* because both are attributes of color. Color is not only a stimulus we perceive, but it is truly a part of our psyche. If it were otherwise, how could we judge color in the first place? How could we express with color? How could we create art, for example?

The artist is more than just a photographic copier of nature. The starting point may be taken from the exterior world, but from the inner world the artist brings his or her interpretations, feelings, and impressions to canvas through form and color. Paul Cézanne felt that colors were personified ideas; they have personality and life. Pablo Picasso declared that he paints things not as he sees them, but as he thinks of them. Frieling feels that the power of color comes from the mystery that lives in them.

Paul Gauguin was one of the first artists to recognize the emotional power of color. Leonard Shlain wrote about him: "Paul Gauguin . . . discovered by trial and error that color could be used as a silent language to evoke visceral reaction antecedent to words." Gauguin used color as a component to manipulate the viewer's emotion.

One of the most relevant statements about color's power of expression, and one that is relevant not just to painting, but also to the use of color in the architectural environment, comes from Vincent van Gogh, who stated:

Color expresses something by itself. *Let's say I have to paint an autumn landscape with yellow leaves on the trees. If I see it as a symphony in yellow, does it matter whether the yellow that I use is the same as the yellow of the leaves?* No it doesn't. *(Van Gogh, quoted in Shlain 1991, p. 175.)*

Expression of emotion through color by two such great painters as Gauguin and Van Gogh supports my earlier contention that art and psychology merge in this area. As humans are exposed to the stimuli of color, thoughts and feelings are brought into motion in a chain reaction. As Gauguin realized, color is a powerful impulse and a language that evokes reaction. That form and color in art affect the human psyche is indisputable. We can therefore draw the conclusion that the larger art form, our architectural environment, also affects our psyche.

Color Is Essential for Life

Most people who hear about color psychology for the first time often voice the opinion that it does not really affect them. They claim

Van Gogh felt that color expresses something by itself.

they have their own tastes and preferences, and after all, aren't these re-actions to color all subjective? This is one of the reasons why too often color in the architectural environment is assigned a secondary or cosmetic role. Of course, the subjective feeling an individual has about color plays an important role, as do personal preference and taste. But if we think that is all, we're overlooking something that goes much deeper, and we are confusing cause and effect.

Just where does an individual's color taste and preference come from? This basic question is hardly ever considered. Perceiving color, thereby *experiencing* color, can be both objective and subjective—if the two can even be separated. These people who claim that they cannot be manipulated by color because they view a given situation objectively might be surprised to discover how their objective judgment is nevertheless influenced by the subjective.

Through our evolutionary development as a species we have inherited reactions to color that we cannot control, that we cannot objectively explain, and that we cannot escape. Color is a part of our psychological and biological heritage. One simple fact must be understood: *Color is essential for life,* and its role goes much deeper than is often realized. Color is part of life-giving and life-sustaining processes that have had their influence since the beginning of time, and color has therefore been an influence on man biologically and psychologically.

The "Color Experience" Pyramid

Human beings receive 80 percent of their information from the environment. Color belongs to the environment, and it is therefore a means of information and communication of absolute necessity for the interpretation and understanding of the natural and artificial or architectural, environment. The perception of color in the environment always carries visual, associative, synaesthetic, symbolic, emotional, and physiological effects with it.

To "see" color is a far deeper and more complex process than merely the optical perception of these stimuli and the resulting physiological stimulation of sensory cells in the cerebral cortex. Color stimulation received from the exterior world corresponds with a reaction in the inner world—our psyche. The great Goethe said: "Nothing is within, nothing is outside, because what is within is outside."

To perceive color means to "experience"; to become conscious or aware. A multitude of factors work together in this process, partly on a conscious level, partly on an unconscious level. With so many correlations involved, the "color experience" can't be definitively systematized or classified. However, we may assume that six basic interrelated factors influence this experience. Using a pyramid (as in the illustration on the following page) I start with the base of the pyramid (1) inescapable biological reactions; then go to associations from (2) the collective unconscious; (3) symbolisms of the conscious; (4) cultural influences and mannerisms; (5) influence of trends, fashions, and styles; until we reach the highest level (6) the "personal relationship" the individual has to color. The "personal relationship" is connected with and *influenced by all the other levels.*

These six levels need elucidation, then out of them we can draw findings that point toward some of the universal human reactions to color. These in turn impact importantly on the design of our architectural environment.

Biological Reactions to a Color Stimulus

In a world where color impinges on our every waking moment, and in sleep penetrates our dreams (despite those who say they never "dream in color"), life is governed by the radiation of the sun. We all know that part of this radiation that reaches the world is visible light, and we know that this light is color. Color is a gift of evolution, an inherited characteristic for the survival of vegetable and animal life.

Green plants are green, for example, because they depend on the pigment chlorophyll for photosynthesis; the process by which the energy of light is captured to manufacture carbohydrates from water and

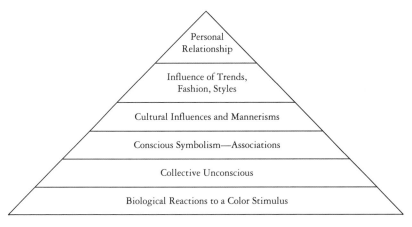

The "Color Experience Pyramid."

Personal Relationship

Influence of Trends, Fashion, Styles

Cultural Influences and Mannerisms

Conscious Symbolism—Associations

Collective Unconscious

Biological Reactions to a Color Stimulus

Copyright © Frank H. Mahnke 1990

carbon dioxide. Chlorophyll provides energy by absorbing red, yellow, blue, and violet wavelengths, but reflecting green. Photosynthesis is a matter of survival.

Survival in the vegetable world also means spreading fertilized seeds or spores. Evolution colored and shaped each vegetable species to offer the strongest attraction to the insects, birds, or mammals best suited to pollinating it. The plants that made it easiest for this transfer of pollen to occur had the best chance of survival. Color became a vivid signal to those particular species whose color vision evolved to pick up those signals.

We know that animals react biologically to colored light and color signals. Light, which is color, affects animals either through the eyes or the skin, or both. Humans are also bound to these biological reactions. In the evolution of the human and certain species of other animals, the ability to see color developed because this power was crucial for survival.

For example, the unripe sloe berries of the blackthorn tree are green and blend in with the surrounding leaves. When they ripen they turn blue and become distinguishable from their foliage—thus signal that they are ready to be eaten. Finches and other birds that feed on sloes are most sensitive to red, but can also see blue. They feed on the flesh of the fruit, carry the seed for some distance, and then discard it to the ground. The seed germinates and so continues the next generation of blackthorn tree, and of course, the bird species for which the sloe berries are a source of food.

The eyes of the Anna's hummingbird are especially sensitive to longer wavelengths of visible light. Flowers that reflect those wavelengths attract the hummingbird and while it is feeding on the nectar, male pollen collects on its beak, to be deposited later on the female stigma of another flower of the same species.

There are countless examples where the signal character of a color in plants and animals contributes to their protection and preservation. In general animals are colored either for display or for camouflage. Color plays a vital role in their search for food and safety from predators. For example, the arrow-poison frog's coloration sends a warning signal to predatory snakes or birds, which rely on vision for hunting, that it would make a deadly meal.

As illustrated on the following page, the frigate bird develops enormous red throat pouches during the breeding season. The red signals threat toward other males, but acts as an attraction toward females. It's interesting to note that we humans also use red as an alert that says *stop* on the one hand, and signals erotic attraction on the other—the reddened lips of a woman being an obvious example.

The messages conveyed by signal coloration are of infinite variety, and we can be certain that they played a critical role in the evolution of the human species. Through color humans learned to distinguish between the edible and inedible. Color helped us to understand and interpret the natural environment surrounding us. Surely the changing colors of the seasons have always given us significant guidance. How much of this biological heritage is still within modern man is a matter of speculation, but as Dr. Nicholas Humphrey, Senior Research Fellow at Darwin College, wrote:

> *Yet I do not believe that our long involvement with color as a signal in the course of evolution can be quite forgotten. Though modern man's use of color may frequently be arbitrary, his response to it continues to show traces of his evolutionary heritage. (Humphrey 1976, p. 96)*

There is also another aspect of biological reaction to color that is unconnected to color as a message carrier. Vision is not the only result of light entering the eye; it also induces biological function in humans and animals. A neural pathway, called the "energetic portion" of the optic pathway, carries light and color stimulation to the hypothalamic midbrain region, and on to the pineal and pituitary glands. These master glands control the entire endocrine system—that is, the production and release of hormones.

For example, studies have shown that green and blue light thwart activity in mice. Under pink light rats have become more aggressive. Chickens have layed more eggs under red light. Humans also show biological effects, not only under monochromatic light, but also to some artificial "white" light sources. Artificial light, whose spectrum deviates strongly from that of natural light (sunlight) but is still perceived as white light, may cause the production of the adrenocorticotropic (ACTH) hormone in the pituitary gland, which in turn causes the adrenal cortex to produce the stress hormone cortisol. Many effects are

During breeding season the red of the frigate bird's throat pouches signals attraction to the females and threat to the males. We humans also associate red with aggression and eroticism.

produced by visible light, from activation of the pineal organ to the entrainment of circadian rhythms (discussed in a following chapter). Colored light also acts through the skin. The use of blue light to cure infant jaundice (hyperbilirubinemia) has been standard medical practice for decades.

Building on the above, let me propose the following: From the energy of light—which is color—plant life, animals, and humans accept what is needed and reject what is not needed. We see this principle at work in the vegetable world. We know too that the color of living creatures, and the colors they perceive, have purpose. *Living creatures only see or sense those energies (colors) necessary for survival.* That is how color vision evolved. Humans may be considered as having *total* color vision, which must mean that the total spectrum is necessary for our survival biologically, and beyond that, psychologically. It is the psychological that affects us emotionally, making things seem sympathetic, provocative, warm, cold, friendly, exciting, tranquil, and a host of other feelings necessary for the survival of our psyche.

This psychological component is to be found in the other levels of the color experience pyramid. To sum up the biological reactions, it may be said that they are those reactions that are beyond our control since they are in the physiological realm that remains outside the scope of how we, as individuals, think or feel about a certain hue, or a group of colors.

Collective Unconscious

Above the base of biological reaction to color lies another level that is also not controlled or caused by the intellect or conscious rational thought. In accordance with Jungian psychology, the "collective unconscious" is that part of our psyche that has nothing to do with con-

We have inherited primordial images from our human ancestors as well as from our prehuman or animal ancestors.

scious or unconscious reactions based on personal experience amassed during our lifetime.

Authors Calvin Hall and Vernon Nordby give this explanation of Carl Jung's understanding of the collective unconscious:

> *First of all, it is that portion of the psyche which can be differentiated from the personal unconscious by the fact that its existence is not dependent upon personal experience. The personal unconscious is composed of contents that were once conscious, but the contents of the collective unconscious have never been conscious, within the lifetime of the individual. (Hall and Nordby, p. 39)*

The contents of the collective unconscious are archetypes, or the original pattern or model from which other things of the same kind are made. They are fundamental images formed in our development as a species. They are predispositions or potentialities for responding to or experiencing our world in the same manner as our ancestors did. The authors explain further:

> *The collective unconscious is a reservoir of latent images, usually called* primordial images *by Jung.* Primordial *means the "first" or "original"; therefore a primordial image refers to the earliest development of the psyche. Man inherits these images from his ancestral past, a past that includes all of his human ancestors as well as his prehuman or animal ancestors. (Hall and Nordby, p. 39)*

We humans do not start our lives as a blank page to be filled in by a learning process through our environment and society. From the be-

Infants are born with inherited memories and experiences. For example, the infant's predilection for two spots next to each other is due to the fact that in their brain the prototype of a human face is already engraved.

ginning of our lives that page has inscribed on it the inherited memories of mankind's entire experience. Modern research into the function of the brain, especially neuroinformation studies, supports the validity of Jung's belief. Millions of years of knowledge are stored in the genetic building plan of our brain. Throughout human life the individual refines this building plan through experience and learning. Without this "inborn" knowledge we would drown in a sea of meaningless sensory information, data, and signals that we could not sort out, recognize, or interpret.

Infants, for example, have a predilection for two dark spots next to each other. Researcher Christoph von der Marlsburg explains the reason: "Because in their brain convolutions the prototype of a human face is already engraved" (von der Marlsburg, quoted in *Der Spiegel.* p. 242).

In the landscape of our soul exist vaguely sensed, prodding, and powerful sources; unconscious images that express themselves in behavioral patterns and reflexes; in our structures of thought and dreams. Colors are also part of these primordial images of archetypal significance. Is it not impossible that within these latent images and experiences there exist the initial feelings and origins of aesthetic qualities that were identified and connected with color over many millenia.

Between this level of the pyramid and the one to follow, I could have included a level entitled "the personal unconscious," which alludes to an individual's own experience with a color or colors, that for one reason or another was erased from his or her consciousness. Imagine a person who, contrary to all research on color symbolism and psychological effect, associates an ice-blue tone with heat, because as a toddler he burned himself on an object of that color. But to draw an absolute connection to that experience through the unconscious would be quite difficult.

Conscious Symbolism—Associations

The third level of the pyramid represents the conscious symbolism or associative power of color—the associations, impressions, and symbolism made on a conscious level—perhaps to some extent also "learned" responses. There are numerous examples of associations that have universal interpretation, where research has shown basic agreement among most people in all cultures: blue with sky and water; green with nature; red with revolution; black combined with gold with luxury and glamour; and so forth.

Application of color association and their symbolic content is of importance in various fields, such as advertising, fashion, product and graphic design. Included, of course, must be architecture, because of the significance color plays in producing mood associations. The associative power of color has an ultimate effect on whether an architectural space is perceived as being friendly, warm, cold, inspiring, sad, dirty, dynamic, harsh, expensive, cheap, aloof, etc.

The symbolism of color has played an important part in human life since recorded history. It has been significant in religion, medicine, healing, mythology, alchemy, astrology, art, and even with ceremonies of birth, marriage, and death.

In colorful metaphors—literally—we find many examples based on color. We speak of "having the blues" when we're depressed; of "rolling out the red carpet" or giving someone the "red-carpet treatment"; of the "green of youth" or "greenhorn," for the inexperienced. From German the expression translates as "He's still green behind the ears."

While many associations are fairly modern, many have been inherited from the past, remain actively in use, and show remarkable consistency in meaning over time.

Cultural Influences and Mannerisms

Color associations, symbolism, impressions, and mannerisms that are characteristic of specific cultures and groups, even down to regional levels, also play a role in how color is experienced and used.

Turquoise, for example, is the national color of Persia. Ancient Persians trusted it to ward off the evil eye by protecting themselves with turquoise charms. In Islam, green has religious significance; the cloak of the prophet was thought to be green, and so it is also a symbol of hope.

Greeks find all colors to be equally refined, while Swedes consider saturated color to be more vulgar than unsaturated ones. The Japanese respond deeply to the gentle colors of water, sky, and wood; whereas Indian arts and crafts have a common theme of vivid color.

Although cultural differences are evident, we know that many reactions to color are universal and cross cultural boundaries. It's often natural to look for difference rather than commonality, but in trying to understand human reaction to color, the basic similarities are of importance, especially when it comes to the design of the human habitat.

Influence of Trends, Fashions, Styles

Every year or two new trends in color appear around the world in fashion and consumer products. In interior design and architecture color changes move more slowly. Color changes are necessary to adapt to the *Zeitgeist,* the spirit of a particular time; to guard against consumer boredom; and particularly to increase sales of certain products—especially in fashion and consumer goods. Temporary as they may be, these color trends are also a part of the overall way we experience color.

My viewpoint on color trends and color cycles has often been overzealously misinterpreted, thereby giving me the reputation of being an enemy of color trends and color forecasting. This is quite an incorrect estimation. I am the first to delight in something "new" in color, especially when it comes to fashion and certain other consumer items.

However, I have great difficulty accepting color trends in the creation of the architectural environment. I advise great caution, because a particular design color trend in current fashion will make it difficult to satisfy all the different aspects, goals, and needs particular to a certain environment. A hospital has a different function from an assembly line; a school has different needs than a shop; and a hot-dog stand is not a gourmet restaurant.

Designers who are unsure in their use of color have a tendency to "play it safe" and copy color trends. Remember the gray-and-violet trend of several years ago (which to some extent is still in use)? Gray was combined with violets, various pinks, rose, and the like, and caught on to such an extent that it made its way into numerous offices, restaurants, building facades, private homes, and even psychiatric hospitals—where it certainly had no business being. Following color trends in architecture also stifles the individual's creative freedom.

Color trends in exterior and interior architecture come and go, and scrutinized a little closer, we find out that there are always two basic directions. There really isn't very much new under the sun. The turn of the century started with delicate pastels. Before World War I there was an explosion of color, and then the trend turned more subdued and quieter during the 1920s and 1930s. It then changed back and forth until the psychedelic color revolution in the 1960s—a period in which many old color rules were discarded. Today we stand between Modernism and the high-tech image, and Post-Modernism.

Seen from the standpoint of architecture, I am hoping that we will stop fluctuating between the one extreme of using hardly any color, and the other extreme of being too colorful. We must find the golden middle, which would not lead to stagnation. Quite the opposite would actually be the result.

Personal Relationship

Our personal relationship to color expresses our like, indifference, or dislike of certain hues. We've all heard someone proclaim to "hate green" or "love red," and were we to ask why, an objective answer would hardly be forthcoming, because how we experience color is made up of the interrelationships among all the levels of the pyramid. As noted earlier, these levels include both the unconscious and the conscious.

Our personal relationship to color and its significance can only be truly investigated through psychodiagnostic color tests, such as those known as the Frieling, Pfister, or Lüscher tests. These tests demand that judgments of which colors we like or dislike are made spontaneously, without an association to any object or prior experience.

Summary

We may summarize the human experiencing of color thus: Color, which is created by light, is therefore a form of energy, and this energy affects body function just as it influences mind and emotion. We know that color affects cortical activation (brain waves); functions of the autonomic nervous system (which regulates the body's internal environment), and hormonal activity; and that color arouses definite emotional and aesthetic associations. In short, our response to color is total; it influences us both psychologically and physiologically.

Chapter Two

Psychophysiological Effects

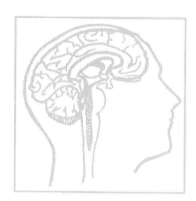

If human response to the environment is to be understood, it cannot be stressed enough that anyone working with color in the architectural environment must first review how the physiological fundamentals of the brain functions, and how information coming from the outside is changed into feelings, thoughts, and actions.

A Neuropsychological Aspect

Brain function still has a long way to go before it is fully understood. It is the last frontier, an awesome territory that contains hundreds of billions of cells, interlinked through trillions of connections with innumerable and imperceptible transactions occurring within the central nervous system at any given moment.

The brain is an efficient processor of information, and it influences human behavior. Neuropsychologists study the nervous system structure and how it relates to organs and other parts of the body. They also seek to discover how information coming from the external world and the internal world affects humans. An understanding of the relationship between the brain and the action of muscles and glands also falls within the realm of the neuropsychologist.

Since color is among the strongest stimuli we receive from the exterior world, it is important to understand the structures of the brain that first receive incoming information, how they interpret, deal with it, and regulate the fundamental processes of the body.

Cerebral Cortex

The cerebral cortex is the gray matter that covers the cerebrum; it contains 90 percent of all nerve cells. It receives and interprets sensory impulses, thereby being responsible for an essential role in perception, memory, thought, mental ability, and intellect. The sensory cortex is a part of the functional regions that make up the cerebral cortex.

Cerebrum

The largest and most developed part of the brain and the seat of reason, imagination, and creativity, the cerebrum is believed to control voluntary and conscious processes. It is where "thinking" takes place. The cerebrum is composed of two hemispheres: The right side controls imagination, insight, art awareness, three-dimensional forms, and music awareness; the left hemisphere is responsible for logical and scientific aspects of thought.

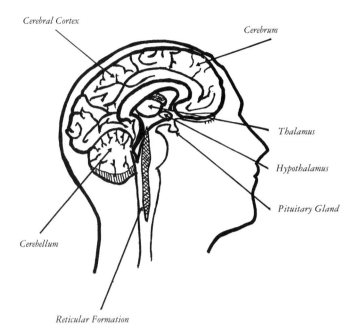

Cerebral Cortex

Cerebrum

Thalamus

Hypothalamus

Pituitary Gland

Cerebellum

Reticular Formation

Schematic drawing of the side view of the human brain.

Thalamus

Four of our sensory impulses—sight, hearing, taste, and touch—converge on the thalamus. These messages are sorted out and then relayed to the appropriate regions of the cerebral cortex.

Hypothalamus

The hypothalamus monitors the changes in the internal environment of the human body; it contains the center for the regulation of blood pressure and body temperature. It is also the brain's intermediary for translating emotions into physical response. When strong emotional reactions such as rage, fear, pleasure, or excitement are generated in the mind, whether by the action of thoughts or by external stimuli, the hypothalamus sends signals for physiological changes through the autonomic nervous system and through the release of hormones from the pituitary gland. It is thought to have major effects on responses to stress, and it also regulates the drives of hunger, thirst, and sex.

Pituitary Gland

This tiny rounded organ is considered the master endocrine gland of the body; its secretion influences the activity of other glands.

Cerebellum

The cerebellum (from the Latin for "little brain") is responsible for sorting out and processing the signals required for muscular coordination, a sense of balance, and coordinated movement.

Reticular Formation

Studies published by G. Moruzzi and H. W. Magoun in 1949 presented observations that proved important in understanding our general reactions to stimulation. The central nervous system (CNS), consisting of the brain and spinal cord, is the major control center for all human behavior. The investigators found that every impulse transmitted by afferent nerves that reaches the higher centers of the CNS first activates part of the brain stem, the reticular formation, which then activates the entire nervous system. The reticular formation seems to affect the entire nervous system's state of preparedness. This has been designated the *ascending reticular activation system* (ARAS).

Humans are subjected to many kinds of stimulation, including information from the visual field, and all of it affects the ARAS. As Rikard Küller has explained: "The ARAS might be regarded as a clearing station for kinds of stimulation ranging from sensory deprivation at one extreme to sensory overload at the other." (Küller 1981, p. 234) Much of the information from the visual field (or visual stimulation) lies in the hands of the designer, who therefore must understand basics of the activation theory. This will become evident in regard to environmental over- and understimulation, discussed later in this chapter.

Moruzzi and Magoun's theory has been revised in various ways. Reticular activation occurs not only through external stimulation but also through mental activity—impulses coming from the highest nervous centers. The cognitive mechanism, perception, memory, and judgment, is also triggered to deal with a great part of incoming information. These impulses descend from the cortex on the reticular formation. Therefore, there are two functional systems; in addition to the ascending reticular activation system, there is the *descending reticular activation system* (DRAS). The arousal level of humans may be influenced via the ARAS, before the impulse has reached the cortex, or via the DRAS, after the cortex has had time to make an analysis.

Activation is divided into two components called *phasic arousal* and *tonic arousal*. Phasic arousal implies the immediate response to stimulation, while tonic arousal is the response level averaged over a prolonged period. The tonic arousal level changes gradually either upward or downward, depending on the occurrence of phasic arousal reactions. The participating reticular formation seeks to maintain a state of normalcy in the arousal level during this process, but it can also malfunction, as has been shown in experiments on sensory deprivation and in stress research.

In sum, every impulse, whether originated externally or internally, results in a short, temporary arousal reaction (phasic). Repeated effect will alter the tonic arousal level either upward or downward. At that point there are changes in the individual's emotional state.

Unity and Complexity Balance— Variety Within Reason

If we measure balance by the visual information rate contained in a space such as a room, as it is perceived through the optical system, we can identify two opposite poles called unity and complexity. Unity involves various components and parts fitting together into a coherent unit. Complexity involves more variation. (See Figures C-1, C-2, C-3, C-4, and C-5.)

Extreme unity (monotony or sensory deprivation) can lead to understimulation, and extreme complexity to overstimulation. Exposure to overstimulation can cause changes in the rate of breathing, pulse rate, and blood pressure; increase in muscle tension; psychiatric reactions of varying types; and probably compounded medical consequences, such as increased susceptibility to infection, coronary disease, and ulcers. The "stress research" conducted shows these symptoms as typical effects on those persons who have been subjected to overstimulation.

Rikard Küller (1976) conducted an experiment on the effects of two opposite environments. For three hours, six men and six women were placed in two rooms that differed in visual complexity and visual unity. One room was gray and sterile; the other, colorful and diversified. The experiment demonstrated that the coloring and visual patterning of an interior space can have a profound effect on an electroencephalogram (EEG) and pulse rate, as well as on the subjective emotional feeling of a person. This corroborates the fact that the ARAS affects not only the cortex but the entire nervous system.

The chaotic visual impact in the more complex and colorful room made the subjects feel silent and subdued—a surprising result which I'll address shortly. The alpha component (alpha brain-wave activity) was lower in the complex room, which may be explained in terms of cortical arousal. Alpha brainwaves are produced when we are in a more alert condition than during the production of theta rhythms, these making their appearance when we become sleepy. During the production of alpha rhythms we are fully conscious. Beta rhythms are connected with full alertness, whereas the lowest and slowest frequency are

*Complex and incongruous
visual patterns evoke an
increase in phasic arousal
level.*

the delta wavelengths which are produced when we sleep or are unconscious.

The subject's electrocardiogram, (EKG), showing heart rate, was slower in the more colorful room than in the gray room, which Küller explains "is in agreement with the hypothesis of Lacey, Kagan, Lacey, and Moss, 1963, i.e., intense attention might be accompanied by cardiac deceleration." (Küller 1981, p. 101) Stress reactions were more noticeable in men than in women. The men were more bored in the gray room than the women were. Perhaps they couldn't achieve the same degree of mental relaxation as the women did.

As noted earlier, I find it especially interesting that the heart response was lower in the colorful room than in the gray room. Therefore, we may conclude that a dull environment tends to make us turn to our inner self, since the exterior provides no stimulation. This, in certain circumstance, may induce anxiety, fear, and distress—dependent on the particular situation we are dealing with, and the nature of our thoughts.

Persons subjected to understimulation show symptoms of restlessness, excessive emotional response, difficulty in concentration, irritation, and in some cases, a variety of more extreme reactions. This conclusion should be considered very seriously by those who propose a

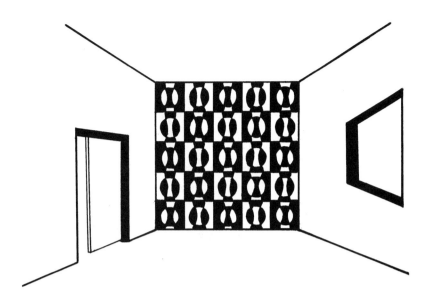

Too much visual pattern will overstimulate an environment.

white or neutral environment; such environments are anything but neutral in the effects they have on their occupants.

Just as light and color affect the ARAS, so does visual pattern. A number of studies have been conducted to investigate the arousal effect of pattern. How does a pattern's size, color, contrast, shape, and brightness impact on a viewer? Berlyne and McDonnell, for example, found that more complex or incongruous visual patterns evoke an increase in phasic arousal level.

Trends come and go, and some hang on forever. In the past there used to be—and perhaps some designers still follow these trends on occasions—a marked tendency toward the use of stripes, geometric patterns, brightly colored designs, and strong hues in general. Previously discussed problems of the overstimulated environment will manifest themselves as a result of this practice. Overexcitation *is* distracting and fatiguing. Strong color, too much visual pattern, and high brightness demand voluntary and involuntary attention. Vivid design in work areas can impair productivity by seriously interfering with work tasks that require visual concentration. (See Figure C-16.)

On the other hand, we know now that the *under*stimulated environment is as unacceptable as the *over*stimulated one. Monotonous and achromatic environments, especially evident in the so-called hi-tech image design that so many office environments adopt in order to appear sleek, sophisticated, up-to-date, are totally misplaced for the well-being of the user from both psychological and physiological standpoints.

Taking all research collectively, it is safe to conclude and suggest that color variety is psychologically most beneficial. It is not just that one color is better than another for a specific purpose, that one may be considered psychologically exciting or another calming. Indeed a variety of visual stimulation and change in atmosphere or mood is required in establishing a sound milieu. British psychologist M. D. Vernon has written:

> *Thus we must conclude that normal consciousness, perception and thought can be maintained only in a constantly changing environment. When there is no change, a state of "sensory deprivation" occurs; the capacity of adults to concentrate deteriorates, attention fluctuates and lapses, and normal perception fades. (Vernon, quoted in Birren 1982, p. 28)*

In the total environment there must be colors in changing degrees of lightness (light and dark), temperature (warm and cool), and intensity (strong and weak), and the complementary of the dominant color should be present to some extent. Maximum favorable color effects depend on variety and contrast, *but within reason.*

The need for variety has been summed up best by Faber Birren:

> *In response to environment, people expect all of their senses to be moderately stimulated at all times. This is what happens in nature, and it relates not only to color and changing degrees of brightness, but to variations in temperature and sound. The unnatural condition is one that is static, boring, tedious and unchanging. Variety is indeed the spice—and needed substance—of life. (Birren 1983, p. 167)*

The need to balance unity and complexity is one of the major challenges designers face. Finding that solution is of great importance. The concept is not new. Writers on the subject of color have expressed similar views over the years. It matters little whether their conclusions were based on research of the day or keen observation, since present-day scientific investigations validate their pronouncements. As color specialist Frederick M. Crewdson wrote in 1953:

> *Balance is the securing of unity in the midst of variety. Both variety and unity are necessary to sustain interest, and these opposing forces must be balanced. Variety is necessary to attract and arouse interest; unity is essential to create a favorable impression and to satisfy the moods and desires. Variety overdone is confusing and unpleasant; unity overdone is monotonous. The mark of good color arrangement is in knowing where to stop between these extremes. (Crewdson, p. 121)*

Ten years later color specialist Richard Ellinger had this to say about complexity:

First of all, as human beings exposed to the visual stimuli, we are, let us admit, easily confused. Disorder occasioned by unrestrained diversity can be nothing but emotionally repellent. We have a limited tolerance for diversity. (Ellinger 1963, p. 27)

In regard to unity, the same author commented:

A second human demand is rooted in our emotional response to tedium. We are easily bored. We can easily get too much of anything. Emotionally, we demand relief whenever monotony threatens. We demand the play of opposing forces. (Ellinger, p. 27)

Judging where "balance" is achieved depends on the degree to which the designer has developed his color faculties and sensitivity. This demands knowledge of relationships among harmony, contrast, and the affective values of color. It cannot be stressed enough that the balance between unity and complexity *is the first and most important rule* in the design of beneficial environments.

Personality and Reaction to Stimulation

Another important consideration in creating beneficial environments is the relationship between personality and reaction to stimulation. From a practical standpoint this applies more to the design of an environment for a particular individual (private home or office). How is an individual's reaction tendency to stimulation influenced by his or her personality? All people have pleasant or unpleasant arousal reactions, but they experience them in varying degrees. Psychologist H. J. Eysenck designated these reactions as *extroversion* and *introversion,* terms that express the degree of excitability.

There is a fallacious belief among some designers that prescribing passive environments for extroverted temperaments will calm them down, and active environments for subdued and introverted personalities will draw them out of their introspection and boost their spirits. Quite the opposite will occur. People will not be happier in surroundings that conflict with their personalities. The nervous system of the introvert is more excitable than that of the extrovert. The afferent flow of stimulation, regardless of its origin, is facilitated in the introvert but obstructed in the extrovert. In other words, there is a difference in the amount of stimulation passing through the cerebral cortex for each of these personality types.

In general terms, this means that the extroverted personality type has a greater inclination toward more intensive stimulation, and consequently enjoys more colorful surroundings. In fact, monotonous or low-stimulus environmental conditions for the extroverted personality can lead to a lack of interest, boredom, and an exploratory mode of behavior that in very extreme cases can become a stimulus craving with pathological side effects. On the other hand, because introverts are very sensitive to stimulation and have a great need for privacy and calm, they manage best in environments with a lower degree of stimulation. For them, overstimulated environments will lead to intensive anxiety or psychosomatic symptoms.

However, wrong conclusions should not be drawn from these facts. The extroverted personality type at times also needs to find tranquility, including visual tranquility.

Carl Jung also made a distinction between two basic personality types or basic attitudes. In his system of classification he used the key terms *extraversion* and *introversion.* He believed that the psychic energy of the extravert is channeled toward the objective external world—thoughts and feelings about objects, people, animals, and other environmental circumstances and conditions. On the other hand, the introvert explores and analyzes his inner world, being withdrawn and preoccupied by his internal affairs. But Jung points out that although one attitude predominates, a person may be extraverted on some occasions and introverted on others. This conclusion again points toward the need for variety in design within reason. For the extraverted, perhaps an overall degree of higher stimulation is necessary, yet with elements of lower stimulation being included. For the introverted personality type the reverse procedure would be beneficial.

Although for most people it's preferable that their surroundings match rather than contrast with their personalities, Birren wrote in 1967 that for people with some forms of mental illness this method might have to be reversed. Color has been used therapeutically in treating emotionally and mentally ill patients, in the belief that manic and aggressive patients need cool or low-stimulus colors to calm them down, while depressive and suicidal patients need warm and exciting colors in their environment to compensate for their melancholic inner state.

Patients in a frantic or manic state may be sedated by the use of cool hues and dim illumination, just as depressive patients may have their spirits bolstered by compensating warm and stimulating hues, to direct their attention outward toward the environment, away from their inner state. But these are immediate therapeutic effects of temporary duration. Visual sedation or stimulation, whichever the case may be, cannot be prolonged, because it will lose its effectiveness in a relatively short time. Also, the concept of unity and complexity balance indicates that color reactions require constant change if they are to be beneficial and actively maintained.

It should not be difficult to set aside certain areas where color can have an immediate therapeutic effect. Most psychiatric facilities already have rooms set aside for distraught patients. These rooms should be color-treated to achieve the desired therapeutic effect.

Effects of Red, Yellow, Green, and Blue on Humans

Since the 1949 study by Moruzzi and Magoun, there have been numerous investigations of the effects of visual stimulation upon the ARAS, especially color. Perhaps the studies best known in the design world are those that compare the light (color) of long wavelengths to that of short wavelengths, or red and yellow versus green and blue.

The renowned American color authority Faber Birren once wrote: "The story of color is almost the story of civilization itself." (Birren 1963, p. 11) From time immemorial man has shown his fascination with color, perhaps the richest sense experience of all, universally present, flooding us with sensations and information that reach our mind, soul, and body. To understand the total concept of human reaction to color stimuli as well as the particular effects of various colors on a psychological and/or physiological basis, one influencing the other, we must explore the fascinating history of color—especially how it was used in healing.

Color in Healing—from Past to Present

The history of color teaches that ancient man had symbolism, mystery, and magic in mind when using color. He was not concerned with giving free fancy to his imagination or aesthetics. It was not until the Renaissance that color changed from sacred formulas rooted in mysticism to the artist's individual expression of beauty.

Since the beginning of recorded time (and probably before) man has believed in the healing power of color. The power of the sun and rainbow were related to divine forces. In many primitive religions the sun was worshiped. Sunbathing was even practiced in ancient times. Early in time our ancestors observed that sunlight sustains all life, and that without it there would be death.

The ancients knew little about the functioning of the human body or the diseases that affected it: "For him, flesh and blood were a combination of earth, fire, water and air animated by the spirit of some supernatural deity." (Birren 1963, p. 51) This deity did not only create

*Ancient Egyptians
prescribed color in healing
in various ways.*

the elements of man, but also those of the universe. It was believed that the only way to avoid illness and death was to bring the elements of man in harmony with the harmony of the universe and the gods.

Ancient physicians revered color, diagnosed through it, and prescribed color through chemicals, organic and inorganic potients, amulets, and rituals. One of the oldest medical documents is the *Papyrus Ebers,* named for the Egyptologist who discovered it. Dating back to 1500 B.C., this document reveals that ancient Egyptian healers prescribed colored minerals, such as malachite, red and yellow ochre, and red clay. White oil, black lizards, testicles of a black ass, and indigo were also mentioned. Verdigris, a green copper salt, was mixed with beetle wax to treat cataracts; constipation was cured with red or white cake; and a plaster of raw red meat healed a black eye.

Sometimes these color cures actually did work. For example, the Greeks used Tyrian purple, obtained from the murex shellfish, not only to dye the cloaks of kings, but as a remedy for ulcers and boils. Owing to its calcium-oxide content, it did indeed have ameliorative effect.

The ancient Greeks adopted many Egyptian theories. Pythagoras (c. 580–500 B.C.) also taught harmony and unity. For him God was living and absolute truth clothed in light, his body composed of the substance of light. Pythagoras' medical practices are not known, but it is believed that he cured illness with the aid of color, music, and poetry.

The founding of modern medicine is generally attributed to Hippocrates (c. 460–377 B.C.). He took a more diagnostic and critical atti-

Galen's teachings were not seriously challenged for fourteen hundred years.

tude toward healing than a mystical one, concerning himself with the beating of the heart and the pallor of the skin. Perhaps the practice of color diagnosis started with him—color as an outward expression of an internal condition. His prognostications of the sex of an unborn focused on the mother's skin tone: "A woman with child, if it be a male, has a good color, and if a female, she has a bad color." (Hippocrates quoted in Birren 1963, p. 56)

Celsus, who lived in the first century A.D., followed the doctrine of Hippocrates. Instead of being occult, his attitude toward color was also more practical. However, he prescribed medicine with color in mind, especially from flowers: iris, violets, lilies, saffron, narcissus, roses, and so forth. He also used plasters of black, green, white, and red. In regard to red he wrote: "There is one plaster almost of a red color, which seems to bring wounds very rapidly to cicatrize." (Celsus, quoted in Birren 1963, p. 56) How interesting that modern science has also shown that red, in the form of light, promotes improved scar formation on the skin.

The Greek-Roman scholar Galen (Claudius Galenus, A.D. 129– c. 199), court physician to emporer Marcus Aurelius, wrote some five hundred treatises that remained undisputed for several centuries. Galen separated man into four different temperaments and humors (bodily fluids): the melancholy (black bile); the choleric (yellow bile); the sanguine (blood); and the phlegmatic (phlegm). He classified each one of the four personality types according to the dominant humor, and specified which illness each type would be prone to. For example, circulatory disorders for the sanguine type, gallstones for the phlegmatic. Galen also made mention of the color preferences for each type: the choleric red, the sanguine yellow, the melancholic blue, and the phlegmatic green. Even today these color concepts are valid to some extent—at least in the symbolic sense.

The link between color and medical diagnosis is most persistently expressed through the *Doctrine of Humors.* Not only Romans and Greeks adhered to it; also the Chinese and Hindus in one form or the other. Medieval Western Europe acquired its version from Islam.

Progress in medicine passed from Rome to Islam during the Dark Ages. The physician-philosopher Ibn Sina of Persia (980–1037), known in the West as Avicenna, wrote a masterpiece of its time: *Canon of Medicine.* Color held great significance for Avicenna, worthy of profound study. He diagnosed diseases through color: the color of skin, eyes, excrement, and urine. He also had great confidence in color therapy. Especially compelling and remarkable are his words: "Even imagination, emotional states and other agents cause the humors to move." (Avicenna quoted in Birren 1963, p. 57) The reference to imagination and emotional states finds its counterpart in contemporary psychosomatic-medicine theories. Just as prescient is Avicenna's declaration that blue light slowed the movement of the blood and red light stimulated it. This observation, made almost a thousand years ago, is somewhat substantiated by modern studies on the calming effects of blue and stimulating action of red.

The more objective and scientific methods of investigation introduced by Hippocrates and carried on by Celsus, Galen, and Avicenna were lost in the Middle Ages. To the fore came a brotherhood of mystics and alchemists whose emphasis was on God, natural laws, philosophy, and the harmony of divine forces. It was a return to the mystic. Alchemy is a story by itself, whose origin is surrounded by mystery. It is possible that alchemy's roots are found in Egypt or Khem (the land of dark soil). In Islam it was known as "al Khem," and through Islam the word *alchemy* made its way into Western civilization.

Alchemy devoted itself to the transmutation of metals, but more than that it was a mystical and occult science. Although theories differed, most alchemists saw in the "Philosopher's Stone" the divine harmony of the four elements earth, fire, water, and air. They believed that if these four elements could be united, a substance could be derived capable of transmuting baser metals into gold or silver. More than that, it would be used as a medicine to cure all diseases. Alchemy abounds with references to color. Even the various stages necessary for the creation of the Philosopher's Stone were marked by the emergence of certain colors. If those colors did not appear, the process was deemed a failure.

Alchemy lost favor, and at some point color also was set aside as a therapeutic tool. Out of the questioning period came the medical sciences as we know them today—a rational approach with the help of electronic microscopes, X rays, lasers, and diagnostic computers. However, there was a brief interlude to this purely rational approach during the 19th century, an interruption caused by the Americans S. Pancoast and Edwin Babbitt.

Pancoast wrote the book *Blue and Red Light* (1877), in which he attacked the medical profession of his time, and praised the ancient mystics. He boasted of miraculous cures he had devised which were based on rather simple methods. He passed sunlight through panes of red or blue glass; "to *accelerate* the Nervous System, in all cases of relaxation, the *red* ray must be used, and to *relax* the Nervous System, in all cases of excessively accelerated tension, the *blue* ray must be used." (Pancoast quoted in Birren 1963, p. 61) Although my critique of color healing will be presented later in this chapter, I must concede that in general, Pancoast's pronouncements are not too far removed from what modern research has discovered: Red light is indeed a stimulant; blue light is a relaxant.

In 1878 Dr. Edwin Babbitt published his 560-page book *The Principles of Light and Color* (a second edition followed in 1896). Babbitt promptly became world-famous, his book having been translated into several languages. Even today Babbitt's chromotherapy is practiced by many followers. As far as I know, chromotherapy and the sale of chromotherapeutic equipment is forbidden in the United States, but not in Europe and other parts of the world.

Babbitt spoke of such things as thermal and electrical colors and the relationship among colors, elements, and minerals. He prescribed red for illnesses such as consumption, physical exhaustion, chronic rheumatism, and paralysis. He believed that red shared properties with the warming elements of the sun. He declared it to have an especially rousing effect upon the blood, and to some extent upon the nerves, especially when strained through some grades of red glass that also admit yellow rays. Babbitt classified yellow and orange as stimulants for the nerves, yellow also being described as a laxative, an emetic, and a purgative. Yellow mixed with a little red was a cerebral stimulant, and with a considerable amount of red became a diuretic.

Babbitt felt that blue and violet were to be considered cold, soothing, and possessing contracting potencies. He employed them against all inflammatory and nervous conditions, such as sciatica, hemorrhage of the lungs, cerebrospinal meningitis, neuralgic headaches, nervousness, nervous irritability, and sunstroke.

Largely because of Babbitt, who was popular among mystics but attacked, disputed, and renounced by the medical profession, color became discredited as a therapeutic agent. A vast clique of fraudulent color healers of Babbitt's time compounded adverse reaction by the medical profession. The American Medical Association and the U.S. Post Office subsequently put many a chromotherapist out of business. The respected American medical doctor, researcher, and professor of pediatrics Thomas Sisson, once declared: "Medical uses of the visible spectrum have been virtually ignored by physicians for the past 90 years." (Sisson quoted in Birren, 1978, p. 91)

However, light and color *are* working themselves back onto the modern medical field. One example of this is the established use of visible blue light in the treatment of infant jaundice (hyperbilirubinimea). The antiseptic qualities of ultraviolet light are used to cleanse the air in operating theaters. Sunlight, containing all the colors of the spectrum, is known to be a nutrient; lack of it causes diseases of the bones, rickets, and other illnesses. Researchers in medical, photobiological, and psychological fields are continually investigating the effects of color and light on the human organism.

Before I discuss the findings of research that has been conducted in more recent times, let me interject a few words about "color healing," often also called "color therapy," by which I mean a direct method of treating specific illnesses. As I stated before, to the best of my knowledge, color healing is not legal in the United States. However, I would not rule out that there might exist private groups or individuals—apart from the medical field—who discuss, experiment, or suggest methods of healing with color.

The theories of the majority of adherents of color healing are based on the "human aura"—those emanations which psychics claim to sense surrounding the human body. Auras were seen and believed in for centuries before electromagnetic energy was known. Color healers believe that the health of the body and mind depend upon a balance of aural colors, and should a color be missing or overdominant, it must be compensated for by chromotherapy.

The human aura is one realm where the mystic's belief has been substantiated by modern research. The human body transmits a series of electronic or magnetic fields, whose emissions can be measured with modern equipment, such as the electroencephalograph (EEG) which measures brain waves.

Semyon and Valentina Kirlian brought credibility to the existence of the aura by photographing energy fields surrounding animate and inanimate objects. One such photograph recorded the discharge emanating from a healer's thumb placed on a photographic plate through which a powerful electrical charge was passed. Russian and English researchers found that a leaf cut in half still registered the whole leaf on the photograph. The energy that emanated from the leaf did not show the amputation.

Further evidence of the existence of the aura has been supplied by a new method of "aura-photography," which makes the energy field surrounding the body visible in color. In his book *Aura Visionen* (Aura Visions), the German author and aura photographer Johannes Fisslinger shows many photographs taken of people's auras.

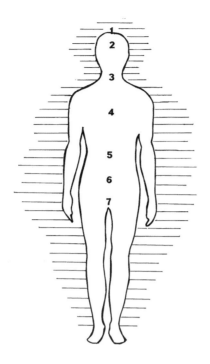

Researchers claim to be able to diagnose physical and emotional states from the colors and condition of the human aura. "In psychosomatic medicine, in which environmental conditions may lead to tension, fear, depression and in which these in turn may lead to a number of physiological ailments, a study of the aura may be of great aid in diagnosis." (Birren 1978, p. 77)

Color healers also believe in *chakras,* energy centers that exist outside of our body, but within the aura. The energies of the chakras are in communication with the autonomic nervous system and the regulation of hormone secretion. These energy centers are divided into seven chakras; each chakra corresponds to one of the seven spectral colors as in the illustration above:

1. *Vertex chakra (violet) stands for wisdom and spiritual energy. It influences the pituitary gland.*

2. *Forehead chakra (indigo) stands for intuition (the third eye), and influences the pineal gland.*

3. *Larynx chakra (blue) stands for religious inspiration, creativity, language, and communication. It influences the thyroid gland.*

4. *Heart chakra (green, pink) stands for love, sympathy, and harmony. It influences the heart and the thymus gland.*

5. *Solar plexus chakra (yellow) stands for knowledge, intellect, and is also the seat of tension. It influences the solar plexus and the adrenal body.*

6. *Spleen chakra (orange) stands for energy, and it influences the spleen and pancreas.*

7. *Basis chakra (red) stands for life and reproduction. It influences the sex glands and sexual organs.*

If the energies of the chakras are not in balance, meaning that there is too much or too little energy in each, emotional well-being and personality are affected. Proper balance is restored through color therapy.

In a fascinating 1989 book entitled *Farbtherapie—Mit Farben heilen—der sanfte Weg zur Gesundheit* (Color therapy—healing with color—the gentle way toward health), the author Christa Muths explains the nine methods of color healing that supposedly heal or help heal numerous illnesses such as high blood pressure, low blood pressure, allergies, depression, cancer, and others:

1. *Color intake through foods.*

2. *Irradiation with the inherent color (irradiating food with its inherent color).*

3. *Color intake through drinking (color irradiated water).*

4. *Bathing in colored water.*

5. *Sunbathing in color.*

6. *Irradiation with color (specific parts of the body).*

7. *Visualizing color (breathing exercises coupled with the visualization of color in sequence of the rainbow colors).*

8. *Breathing color (a visualized color is inhaled and exhaled).*

9. *Color meditation.*

In my early years I denounced color healing on the basis that many of the above points are too far-fetched and unscientific. Now that more than two decades have passed, I have softened my view on color healing. The world is full of mysteries that have no patent explanation, particularly phenomena associated with psychological and subsequent physiological reactions. Skeptics often see things as having to be neatly packaged either white or black—ignoring the gray areas. These gray areas may be the black or white of tomorrow. Although something defies rational explanation or scientific proof, it should not be ruled out completely. This latitude also pertains to color, a subject where an abundance of scientific proof, empirical observations, and also the unexplainable must be weighed to form the overall picture. To broaden our understanding of anything in this world often demands an open mind (and a small ego). We should all try to practice what the Germans call *gesamtheitliches Denken;* totality of thought.

However, I stand in the middle: the hard scientist finding me perhaps too much oriented toward the *soft* science of psychology, and the mystic denouncing me as being too scientific. I have experienced and known of many "color miracles," the most amazing being a remission of a cancer tumor by the placement of a colored patch over the affected area.

However, through interdisciplinary training, the color specialist must also be able to recognize and reject certain pronouncements that are made about color. There is some truth to some aspects of color healing or, I should say, *plausibility.* Let me make it perfectly clear that I am talking about color healing as presented through the nine methods listed above. To analyze some of these methods: color intake through food and drink (methods 1–3) I will not argue for or against. I see no harm in certain natural foods that color healers suggest. Visualizing color (method 7) is actually practiced in "imagination therapy" to relax the patient. Color meditation (method 9) may be in line with many self-regulating techniques such as meditation and biofeedback that have a wide range of clinical uses.

I see no health risks in any of these methods, nor in the methods of breathing color or bathing in colored water. However, I am skeptical of their efficacy, and under no circumstances should color healing replace sound medical diagnosis and treatment of serious illnesses and diseases.

I do object strongly to and warn against the use of colored light treatment where the possibility exists that the monochromatic light (regardless of color) may enter the eye. As I pointed out previously, we know that light entering the eye not only activates vision, but that it also induces biological functions in both animals and humans. This occurs via the energetic portion of the visual pathway and results in signals sent to the hypothalamic midbrain region, thereby influencing the production and release of hormones. Modern research in this area points out that there are biological implications in some artificial *white* light (in contrast to natural light) due to the fact that its spectral composition differs from that of sunlight. Here we are talking about so-called white light, so what of specific wavelengths, such as a red or green light? How dangerous could they be? We know that red light, for example, will increase blood pressure in a very short time; that rats become highly aggressive under pink light and so forth. *Unless the use of specific therapy with a monochromatic light is performed by trained personnel and medically approved* (as is the practice of using blue light to cure infant jaundice, which, by the way, is done with the baby's eyes covered), *we should keep our hands off light therapy.* Especially unfortunate is the fact that in Europe a book is available that contains plastic-colored filters to be fitted to a desk lamp for the purpose of instant self-help color therapy.

I would like the reader to observe the difference between color healing and color therapy—*psychotherapeutic effects of color* to be exact. Let there be no doubt that color can be a therapeutic agent, but it does not involve sleeping in blue sheets to relieve backaches, breathing pink to lose wrinkles, or drinking water illuminated with yellow to relieve constipation. These pronouncements do little to sway people who are skeptical about color's effect on humans in the first place. It makes it so much more difficult for those of us who take a more rational approach to color, but are too often being linked with the esoteric as soon as the words *color therapy* fall.

An excellent example of how color can be an important element in psychotherapeutical treatment was reported in the July/August 1992 issue of the the German medical journal *TW Neurologie Psychiatrie.* Dr. Heinrich Frieling of the Institute of Color Psychology successfully treated two cases within a few months, although prior traditional treatment by others had been unsuccessful.

The first was a serious case of hydrocephalus, where repeated operations resulted in trouble with memory, a loss of the sense of smell, and with depression. After treatment the patient rediscovered himself, built up hidden abilities, and learned a new way of concentrating.

The second case was a mentally deficient boy with anxiety neurosis, whose terrible nightmares disappeared after treatment. Frieling used a previously unknown psychotherapeutical treatment where not only art therapy was applied in accordance with Jungian psychology but also the use of experiences with the *afterimages of color.*

Modern Findings

Modern research has conducted many studies to investigate whether or not there exists a difference in the physiological and psychological reactions among major hues. Taking all studies collectively, it is evident that there is a difference indeed. Overwhelmingly, research studies substantiate this difference, although some studies proved to be inconclusive.

As early as 1942, K. Goldstein published his observations on color's influence on the functioning on the human organism. His work also pointed out some normal effects on motor behavior. Perhaps his most classic study was that of patients suffering from Parkinson's disease. It showed that red colors had a tendency to worsen a patient's pathological condition, whereas green seemed to improve it. Goldstein also found, among many observations, that brain-damaged subjects responded excitedly to red and calmly to green. Although his theories have been attacked because his subjects were brain-damaged, his overall findings have withstood challenges.

R. Gerard found in 1957 that red had a more arousing effect than did blue on visual cortical activity and functions of the autonomic nervous system. M. R. Ali in 1972, using electroencephalogram analysis, demonstrated greater arousal following red light than blue light. The colors were thrown directly into the eyes of the test subjects with a projector for a maximum time of six hundred seconds. Jacobs and Hustmyer noted in 1974 that red was more arousing than green, and green more arousing than blue or yellow. Each color was presented for one minute.

In his 1990 book *Gesetz der Farbe* (Laws of color), Frieling presented the results of an investigation with colored light that not only recorded physiological reactions, but also psychological responses. Subjects were asked to look into red, yellow, green, and blue light. Their comments were tape-recorded and presented in accordance with Wundt's "wind rose of emotions." The windrose separates emotions into the categories of arousing-calming, pleasant-unpleasant, tension-release. Major reactions may be condensed as follows:

Red Light   Red was found to be arousing, with blood pressure becoming inconstant, pulse increasing, and an unpleasant feeling of tightness gripping the throat. The dazzling glare was found unpleasant and produced headaches (one test subject asked for a discontinuation of the experiment after only two minutes). Pleasure components were not detected. It was noticed that during the time subjects were standing, they had a tendency to step backward and to move their frontward-stretched hands outward.

Yellow Light   As far as tension was concerned, subjects felt the yellow light was "mighty," "sunlike," and that there was a vibration within the core. Calming and pleasant components were not detected. During illumination with the subjects standing with arms outstretched, a nervous twitch and pushing movement was noticed, and also a subjective feeling in the palm of the hands.

Violet-Blue Light   Subjects found the blue to be pleasant. In regard to the calming effect, subjects said it was very restful; they found it a good object for concentration. Unpleasant and arousing components were not found.

Green Light   Green light was found to be pleasant, agreeable, and in reference to the calming effect more calming (in comparison to red). Subjects found it to have "something compelling" and that it subjectively felt moonlike with wide radiation.

Frieling writes that the statements made actually distributed themselves among all "wind rose" directions, indicating balance without arousal. He further stated that in literature there are different results reported as to blood pressure, but mostly in terms of a lowering of blood pressure. Green acts similarly to diffuse daylight, whereas red acts more like darkness. Motor activity is inhibited.

To condense the overall findings:

1. Red stimulates; it is comparable to a sympathomimetic stimulus.

2. Yellow is tensing but releases at the same time, and it raises motor activity.

3. Violet-blue (and blue) increases inner reactivation and leads to calm, and the ability to concentrate.

4. Green has an effect similar to a light stimulus that balances heterogeneous tendencies.

In 1994 I conducted a very informal experiment (without blood pressure measurement) during my seminars with approximately 38 participants, asking them to note their psychological and physiological reactions. Reactions were generally similar to those observed by Frieling. Several participants also reported anxiety under illumination with red light; blue and green overwhelmingly produced calming feelings of relief after the illumination with red light; while orange evoked feelings similar to those of red, but the effect was less arousing and more pleasantly stimulating. The yellow filter was too tinged with green to be useful in the experiment. Violet, which I also used, was reported to produce a profound "mystical" feeling. The exposure time for each light was about two minutes.

Many investigations, of which I have described a few, were mostly done utilizing colored lights, or in some cases color samples. Fewer studies have been conducted with the effects of surrounding color—that is, colored rooms. One of the earliest studies reported by Louis Cheskin, former associate director of the now defunct Color Research Institute of America, compared four rooms decorated entirely in one color: red, blue, yellow, or green; furnishings (typewriters, chairs, desks) in each case were colored to match the room.

In the red room an increase in blood pressure and pulse was noted. Subjects had difficulty working, or even remaining in the room for any length of time, due to overstimulation. The opposite effect occurred in the blue room—blood pressure and pulse declined, and activity slowed down. The bright yellow room produced no effect on blood pressure and pulse, however there were complaints of eyestrain which made many activities impossible. No abnormal reactions were detected in the green room—with the exception that it produced monotony.

In 1971 Dr. Hans Jürgen Scheurle conducted color therapy experiments at a clinic (Lukasklinik) in Arlesheim, Switzerland. The experiment was a "pilot study on color therapy with environmental (surrounding) colors" recording patients' blood pressure, pulse, rate of breathing, bodily sensations, effects during pain, and psychological reactions.

The experiment was conducted with one room in red and the other in blue. Colors were applied to walls, ceiling, and floor through the transparent painting method, meaning transparent layers or washes of color were applied to surfaces to give them a less opaque look, leaving the rooms lighter. But due to better light reflection and the surfaces reflecting off each other, a more intense color effect was achieved.

The study is quite voluminous and detailed, which leaves me to report only the major findings. One surprising effect was a lowering of blood pressure as soon as the patients entered the rooms, not only in the blue room, as was expected, but also in the red room. Blood pressure rose after the subjects left the rooms. In regard to the red room this seems quite contrary to other investigations. But I propose the theory that the unusual surroundings confronting patients upon entering the room prompted concentrated attention to the environment, which according to Lacey et al's hypothesis cited earlier results in cardiac deceleration.

Upon entering the red room, four persons felt physically unwell mainly because they developed headaches. Two of those patients also started perspiring on the face, neck, and palms. Headaches were not developed in the blue room, with the exception of the two patients who had shown more extreme reactions in the red room; in the blue room they also felt unwell.

Psychological reactions swung from sympathy and antipathy. One group of patients found the red room "beautiful," "light," "sunny," others found it too "glaring," "arousing," "exciting." Calmer emotions were generally noticed in the blue room; some patients found it "pleasant," "calming," "restful." Especially obvious were repeated remarks: "It's easier to concentrate, think, meditate." Other patients found the blue too "cool," "depressing," "sad."

As will be discussed in a later chapter, the psychological reactions to a major hue vary between positive associations and impressions and negative ones. It must be remembered that in practical design not only one color is present in a space.

A similar study was conducted in 1977 for a dissertation by Frank Gebert about the psychological and physiological effects of surrounding colors. Four chambers (about seven feet high, wide, and long) were colored respectively in red, yellow, green, or blue. The subjects were students and academicians between the ages of 20 and 40.

Gebert summarized his extensive study with the observation that physiological measurements showed definite and constant results only in the red chamber (increase in arousal). In regard to psychological effects, the results showed agreement between most subjects as to mood values and judgments of color. Red and yellow were considered stimulating; blue and green, calming.

Rikard Küller (1977) remarked that there seems to be an unresolved problem of color and arousal. When red, yellow, green, and blue color samples are judged on a scale ranging from calming to exciting, the more intense color will be judged more exciting regardless of hue. On the other hand, physiological measurements show that red hues are more arousing than green and blue hues. Differences have been found in EEG, blood pressure, respiratory rate, and reaction time. Küller proposes the hypothesis that two separate mechanisms are at work: intensity functions increase arousal and different hues contain particular information for the human body, perhaps of profound biological significance.

Avoiding Inflexible Conclusions

Taking all studies collectively, including the few I have just mentioned, we can conclude that colors richer in long wavelengths are more arousing than those of short wavelengths. However these findings should not be erroneously interpreted or used. Human reaction depends on a multitude of factors. First we must consider that in choosing appropriate surface colors much depends on the specific hue, its value, and intensity. Also *where* color is placed, how much of it (a red chair isn't going to increase blood pressure), for what purpose, and for what length of time should all be taken into account.

It would be erroneous to think that color design for interiors can or should be geared to a *specific physiological effect*—such as lowering the blood pressure of a person suffering from hypertension. Let me emphasize: *Specific physiological effects* (such as in color healing) *should not be the designer's objective.* This would be a crude stimulus-reaction game—a risky game to play because it doesn't always take the psyche into consideration. As Heinrich Frieling wrote:

> *Everyone knows that a rise of blood pressure also causes a specific attitude of mind, but it is also known that certain behavior will cause the blood pressure to rise; further it is known that irradiation with color also affects blood pressure. So where is there the beginning and the end of the chain reaction? (Frieling 1990, p. 184)*

It should be made quite clear that any strong color will cause an immediate reaction that can be physiologically measured, but the duration of the effect is not continuous. Red may increase blood pressure, but after a length of time the body will normalize this condition, or even show an opposite effect. In addition, I doubt that any color designer with a bit of sensitivity will create interior spaces in bright primary hues as the dominant theme (especially in workplace, school, and health-care facilities).

Does this mean that we cannot design stimulating or calming environments? Does this imply that it really makes no difference how an environment is designed? Of course we can design environments that serve a specific function, and of course it makes a difference how we use color, but it does not work through the method of trying to create a stimulus that only calls forth a *physiological* reaction of some type.

We must consider the human psyche with its potential for inducing physiological reaction. In the majority of cases we are working with surface colors to create a "room experience." This setting not only features color, but many other integrated design elements. The colorist who yields to generalities, such as red excites and blue calms, without an understanding of psychological/neuropsychological interconnections will soon find out that the desired effect cannot be achieved. It reminds me of the story of the designer who was asked to create a soothing milieau in a mental health facility. Resorting to a misguided generality, he made it a predominant blue throughout, resulting in a monotonous environment that produced a precisely reverse effect.

When designing with color we must always see it in context, and not apply it through generalities. Although they might work in some cases, we must analyze cases individually to see if generalities pertain to a particular situation.

Chapter Three

Psychosomatics, Emotions, and Design

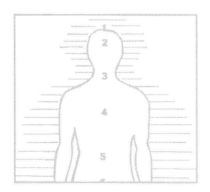

Designers rarely understand that our architectural environment influences our human psyche beyond aesthetic impressions. It is generally assumed that as long as an architectural space is aesthetically pleasing it satisfies the need and function of the environment. This is somewhat of an illusion because the term *aesthetics* is rather elusive. Basic rules regarding aesthetics do exist in very broad interpretation. There are some universal standards and interpretations of beauty and ugliness, of "class" or "kitsch."

Architects might be very surprised to know that their aesthetic interpretations differ from those of the general public, or should we say the user public. Studies indicate that the general public approaches, evaluates, and views an architectural environment from a different starting point than the architect. The subtleties of design that the architect enjoys through training are not necessarily understood or appreciated by people who have no training in the field.

Therefore, we may speak of a different set of rules between the two. The user is more concerned with basic instincts, which can be expressed in terms of comfort, friendliness of an environment, or that it just "feels right" because it seems appropriate to the given situation, and is easily understood. The architect, on the other hand, develops personal aesthetics shaped by training so while his or her basic instincts are satisfied, the aesthetic judgments are nonetheless influenced by professional training.

I am often reminded of this distinction during seminars and lectures where the audience is a mixture of architectural students, persons who are interested in color but not necessarily being trained as architects, interior designers, and architectural color consultants. In one such situation, the speaker, a well-known architect, proposed a color scheme that was applauded by the architectural students, but found to be inappropriate by all others.

The aware architect is able to fulfill his artistic professional tastes and aspirations, and still satisfy the tastes and needs of the user group. In *Inscape,* edited by Sir Hugh Casson (London: The Architectural Press, Ltd., 1969) this statement makes the point: "An interior (or a building or a city) that carries too heavily and forever the professional signature of its designer, and permits no contribution from its user, may be a fine monument, but it is nevertheless a tomb." (Quoted in Kleeman, 1981)

Bringing the two together for an "ideal" situation demands understanding that our architectural environment does produce emotions: These emotions do have psychosomatic effects which must be considered, and cannot be satisfied by current aesthetics alone. By *current* I mean the zeitgeist or spirit of the time.

Environmental Influence on Emotions

Professor Sune Lindstrom once stated: "With every particular architectural product is the spontaneous emotional reaction that is of importance to us." (Lindstrom, quoted in Hesselgren) The internationally respected architect Sven Hesselgren came up with the term *emotional loading* to characterize an element of architectural design inherent in any interior or exterior environment. Since it must be our goal to create places and spaces that will not unnecessarily burden the mental and physical well-being of their inhabitants, we will have to look further into the subject of emotions and how they are important in psychosomatics.

The word *mind* means something more than just intellect. It also includes the emotions and all the other qualities that give each one of us our distinct personality. The Greeks summed it up with the word *psyche* (spirit, soul, life), which has become the prefix in *psychology, psychophysiology, psychobiology,* and almost every word that has to do with the treatment or study of the mind.

Psychosomatic Medicine

In their 1972 book *Psychosomatics,* authors Howard R. and Martha E. Lewis tell the story of a four-year-old girl who was to undergo the extraction of some baby teeth. Earlier, the little girl had had a bad experience with a local anesthetic for stitches on her forehead. The dentist who was going to extract her teeth had difficulty with the struggling child and gave her a sedative before he could proceed. Shortly after the extraction, the child had a heart attack, and died two days later after having been rushed to a hospital. The coroner attributed the heart attack to an excess of adrenaline in the bloodstream triggered by fear.

Certainly I won't be so naive or bold to state that color in the environment would have made any difference in this case, especially since no information about the design atmosphere in the dentist's office is available. However, we may aver that environmental design does have an impact on human emotions. As the authors Lewis point out: "Tracings show that through circuitry from your sense organs, the limbic system can receive external stimuli—sights, sounds, tastes, smells, and touches that can evoke emotions." (Lewis 1972, p. 19)

Designers are at least responsible for the "sights" of external stimuli. This in essence means that we can create environments that will

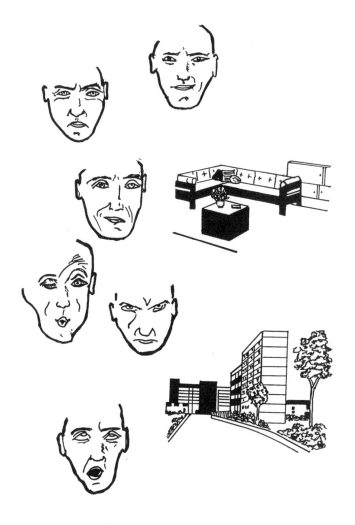

not unduly promote anxiety: surroundings that give the visual impression of being inviting, personal, and nurturing. These attributes are important in reducing anxiety.

Psychosomatic medicine sees man in his totality of mind and body, thereby emphasizing treatment of both mind and body. Physical disorders may originate through psychological factors, be aggravated by them, and vice versa. In his recent book on the subject, Paul-Heinz Koesters declares that almost half of all patients suffer from somatic, or bodily, illnesses whose origins are not found to be organic. Psychosomatic medicine therefore concludes that the mind is responsible for many illnesses.

All of us know from direct experience or from observation of others that stress causes headaches; anxiety makes the heart beat faster; and that anger and distress may affect the stomach. Examples of physical disorders that may originate through, or be aggravated by, psychological factors, include: stomach ulcers, high blood pressure, heart palpitations, migraine headaches, rheumatoid arthritis, infertility, and impotence. Should the design community concern itself with these facts? Since our professional responsibility is to create environments that do not put unnecessary strain on psychological and physiological well-being, yes, we must familiarize ourselves with psychosomatics. Decisions about visual design in our environment should be based on an understanding of aspects of architectural psychology—especially color psychology.

Psycho-Neuro-Immunology (PNI)

A most interesting, relatively new research science called Psycho-Neuro-Immunology gives further proof that a close relationship exists between the psyche and physical well-being. Neurobiologists, biochemists, and immunologists all over the world are increasingly discovering new networks of nerve fibers and molecular bridges that connect the psyche and the body with each other. It has become evident that emotions penetrate completely into the cell of the organism. PNI research indicates that a *positive* emotional mood strengthens the body's defensive system against illness, whereas a negative frame of mind has a weakening effect. Quite relevant to designers is a statement in *Psychologie Heute,* May 1994, by David Felten, professor of neurobiology and anatomy at the School of Medicine, University of Rochester. When asked, "When does the interaction between the mind and the body commence?" Felten answered, "The moment we begin to perceive sensory stimulation."

A System of Emotions

Emotions are to a great extent unconscious processes which cannot be classified to show a logical plan that links various parts together. However, in his book about architectural theory based on psychological research, Sven Hesselgren discusses the work of the American psychologist Robert Plutchik whose approach to the problem seems plausible.

With the help of results obtained by other researchers, Plutchik identifies eight behavioral patterns: destruction, reproduction, incorporation, orientation, protection, deprivation, rejection, and exploration. The behavioral patterns form the foundation for the following primary emotions:

Anger

Joy

Acceptance

Fear

Sorrow

Rejection

Expectancy

The primaries build four pairs of opposites:

Anger—Fear

Joy—Sorrow

Acceptance—Rejection

Surprise—Expectancy

These primary emotions appear in various intensities, listed in descending order from strongest to weakest:

Anger: rage, wrath, anger, annoyance, irritation

Fear: terror, fear, apprehension, timidity, diffidence

Joy: ecstasy, rapture, joy, happiness, pleasure

Sorrow: anguish, grief, sorrow, dejection, pensiveness

Acceptance: love, affection, fondness, acceptance, tolerance

Rejection: loathing, aversion, dislike, boredom, tiresomeness

Surprise: amazement, astonishment, surprise, strangeness, bewilderment

Expectancy: suspense, anticipation, expectancy, attentiveness, interest

Notice that Plutchik has not always chosen to designate a primary emotion by its strongest intensity, but by the intensity in which it most commonly occurs. He also points out that in everyday life we generally experience mixed emotions, and not always pure primary emotions in their various intensities. This is only a very short outline of Plutchik's work. It is interesting that he also devised an emotional wheel in the form of an eight-part color wheel. The mixture of two primary emotions creates a third emotion. For example, joy and acceptance form love.

Communicators = Perception = Impression = Emotional Reaction

The sum of all elements—color, light, pattern, furnishings, accessories—in an architectural space communicate an overall impression to the viewer. That impression engenders a reaction that carries some type of emotional content.

Let me illustrate with an imaginary setting—yet one that I have encountered often. Picture a small room with a very light floor, white walls, spartan furnishings, and the customary overhead fluorescent lighting. For the sake of argument, we will assume that it is a hospital patient room or examination room, which the patient enters in a disposition not exactly filled with joy. We can categorize this room according to the above formula which leads from communicators to emotional reaction:

Communicators: small space, white walls, light floors, spartan furnishings, bright, unrelieved sameness of light

Impression: cell-like, empty, emotionally cold, unattractive, depressive, hostile, harsh, discouraging

Possible emotional reaction (using Plutchik's system):

Primary Emotion:	*Intensity:*
Anger	Initial annoyance
Fear	Apprehension
Rejection	Dislike, boredom
Sorrow	Sorrow, pensiveness

It is obvious that this room has not fulfilled its design goal in regard to human emotional reaction.

We can pin down at least some basic impression of a space through the use of a semantic differential chart, also known as a polarity profile. This most efficient tool will be explained in a following chapter. The polarity profile allows us to analyze different sections of an environment to set the requirements needed for an ideal ambiance, projected function, and expectation of a particular space. This analysis identifies environmental conditions and helps the designer analyze reactions to them. It must be the designer's goal to avoid choices that will trigger negative emotional reaction.

For a concluding example to the above premise, let's take the emotion *anger.* Even to avoid its lowest intensity on the rating scale, *annoyance,* the environmental impression must be calming, relaxing, friendly, personal. Conversely, it must not be agitating, irritating, unfriendly, or impersonal.

Characteristics and Effects of Major Hues

Color not only produces mood associations and subjective and objective impressions, but also influences our estimation of volume, weight, temperature, time, and noise. Collective findings have shown that there are basic reactions to color common to most people. It may be said that color is a universal language.

Numerous studies have been undertaken that show the affective values of certain hues, thereby making it possible to assess mood-tones of colors with reasonable accuracy. This indicates that in design—whether it be for architecture, marketing, product packaging, or any other business—an understanding of the different impressions, associations, and characteristics of a color is of immense value for the color specialist.

It has often been questioned whether cultural heritage influences the effects of color, thus rendering any reasonable conclusions about color's psychological effect meaningless. Each color has its own color and pattern traditions, each has economic, geographical, and religious factors, and each has fluctuations of taste and educational levels.

As we learned from the "Color Experience Pyramid," many factors contribute to the way we judge, respond to, and form associations with color. As I had indicated, reaction to color is both innate and learned, but perhaps to the greatest extent innate, therefore archetypal, which means universal reactions.

A fair amount of research has been done on this subject, and we can safely state that it *is* possible to find universal appeal in color application where broad acceptance as a practical necessity is the desired goal. Küller summarized it very well:

> *One of the most striking features of the results concerning preferences, connotations and color-mood associations is the consistency from one individual to another, from group to group, and cross-culturally. There has been a great number of cross-cultural studies comparing subjects in America, Lebanon, Kenya, Botswana, Greece, just to mention a few. Monkeys have been compared to Man, men to women, children to adults, laymen to architects. As one author concludes: "It would indicate either that our heritage is such that we learn the correct responses, or that there is some innate mood reaction to different colors." (Küller 1981, p. 164)*

Example of a Color Association Study

One of my studies with participants of the International Association of Color Consultants seminars in the United States and Europe showed very little difference between input from Americans and Europeans.

Usually color association tests are performed by asking the subjects to pick from color chips the one they feel best expresses a specific mood or association with a specific term. I decided against the color chip method since their predetermined range limits the participants' choice. The people taking part in the study were allowed to use paints or colored pencils. The instructions were as follows:

> *Please assign colors to the below listed terms without thinking about specific objects (such as clothing, flowers, tapestries, rooms, and the like). We are interested in the association you make with the concept or idea of the terms. Don't stop at only one color that you feel is closely allied to the term listed or gives the best color expression of the term; select a second if you so wish.*

The study in the United States was conducted with several different groups between April 1991 to April 1993. Participants not only came from the United States, but also from Canada, Australia, and Japan, and range in age from 25 to 60 years.

The single colors chosen were then paired with others to show that color associations are not necessarily made with only a single tone; i.e., that red was not the only color associated with the word *love;* it was also connected to red-violet. Therefore, the colors chosen and viewed as a group are important in creating a certain mood or the passing of a certain message, as in advertising.

The results were as follows:

Term	Colors Chosen	Percentage
Love	Red, Red-Violet	81 %
Hatred	Black, Red	89.6 %

Many of the 89.6 % of the subjects showed black and red as a combination representing hatred.

Term	Colors Chosen	Percentage
Peace/Tranquility	Blue, Blue-Green, Green	93.6 %

The high result was not surprising. These colors have always been considered calming.

Term	Colors Chosen	Percentage
Mourning/Sorrow	Black, Gray	86 %
Happy	Yellow, Orange	63 %
Jovial	Orange, Yellow	50 %

Note that *jovial* produced the same predominant combination as with the term *happy,* however, orange predominated slightly over the yellow placing it in first position—the stronger color denoting the stronger feeling—*jovial* being a stronger expressive form of *happy*.

Term	Colors Chosen	Percentage
Life	Green	73 %

Green was associated with the power of nature (plant life); without it life would not exist. *Red* was also chosen by some subjects to represent life—blood being the life-giving juice of our bodies.

Term	Colors Chosen	Percentage
Luminous	Yellow	65 %
Noble	Blue, Blue-Violet, Violet	81 %

The same test was conducted in Europe in 1993. Those participants came primarily from Germany, Austria, and Switzerland, and were in the age group of 20 to 60 years. In this study we did not group colors but showed percentages for each hue. The choices were similar to those in the American study—in some cases higher than in the United States for some terms (when the two highest percentages are added together as was done in the American study).

Term	Colors Chosen	Percentage
Love	Red	72 %
	Red-Violet	27 %
	Pink	15 %

Combination red and red-violet: Europe, 99 percent; United States, 81 percent—a difference of plus-18 percent

Term	Colors Chosen	Percentage
Hatred	Black	58 %
	Red	36 %
	Yellow-Green	18 %

Combination black and red: Europe, 94 percent; United States, 89.6 percent—difference of plus-4.4 percent.

Term	Colors Chosen	Percentage
Peace/Tranquility	Blue	56 %
	Green	42 %

Combination blue and green: Europe, 98 percent; United States, 93.6 percent—difference of plus-4.4 percent.

Term	Colors Chosen	Percentage
Mourning/Sorrow	Black	76 %
	Gray	30 %
	Brown	18 %
	Violet	18 %

Combination black and gray: Europe, 106 percent; United States, 86 percent—difference of plus-20 percent.

Term	Colors Chosen	Percentage
Happy	Yellow	61 %
	Orange	45 %
	Yellow-Green	24 %

These results were rather surprising. The grouping of yellow and orange is for 100 percent of the European subjects symbolic of *happy,* while in the United States only 63 percent (although still a large majority) of the subjects chose those colors.

Term	Colors Chosen	Percentage
Jovial	Orange	48 %
	Yellow	21 %

Combination orange and yellow: Europe, 69 percent; United States, 50 percent—difference of plus-19 percent.

Term	Colors Chosen	Percentage
Life	Green	68 %
	Red	41 %

Europeans chose decidedly more red than in the United States study. However, green predominates in the United States with 5 percent more subjects choosing it.

Term	Colors Chosen	Percentage
Luminous	Yellow	62 %
	Yellow-Orange	21 %

Yellow: Europe 62 percent; United States, 65 percent; difference of plus-3 percent.

Term	Colors Chosen	Percentage
Noble	Violet, Red Violet	41 %
	Blue	41 %

As in the United States study, violet and blue predominate, with the Europeans leaning more toward red-violet and the subjects in the United States toward blue-violet. The percentage of the grouping of blue to violet is within one percentage point the same.

The results of these studies do show a striking similarity in the dominant color groups chosen by participants in the United States and Europe. The hues chosen also conform to general selections made in color-psychology tests on their associative-symbolic content.

Innate or learned responses? Surely a combination of both. How interesting it would be to compare children with adults, using the same mood terms. So far I have only been able to test one eight-year-old girl. The results speak for themselves:

Love	Red
Hatred	Black
Peace/Tranquility	Mid and light Blue
Mourning/Sorrow	Black
Happy	Yellow
Jovial	Orange and Yellow-Orange
Life	Green, Olive
Luminous	Yellow
Noble	Blue

What Is Color Psychology?

The psychological effects of color, or color psychology, is a vast and complex field. I like to separate the concept of color psychology into two branches, not each a distinct branch divorced from the other, but two interrelated branches each having its task. One branch is *applied,* or practical, color psychology. Applied color psychology is what most professionals practice in their design of the architectural environment; it is also used in marketing. The psychological effects (associations, impressions, character) of colors are predetermined to produce a visual ambience that will benefit the psychological, and therefore physiological, well-being of the user. In marketing, of course, it pertains to the presentation and selling of products.

The second branch involves the use of color in psychology itself. For lack of a better term I call this *depth color psychology.* This branch includes the various psychodiagnostic color tests that probe people's character or personality traits, and the psychodiagnostic interpretation of an individual's use of color in art therapy and the like. It includes any activity that incorporates color as a tool in psychotherapy.

If you work as a designer, I hope you will keep in mind the "Color Experience Pyramid" at all times. The six basic levels of how we experience color, or become conscious of color, has validity in both branches of color psychology.

The psychologist Ingrid Riedel makes the interesting point that nature's colors probably have the most indelible influence on the "experiencing of color." For example, the experience of new green or fresh growth in nature is synonymous with continuity, rebirth, and therefore, hope. By extension, this association of green with hope has powerful religious symbolism: the spirit of hope as represented by the Holy Spirit, Pentecost, Palm Sunday—Christian rituals that incorporate the greens of nature.

Valuable information about emotional content of colors comes from a series of separate psychological experiments conducted by Frieling, Pfister, Lüscher, Stefanescu-Goanga, and others. Comparisons were made between color symbolisms found in different culture groups ranging from European-Christians to old Egyptian, ancient Chinese, and early Greek. All evidenced ritual symbolism based on the experiences of color in nature. These transferred to and evolved into major emotional associations stimulated by certain colors. These in turn were transferred to sociological-cultural and religious experiences.

Deeply ingrained conscious-unconscious connotations of color are therefore not just a matter of individual interpretation, but part of our collective heritage. All connotations are derived from certain primary associations.

This may be illustrated with the color *red* as an example. One of the earliest investigations was conducted by Stefanescu-Goanga in 1912. He found that red primarily evoked images of heat, fire, and blood. Birren, whose investigations were also among the earliest in this field, mentions the same three red symbols: heat, fire, and blood.

From primary associations with red, secondary suggestions derive: from *red* evoking *blood* the mind quickly sees wounds, pain, war, victims, revolution. But energy and sexuality (life, love, eroticism) are also connected with the red of blood. For the association with fire: warmth, sunset, heat, tropics, excitement, enthusiasm ("He gave a fiery speech") and similar positives.

The scale of red reaches its emotional expression from aggression, destruction, and death, to love, sacrifice, and devotion. We see this reflected in widespread mystical, religious, and cultural symbolism. For example:

In astrology   Red is assigned to the impatient, hot-tempered, trailblazing leader Aries. Assigned to Aries is also the planet of Mars, the god of war, also symbolized by the color red. It is interesting to note that the four elements and temperaments proposed by Pythagoras and Hippocrates of ancient Greece assign red (and yellow) to the choleric (hot-tempered) person and the element fire.

In ancient Egypt   Those who had great energy and skill; also connotes the demonic, desert, and blood atonement.

In China   Red was the symbol of pleasure, joy, festivity, fire, southern regions, and the expulsion of demons.

In Mosaic Cult   The color scarlet symbolized blood and life.

In the Eastern or Orthodox Church   Red symbolized blazing love. The close link between psychological association and symbolism across all cultures is self-evident. How logical that the physiological effects of red coincide with such associations-symbolism. Physiologically, red is a stimulant; initially it raises blood pressure and actually produces excitation, especially on the sympathetic branch of the autonomic nervous system. This is the case not only with red: The same holds true for all major hues. If we take all the elements of color into consideration—such as associations and symbolism with their origins in nature and their physiological effects—we see amazing similarities in the expressive (associative) and affective (physiological and psychological) force for each color.

Hue Effect—Impressions or Associations—Character

Color impressions and associations and the character of each major hue is a vast subject, vast in the sense that a single chapter can not treat all variations in depth. Instead, regard the following as an overview and convenient reference guide to the general effects and efficacy of major hues.

Red

Red is an arousing, exciting, and stimulating color with the positive associations of passion, strength, activity, and warmth. Negative impressions include aggressivity, rage, intensity, fierceness, and blood.

Its aggressive masculine nature is often linked with combat, dominance, and rebellion. The Roman legions hoisted a red flag to signal an attack. It was called the blood flag, since blood would soon flow. Red military uniforms were meant to charge the spirit, with the practical bonus that blood didn't show too much on red fabric. Red is a sign to the enemy of active resolution and provocation. Revolutionaries often display red. We automatically think *red* when we think of Russian and Chinese Communist revolutions—the Reds. During the French revolution the Jacobin liberty caps were red. In Italy the red shirts and flags of Garibaldi's men signaled revolution. The symbolic color for Mars, the planet and god of war, is red. In modern idiom we say someone has been caught red-handed, meaning with the blood of his victim still on his hands.

Red also signifies life and living. Understanding the connection between life and blood probably goes back to the earliest of times. We can well imagine the scenario: The ancient hunter or animal has been wounded and lies dying, a red substance flowing from the body. Ancient Homo sapiens realized that this red substance gave life and meant life; hence red symbolizes life. Being alive means health, energy, confidence, and strength—all terms that reflect the symbolic meaning of red. In the United States we call someone who is high-spirited, strong-willed, vigorous, and lusty *red-blooded.*

Red is also the color of love. In ancient mythologies red robes were worn by the Greeks to symbolize sacrifice and love. In the Christian religion red stands for the blood of Christ, at the same time a symbol for love. The crimson robes of the cardinals represent the godly and fatherly. For the ancient Hebrews, on the other hand, it meant sacrifice and sin. Passionate, sensual, and erotic love (more than the platonic) is also characterized by red. We speak of "red-light" districts (not blue ones); even in antiquity red was the mark of prostitutes.

Red is perhaps the most dominant and dynamic of all colors. It grabs the attention and overrules all other hues. The lens of the eye has to adjust to focus the red light wavelengths; their natural focal point lies behind the retina. Thus red advances, creating the illusion that red objects are closer than they are.

The masculine and dynamic nature of red changes dramatically where the color turns pink. It changes its gender to feminine and appears gentle and acquiescent.

Orange

Orange has an identity crisis; it really plays second fiddle to red. Bright orange appears exciting and stimulating; a light orange is cheering. The positive associations and impressions of orange are jovial, lively, energetic, extroverted, and sociable. When the color is highly saturated it associates with the terms *intrusive* and *blustering.*

The color is mellower and less primitive than red. It has almost no negative cultural or emotional associations. Orange is the natural color of fire, but red remains its symbol. It is also the dominant autumnal color of nature, brilliantly displaying itself in autumn foliage. Nature features orange in craggy formations such as those at Bryce Canyon. Sunsets dazzle us with orange hues. Aesthetically, unsaturated tones of orange may appear weak, languid.

Brown is a darkened orange. It is not a spectral hue, but it is the last word in natural colors, encompassing all hues of earth and wood. Brown also has a gustatory association, such as coffee and chocolate.

Psychologically, brown is linked with comfort and security. It is earthly, suggesting stability. It is motherly and dependable. In the Middle Ages it was the color worn by peasants and farmers. Certain nuances of brown may appear glum, grubby, and drab.

Yellow

Reflective and luminous, yellow is the happiest of all colors. In its positive associations and impressions it is cheerful, high-spirited, and suggestive of the life-giving sun. It represents a bright future, hope, wisdom, and it is expansive—not earthbound.

Yellow is used in packaging and advertising to express activity and cheerfulness. For example, Kodak film boxes are yellow, and it's the featured color in many of their ads, to suggest golden sands and faraway places. The logo of the Shell company is red and yellow; yellow to signify the search for new horizons; red for the fuel to power vehicles.

Yellow's expansiveness means communication. It is the symbol of Mercury, the messenger of the gods. In many countries mail boxes are yellow. Communication also means mental and spiritual enlightenment.

Yellow is cheerful, surely, but when it is too strong and glaring it becomes egocentric and reminds us of "insane laughter" as Kandinsky described it. It is a comparatively light color; as it loses its lightness, when modified, it ceases to be yellow.

Green

Green is a mixture of the gaiety of yellow and the dignity of blue. In its effect light green is retiring; in its pure hue, relaxing. The positive associations with green are that it is tranquil, refreshing, quiet, and natural. Since the eye focuses green exactly on the retina, it is also the most restful color to the eye. The negatives may be expressed with the words *common, tiresome, guilty.*

As reviewed in some detail earlier, the most obvious associations we make with green are those of nature and vigorous growth. In this sense green is the quintessential color of life. Early humankind's rituals were centered on the green of fresh vegetation, and the expectation of harvest, which meant food—hence, life. In ancient Palestine brides wore green as the color of hope for a happy life and fertility.

In Islam the prophet Mohammed embodied hope through his green gown, and under a green banner led his believers in holy war. Islam still embraces green as a holy color and favors it for interior décor. In Christianity green is the color of spring, hope, resurrection, and immortality.

There is also a contradictory side to green. Just as it is the color of nature and life, it is also the color of mold, decay, sickness, and death in humans. If we ask for a color that would describe poison, most people would choose green. In German a bilious-looking green is described as *Giftgrün,* or poison green (as it is in English). In the 19th century an arsenic-laced pigment, known as Paris green, was used in wallpaper and led to numerous deaths. Could that dreadful occurrence be responsible for the coinage poison green? It's doubtful, since there is evidence that as early as the Middle Ages green was identified with poison.

A neutral green exactly between the poles of blue and yellow is calming. When it slips considerably toward yellow it becomes more stimulating, lighter, and less serious. Toward blue it turns colder, more fastidious, and sensitive, and as a light bluish green it becomes much more refreshing.

Blue

Blue is somewhat the peacemaker of color; not many people dislike it. It has a relaxing effect, and light blue seems retiring. Its positive impressions are calmness, security, comfort, sobriety, contemplation. On the negative side it may be frightening, depressing, and cold. Spontaneous associations evoked by blue are usually passivity, quietness, wetness, cleanliness, odorlessness, mental reflection, melancholy, sadness, sea, sky, and yearning (especially stirred by light blue).

Blue is tranquility and truth that cannot be subverted. It is the color associated with spirituality and wisdom. In Rome it was the color of the philosopher's academic robe. To Christians blue meant hope and piety, and in their art it signified spiritual and pacific virtue. Blue was the color of holiness for the Hebrews. For the Hindus Krishna is exclusively blue. In China blue symbolized the power of heaven and immortality.

Blue is a noble color representing dignity, poise, and reserve. It's awarded to winners: the blue ribbon. In advertising dark blue is often employed to inspire confidence, trust; it suggests security and high quality.

But blue is also synonymous with things cold and melancholy. How often do we express sadness by saying, "I'm blue," or "I have the blues." Blue is the only color that has a rich art form named after it—those melancholy jazz and popular songs known to millions as *the blues*.

But never say you are blue in Germany—because it means you are totally drunk. The generalization that blue is a cold color, especially since it also appears on the "cool" side of the color wheel, is true to some extent. Light blue is cold; however, some middle-value blues and deep blues may appear much warmer. The material a blue appears on also influences the extent to which it is considered colder or warmer. Deep blue in carpet, a thick textile, or a coarser surface in comparison to a slick one will always make blue seem warmer. (See Figure C-54.)

Purple/Violet

Purple is a blend of red and blue; the two colors that are physically and psychologically opposed to each other. Violet is a lighter shade of purple and a pure spectral hue. Purple is a mixed color. They encompass vast differentiations in hue.

Positive associations and impressions can be made with purple in the sense that it is regal, dignified, and exclusive. On the negative side it may prompt lonely, mournful, or pompous associations.

Purple is a clerical color worn by priests. It suggests the integrity of blue and the strength of red. Very dark shades of it appear strict, foreboding. It also symbolizes internalization and depth of feeling, dignity, wealth, mysticism, and magic.

Lighter and closer to red, it becomes sensual, seductive, and secretive; also sweet, cosmetic, and intimate. Certain nuances may appear unsettling, degenerate, morbid, and narcotic.

White

White represents light, the celestial, spiritual, hope, holiness, and innocence. In the Christian religion white stands for chastity, innocence, and purity; to the Jews it signifies purity and joy.

In opposition to black, white is goodness—black is evil; white is *yes*—black is *no*. A lie that is not vicious, but meant to spare someone's feelings, is called a white lie. Black magic is meant to hurt; white magic is benign.

The white flag of submission means an end to hostilities, and the new beginning for a peace (white dove of peace). It is the color of nirvana—the state of perfect blessedness through the absorption of the soul into the supreme spirit. In Asia the color of mourning is white, because it signifies the beginning and not an absolute end to existence. Christians also believe in an afterlife, and black is really the wrong color for mourning (actually, black only became the color of mourning after Louis XII of France declared it to be so).

White means *clean*. Brand-X detergent washes the whitest white. We expect white to *be* white, and it especially disturbs us to see a dirt spot on white clothes and other objects. The same with snow. Isn't it disturbing when freshly fallen snow is sullied by yellow spots left by a dog that went about its business?

With so many positive feelings for the color white, why then is it on the bottom of the list in color-preference tests or psychodiagnostic color tests? Hardly anyone will choose white over "color." But note one big exception: interior design, where white seems always to make its appearance.

From a psychological viewpoint white, in its cleanliness, is sterile. But using it in hospitals, for example, to denote hygiene is nowadays misplaced application. White has no psychotherapeutic effect. It makes us think of unemotional clinical practice rather than involved human caring. Life is color—not detachment.

Black

"Black is the power of darkness, or expressed differently, darkness is a power—and in our impression of it, black is a representative of this power." (Frieling 1988, p. 159) Black is ominous, the fear of the unknown, the dark of night, grief, and death. Many expressions of speech carry negative connotations for the color: blackguard, black humor, blackmail, black market, black sheep.

Black identifies power, the power of the mighty to induce fear; the black uniforms of Hitler's SS troops and Mussolini's Blackshirts come to mind. My color association survey showed clearly that the combination of black and red was considered the ultimate expression of hatred. Punks wear black leather jackets and combat boots—along with skull decorations, razor blades, and chains—symbols of defiance, telling us that they are the no-future generation. It is interesting that psychological preference tests among teenagers shows a greater tendency to accept the color black. A sign of defiance in the search of independence from parental and society's rules? Perhaps, but actually in this case, I'd say it's just a normal choice in the course of growing up. Priests wear black—of course not for the same reason as do the defiant, and many nuns still do—as a sign of self-denial.

In fashion black usually expresses status, elegance, richness and dignity: black limousines, black tails, black gowns, black business suits. Black can set one apart, a mode begun in the Burgundy court of France where during the reign of Louis XII black became the official color of mourning, and was also worn earlier by the aristocracy to separate itself from the common "colorful" folk. The combination of black and gold is the ultimate expression of sophistication, luxury, and quality.

Black heightens colors and makes them appear more luminous. Perhaps the reason why it also has an erotic aspect, as in black lingerie, is because it sets a contrast to the color of white skin. In ancient Egypt women would outline their eyes in black to make their expression more mysterious.

Gray

Pure gray is conservative, quiet, and calm, but also dreary, tedious, passive, and without life. It is the bipolar between light and dark; it is neither tension nor relief. In the gray zone there is no clarity in any direction—it is neutral. In German the term *grauer Alltag*—the gray daily routine—means a day with no high points or low points. In Christian love it represents Christ risen, a blend of white light of divinity and the blackness of sin and death.

Gray lacks energy; it has no will of its own. It does not want to get involved and make a definite statement. In color design it takes on the characteristic of the adjacent color. Gray is often associated with industry; and with modern, man-made structures of concrete and metal.

To Summarize

Keep in mind that this has been a basic overview. Impressions, associations, effects, and symbolism may be altered as these major hues are modified (in hue, intensity, and lightness). This means that their impressions and associations may be modified.

Color Effects in the Interior Space

The location (top, sides, bottom) of a color within the interior space can make a great deal of difference in influencing a room's character, the way it is perceived psychologically, and subsequent reactions to it. A particular hue that is perfectly suitable on the floor may elicit an entirely different reaction when applied to the ceiling.

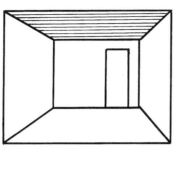

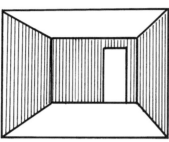

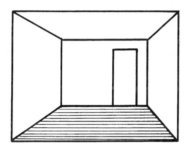

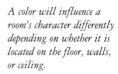

A color will influence a room's character differently depending on whether it is located on the floor, walls, or ceiling.

Red

Ceiling: intruding, disturbing, heavy

Walls: aggressive, advancing

Floor: conscious, alert, perhaps pompous

In practical situations, pure red is seldom used as the dominant color (on walls), but more as an accent. Although physiological arousal may be temporary, red psychologically exhibits emphatic characteristics so far discussed. Therefore, the overuse of saturated red adds to the complexity within a space. Modifications of pure red are much more suitable.

Pink

Ceiling: delicate, comforting

Walls: aggression-inhibiting, intimate, too sweet if not grayed down

Floor: perhaps too delicate, unfamiliar in this location

Pink must be handled carefully. It is generally considered feminine, therefore usable in spaces considered to be in the intimate feminine sphere. Typically it is considered perfect for a young girl's bedroom (pink for girls, blue for boys), but it has become quite a cliché. As an alternative, light blue-green as a dominant color may be used for both genders, but accents can tip the scale in favor of feminine or masculine. With pink much depends on the exact nuance used; a bubble-gum pink will be much livelier and somewhat cheaper-looking than an elegant old rose. (See Figure C-52.)

Orange

Ceiling: stimulating, attention-seeking

Walls: warm, luminous

Floor: activating, motion-oriented

Orange is more mellow than red and is easier to live with. But if it is too bright, it can hardly be used as anything other than an accent. Pastel oranges are appropriate to set cheerful, lively, and sociable moods. In its reflection on skin it may enhance some complexions, especially when its hue position is close to peach (making it an appropriate color in the bathroom).

Brown

Ceiling: oppressive and heavy (if dark)

Walls: secure and assuring if wood; much less so if paint

Floor: steady, stable

There is a great difference between the browns of natural materials such as wood, and brown paint. Brown as a paint is never as comfortable-looking or warm as wood. Brown paint should not be used in certain institutions as not to evoke fecal associations.

Yellow

Ceiling: light (if toward lemon), luminous, stimulating

Walls: warm (if toward orange), exciting to irritating (if highly saturated).

Floor: elevating, diverting

Because of its high visibility, yellow serves many safety purposes, especially in industrial environments. It also appears brighter than white and is useful in poorly illuminated and dim spaces. Pastel yellow can be harmonized with many accent colors, thereby enlivening a space in its predominant mood-cheering and friendly flavor. The accents may then push it toward being either more exciting and warmer (orange, red), or cooler and more calming (green, blue-green).

Green

Ceiling: protective (reflection on skin can be unattractive)

Walls: cool, secure, calm, reliable, passive, irritating if glaring (electric green), muddy if toward olive

Floor: natural (up to a certain saturation point), soft, relaxing, cold (if toward blue-green)

Green, along with blue-green, provides a good background environment for meditation and tasks involving concentration.

Blue

Ceiling: celestial, cool, less tangibly advancing (if light), heavy and oppressive (if dark)

Walls: cool and distant (if light), encouraging and space-deepening (if dark)

Floor: inspiring feeling of effortless movement (if light), substantial (if dark)

Blue tends to be cold and bleak if applied to large areas, especially in hallways and long corridors, and certainly when it is light (also see *blue* under the earlier section headed in this chapter "Hue Effect—Impressions or Associations—Character"). Medium or deep tones are appropriate in incidental areas. Pale blue is refracted sharply by the lens of the eye and therefore tends to cast a haze over details and objects in the environment. This may cause distress to some people confined to a particular area for a long period.

Purple-Violet

Seldom used in interior spaces except for accents or special moods. Psychologically, it may appear disconcerting and subduing.

Gray

Ceiling: shadowy

Walls: neutral to boring

Floor: neutral

As is the case with all neutral hues, gray fails to have much psychotherapeutic application. There has been a marked tendency to use it indoors in conjunction with various accent walls. This defies all logic and many of the principles set forth in this book.

White

Ceiling: empty, no design objections—helps to diffuse light sources and reduce shadows

Walls: neutral to empty, sterile, without energy

Floor: touch-inhibiting (not to be walked upon)

There are psychological and physiological justifications for not using white or off-white as a dominant color in the majority of settings. Some of these reasons have been explained so far, and more will follow.

Black

Ceiling: hollow to oppressive

Walls: ominous, dungeonlike

Floor: odd, abstract

This overview has given general guidelines on color effects in interior spaces. Please keep in mind that it walks hand in hand with the previous section headed "Hue Effect—Impressions or Associations—Character.

Centrifugal/Centripetal Action and Complexity

I must stress that to meet design objectives, the atmosphere of a space can be manipulated to align it with the function of the space. The degree of mood creation depends on particular color usage. Warm and luminous colors with high levels of light produce a centrifugal action, directing attention outward, toward the environment. Such environments are conducive to cheerfulness and activity.

Softer surroundings, cooler colors, and lower levels of illumination produce centripetal action. Such environments encourage inward orientation and enhance the ability to concentrate. This formula can be put to good use where employees are required to perform difficult visual and mental tasks.

As to color and complexity, there is a high correlation between the strength (chromaticity) of a color and the perceived excitement of a space. Studies in full-scale rooms indicate that complexity increases as chromatic strength increases. Regardless of hue, strong colors will make a room appear exciting; weak color has a calming impact. High color contrast also contributes to the apparent excitement of a space.

Estimation of Time

There seems to be a contradiction in regard to the effect of color on the perception of time. It is generally believed that in environments with warm colors, time is overestimated. On the other hand, cool colors produce the opposite effect: Time is underestimated.

Linda Clark tells of an experiment that seems to substantiate this belief. Two groups of salesmen, having removed their watches, were assigned to separate meeting rooms—one group in a red room, the other, a green room. The "red" group guessed that it had spent twice as much time in the meeting, whereas the "green" group thought it had spent less time in the meeting than actually had elapsed.

A study conducted by an American psychologist produced opposite results (reported by Porter and Mikellides). Two identical lectures were presented to two separate audiences—one seated in a blue theater, the other in a red one. The audience in the blue theater felt rather bored and was under the impression that the lecture had lasted longer than it had. The group in the red theater found that time had passed quickly and the lecture had been interesting.

Findings of an experiment performed by a British university were similar. Participants in a meeting held in brightly colored surroundings judged it to have lasted 45 minutes less than an identical meeting held in a subtly colored room.

Although there is as yet no resolution to the question of which hues affect the over- or underestimation of time, it can be concluded from these experiment that color apparently does influence the judgment of time.

Synesthesia—The Unity of the Senses

There is no doubt that a unity exists from one sense to another. Perception is not a mosaic of separate sense stimulations. In Gestalt psychology the entire organism is looked upon as a unity. It seems that the centers for processing sensory information are linked to each other, leading to cross talk between and among the senses.

Colors may evoke associations with odor and taste, appear heavy or light, give tactile impressions, be associated with sound, have volume and temperature associations. These associations are very real and play a very important role in the design of the environment and in advertising—anything where color is used to inform and communicate.

Perception of Volume

Lightness is one of the most important factors in our perception of openness in interior spaces. Light or pale colors recede and increase the apparent room size, as do cooler colors and smaller patterns.

Dark or saturated hues protrude and decrease the apparent size of a room. In general, it may also be said that warm color and large patterns have the same effect.

A high illumination level will enlarge the appearance of volume, whereas a low illumination will diminish it.

Perception of Weight and Size

In general, darker colors appear heavier, whereas lighter and less saturated (pastel) tones seem less dense. If the hues are of the same value and intensity, the tendency is to perceive the warmer hues as heavier.

Good use of these effects can be made in factories and workshops. Bases for machinery and equipment will appear steadier and more solid if they are painted darker than the equipment itself. A piece of heavy machinery painted dark green, for example, will seem imbalanced, shaky, and awkward if it rests on yellow feet.

Heavy objects designed to be moved, carried, or thrown by human effort may be made to appear less heavy with lighter and cooler colors. Cool colors will also make things appear shorter and smaller; warm colors make them seem longer and larger. It is essential that such color design decisions are made on location and with consideration of the whole picture.

In regard to general interiors, extremely high ceilings may be painted in darker and warmer hues—if the objective is to make it seem lower. The heaviness of the darker hue, with its characteristic of advancing, will achieve that effect. Likewise, low ceilings will appear higher if painted in light colors, especially cooler tones.

Perception of Temperature

A long-favored hypothesis maintains that color has the power to suggest warmth or coolness. People are fairly unanimous in their opinion of colors that visually induce either effect.

In his book *The Elements of Color,* Johannes Itten tells of experiments that demonstrated a difference of five to seven degrees in the subjective feeling of heat or cold between a workroom painted blue-green and one painted red-orange. Occupants of the blue-green room felt that 59 degrees Fahrenheit was cold, whereas the temperature had to fall to 52 degrees in the red-orange room before the subjects felt cold.

Another example from Clark's research is that of an air-conditioned factory cafeteria with light-blue walls. Employees complained of the cold, although the thermostat was set at 75 degrees Fahrenheit. The walls were repainted orange and the 75-degree temperature setting, then considered too warm, was reduced to 72.

A Norwegian study produced similar results. People tended to set the thermostat four degrees higher in a blue room than in a red room (Porter and Mikellides).

It's been shown that one will feel cooler in a blue room than in an orange room. However, there are some other elements to be considered regarding warm and cold. In his 1971 study Hans Scheurle reported that most test subjects found the red room to be significantly warmer than the blue room, although temperature settings were the same for both. However, two subjects felt decidedly warmer in the blue room after a certain amount of time had elapsed. Other subjects did not feel the same degree of warmth but did express that after having been exposed to the warm "red room," then to the initially cold "blue room," their feeling of warmth returned to normal.

Scheurle proposes the hypothesis that since the body will always try to normalize a situation (heat, through sweating thereby trying to cool the body; compensation for cold by an increase in the rate of metabolism) this feeling of warmth could be due to the organism's normal reaction. However, if excessive warmth or heat is present in an environment, the body's reaction to compensate may be subjectively supported by the use of a cool color, and vice versa through a warm color in the case of cold.

Colors also absorb and retain heat in various degrees, depending on their light-reflection ratio. The lighter the color, the more light (therefore heat) is reflected; the darker the color, the more light is absorbed. In essence this would mean that indoors (where there is less heat loss than outside—light being reflected outward) a lighter color would throw back more heat from the walls than a darker one. However, this would be minimal, and in practical situations where people are exposed to high temperatures cool colors should be applied and vice versa, as noted earlier. Colors that are considered hot/warm are red, orange, yellow-ochre, pure yellow, yellow-orange. Definitely cool are green, blue-green, and blue (with some blues appearing warmer—as has been explained previously). With other colors, such as pink, yellow-green, and violet much depends on their hue position, and in interior design, on the colors that are used with them as accents.

Perception of Noise and Sound

Phenomena in which sounds will affect color perception have been reviewed by Gestalt psychologists such as Heinz Werner. Krakov, Allen, and Schwartz (quoted in Birren 1982) found that loud noises, strong odors, and strong tastes make the eye more sensitive to green and less sensitive to red.

For design purposes, the designer may profit from the relationship between noise and color that is more in the nature of mental association. Stimulation of the senses, brightness, and loudness are associated with the most active effect of warm colors, the reverse being true for cool colors. People mentally connect a loud red with one of high saturation. Rarely does one speak of a loud blue or green. High-pitched and shrill sounds tend to be compared with saturated and light hues.

These associations can be used to compensate visually for noise problems, especially in work environments such as industrial plants. A noisy atmosphere will be experienced subjectively as noisier or more bothersome if painted with glaring yellows or reds. Shrill and high-pitched sounds may be offset by olive green. Muffled sounds appear more so in darker-hued surroundings, and lighter colors, such as light, clean greens (slightly toward yellow), can be used to compensate.

Heinrich Frieling, director of the Institute of Color Psychology, has done extensive testing with color and their synesthetic effects. He assigns (Frieling 1980) the following sound associations to various colors:

Red: loud, trumpet

Pink: soft, delicate

Orange: loud, major key

Brown: dark, deep, minor key

Gold-Yellow: fanfare, major key

Yellow: shrill, major key

Yellow-Green: high-pitched, minor key

Green: muffled (when dull), shrill (when saturated)

Green-Blue: soft

Blue: distant, flute to violin

Ultramarine: dark, deep, more minor key

Violet: sad, deep, minor key

Light Purple: weak, restrained

Crimson: powerful, stately

Associations of Odor and Taste

Colors that hold pleasant associations with smell are pink, lavender, pale yellow, and green. Tints of coral, peach, soft yellow, light green, flamingo, and pumpkin have pleasant associations with taste.

Some industries (such as food processing or perfume making) produce odors that (whether agreeable or not) may be so penetrating as to become a nuisance. It is almost possible to "taste" the smell. The association of certain colors with particular odors only exacerbates the problem. A solution is to use colors that are contrary in their association to the problem color. (For details, see Chapter 13, "Industrial Work Environments.")

The Institute of Color Psychology under Frieling has compiled a listing of odor/taste associations:

Red: sweet, strong

Pink: sweetish, mild

Orange: strong

Brown: musty, roast

Yellow: sour

Yellow-Green: sour, tangy

Green: sour, juicy

Green-Blue: fresh to salty

Blue: odorless

Violet: narcotic, heavy, sweet

Light Purple: sweetly tangy

Tactile Associations

Colors also give an impression of texture, or sense of touch. Red appears firm and solid; as it is modified and becomes pink the texture turns finer and less solid. Orange appears dry, whereas darkened to a brown it remains dry, but depending on exact hue position it may appear from lumpy to muddy. Sand, a yellow-ochre, gives the impression of being sandy and crumbly. Yellow is smooth and lightlike. Green appears from smooth to damp; it becomes softer, smoother, and watery as it becomes blue-green. Blue is smooth; lighter blues seem less palpable and more atmospheric. Ultramarine, violet, and crimson have a velvety appearance.

The Finer Points of Color Psychology

This chapter has discussed the basic effects, associations, and impressions of major colors. Basic as it is, these primary aspects will help the color designer to start at the fundamentals and from there develop the finer points necessary to find the ultimate (best) color for a specific design situation. In the field of applied color psychology the true professional will always analyze all the different variables involved in conjunction with the various aspects of color's psychological effects.

The color designer must consider that a hue may make the same overall statement as another one, yet it may differ in its expression. For example, the expression of calm or peaceful, in contrast to liveliness and excitement, can be expressed through green and also by gray—it being "nonexciting." However, green carries with it the element or essence of life or life-giving (nature, growth), a relaxation that carries with it the regeneration of energy, the reason we relax in the first place. Whereas with gray, also a color with a low excitement value, there is no vitality, and it is nonexciting due to weakness. Clearly two distinct calm/peaceful statements are made here: one with the element of vitality (healthy); the other with the absence of vitality (weakness, unhealthy).

We can carry this further by forming two mental images to illustrate the point: the "healthy" person relaxing on a meadow, and the other ashen-faced (gray) lying in a hospital bed—both in essence being in a state of nonexcitement of repose. Carrying this over to a particular hospital patient room, for example, which is meant to be nonexciting or nonarousing, ask yourself which is more beneficial to recuperation?

We can carry the same consideration over to marketing and package design. Let's take for example product packaging. Everyone has certain expectations of a product. The color or color combination must meet those expectations. Let us use as an example the packaging for tranquilizers. It is obvious that it would be absurd to package tranquilizers in red and orange colors that symbolize excitement, intensity, and activity. Certainly it's more logical to choose colors that reflect calm and quiet.

Yes, there are many colors that appear nonexciting and calming. But the correct choice should not be so lethargic and weak as to associate it with death. After all, the consumer wishes an "active" effect that helps him reach the state of calmness. The package could be printed in gray, but although neutral and nonarousing, this choice would be an incorrect one. Again, the best choice is a not-too-strong yet refreshing green, because of its characteristic association with relaxation and regeneration of energy. The argument could also be made for a deep blue, a color that carries a high degree of calmness, but at the same time it suggests a sleeping pill. With a tranquilizer the aim is not to sleep, but to change an abnormal level of excitement to a normal state, without losing our ability to function (as would be the case in a sleeping state).

Color psychology is always being accused of generalizing. I think that's an unfair generalization! It is only the novice or inexperienced designer who picks up the obvious sweeping generalities instead of looking at color in detail and context. Unfortunately, authors can only cite the generalities, because we cannot cover all situations case by case. We must trust the reader to utilize the information given (the tool) and build from there through serious thought and analysis. Color is information, just as speech is information. Knowing the alphabet makes it possible to form words to pass on information, but how this is done most effectively depends on the talent of the individual. The information presented in this chapter is color's psychological alphabet.

Chapter Five

Those Achromatic
Environments

For years, the use of white and off-white in interiors was so common that it reached epidemic proportions. The advent of white walls began around 1955 and reached its peak in 1975. After that the practice diminished somewhat—especially in the mid-80s. It resurged shortly after that, along with gray. The neutral trend escalated to such proportions as to permeate all types of man-made environments. Gray or white walls, gray floors, at time gray furnishings, too; an orgy of neutrality evident in homes, offices, banks, restaurants, ice-cream parlors, retail stores, and even health-care facilities.

The neutral trend is still present in most office buildings in order to present a high-tech image. I suppose the purpose is to reflect our modern technological world in terms of unadorned, clean, efficient, impersonal, futuristic surroundings of computer technology. The idea that business efficiency must be reflected by surroundings devoid of color defies logical explanation.

I doubt very seriously if gray and white will ever be replaced by a more rational color approach. The neutrals always make a resurgence after a period of trend tendencies that used too much color. Overstimulation becomes tiring, too, and using color for color's sake, meaning just to be colorful, is also unprofessional. A purposeful approach to color calls for the avoidance of both of these extremes.

First to make my case against white: During my many years of collecting reference material on color and light, I have not yet come across any pronouncement that supports white and off-white on psychological or physiological grounds for prompting its wide use. As early as 1947, Louis Chesking pronounced: "White walls, as we know, are an optical strain and a psychological hazard." Over the years, this simple truth has been echoed again and again by many who have been concerned with color beyond its decorative value. In 1984, a West German government agency issued a study by Heinrich Frieling on color in the work environment. The study's conclusion about white walls: empty, neutral, no vitality.

On a psychological basis, white is sterile. Unless negation is the desired result, it fails to have much psychotherapeutic value. It has been noted that reaction to white is one of bored disinterest. K. Warner Schaie, employing a color pyramid test, found that the incidence of the use of white and black was significantly higher among schizophrenics than among normal persons (quoted in Birren 1978).

It is often argued that white in interiors is an ideal background to set off colored decorative effects. Regardless of accent color distribution, the main impression of the environment more than likely will remain white. Also, the contrast between white and highly colored accessories may require extreme adaptive changes from light to dark—a cause of eye fatigue. (See Figure C-17.) On the other hand, colors of low saturation set against white will look bland and commonplace.

Those who found the "hospital green" of the past unpleasant because of its institutional associations can place white in the same category. Psychologists now are in general agreement that institutions should look anything but institutional. White runs contrary to that school of thought. Its use has tragic effects in old-age or convalescent homes, where many are totally confined indoors or for the greater part of their day.

Especially sad are Alzheimer facilities painted in white. Specialists agree that these patients should not be subjected to sensory deprivation. It is counterproductive for patients with cognitive handicaps that require stimulation to be treated in a low-stimulus environment. Surely, the environment should also not be so overstimulated as to send out conflicting and chaotic signals.

People need sensory variety, and this includes color. Monotony only induces anxiety, tension, fear, and distress. Environments that are predominantly neutral in appearance are beyond any positive value and will always appear static, boring, and tedious. It is also doubtful that a hospitalized person, perhaps already near the mental breaking point, under emotional strain, or recovering from surgical treatment, will have his spirits lifted by a preponderance of white walls.

White, when accompanied by high levels of natural or artificial light, may also play havoc with human vision. High environmental brightness demands fatiguing action of the eye muscles by severely constricting the pupil opening. It handicaps vision by producing distressing glare akin to snow blindness. Prolonged exposure to high brightness can cause damage to the visual organ, or further aggravate existing eye problems.

To illustrate the point, I quote Armando Valladares, a former political prisoner in Cuba, from the August 15, 1983, issue of *Time* magazine:

> *By August, the authorities had built special premises so as to keep me in utter solitary confinement. The walls and ceiling were painted dazzling white, and just above my head, my jailer installed ten neon tubes about five feet long. These were kept on all the time, throwing off a blinding light that caused my sight to be damaged.*

Many complaints of eyestrain often can be corrected by removing the glare of walls without changing light levels. Had architects and designers adhered to recommended light-reflection levels of walls, the use of white and off-white might never have come about. Recommended reflectances for wall surfaces have always been 40 to 60 percent; this can be stretched, depending on lighting conditions, to 70 percent. The minimum light reflection level of off-white, warm or cool tones, is approximately 81 percent, increasing to over 94 percent the purer white it becomes.

Another incorrect belief about white is that it makes interiors brighter. This depends, as shown above, on the light it reflects. In offices and other workplaces light levels remain constant, but in the home they do not. During the day homes are dependent on natural light falling through windows. And as we know, on an overcast or rainy day, white will turn grayish and shadowy. Colors of a certain saturation, however, bring their own luminosity with them that will not turn as grayish or shadowy as white does.

As far as gray is concerned, as explained in the previous chapter, it makes no statement. It is just there and lives in boring neutrality, making the environment neither exciting, nor actively calming, nor inviting. Whether or not the argument of elegance through restraint is sufficient to justify its use depends on the situation. There are so many other alternative choices for establishing elegance in a setting.

White and gray need not be used as predominant colors. Better choices can be established quite quickly through analysis with a polarity profile. White is especially often used as a matter of expediency, or by those not yet sure of themselves in their approaches to color. In this respect, white is considered a "safe" choice, evoking neither positive nor negative comment. People have been conditioned to white by its overabundant use (if things continue, gray will fall into the same category). But does it really justify aesthetically and psychologically sterile environments? For every argument made defending the use of predominant white walls in the environment, the color specialist can find a better solution for the argument "in color."

Color Fundamentals

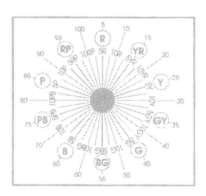

Munsell Color Wheel,
courtesy of MacBeth, New
Windsor, New York.

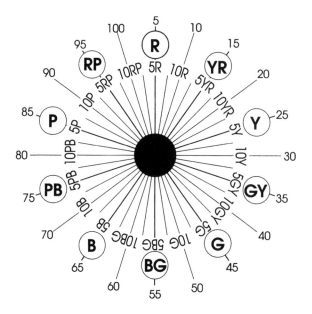

This chapter provides a brief overview of the color fundamentals that designers must know in their everyday work. It is brief because readers have access to entire books on this topic alone. (A list of recommended English and German references appears in the Bibliography; some may be out of print, but copies are available in major libraries.)

The color notations that follow in this chapter are based on the Munsell ten-hue color wheel, illustrated above. Beginning color students are often confused by the differences among color scholars in their notations and explanations of color systems. For example, in some references the complement of red is identified as green, and in others as blue-green. This doesn't reflect disagreement on the basics of color theory, but simply differing ways of positioning color on the wheel and making color identifications. The twelve-hue color wheel, for example, is divided into red, red-orange, orange, yellow-orange, yellow, yellow-green, green, blue-green, blue, blue-violet, violet, and red-violet, while the Munsell ten-hue color-wheel divisions are red, yellow-red, yellow, green-yellow, green, blue-green, blue, purple-blue, purple, and red-purple.

The Color Attributes: Hue, Saturation, and Lightness

Hue is the quality or characteristic by which one color is distinguished from another. The elementary hues that we differentiate are based on the spectral hues red, orange, yellow, green, blue, and violet. All colors are judged to be similar to one hue or a proportion of two of the spectral hues. Thus crimson, vermillion, and pink are close in hue, although they are different colors. Physically, hue is determined by wavelength.

White, gray, and black are perceived as colorless, being neither reddish, yellowish, greenish, or bluish. This lack of color *(chroma)* causes them to be termed achromatic.

Saturation is the second attribute by which a color is distinguished. Also referred to as strength, intensity, or chroma, it designates the purity of a given color, the quality that distinguishes it from a grayed, or weaker color. Two colors may be exactly the same hue, and one no lighter or darker than the other, yet still appear different in color strength.

Lightness, or *value,* is the third dimension in color description. It is the quality that differentiates a dark color from a light one. The lightness of a pigment is a measure of how much light is reflected from its surface. Sometimes brightness is used as a synonym for lightness— which may be confusing. *Brightness* means the intensity of a light source or a luminous sensation when describing light, and it means highly saturated when describing color.

Color Contrasts

The principles or effects of color contrasts determine how a color is perceived, how a color scheme is developed, and how objects are highlighted or partially concealed.

Since the three attributes of color are hue, saturation, and lightness, it is easy to identify the three basic contrasts: hue contrast, saturation contrast, and lightness contrast. What is red cannot be green; a strong green is not a weak green; a light blue is not a dark blue. Within these categories alone, countless possibilities exist for achieving a desired result.

Exploration of these contrasts is a good starting point for effective color design; detailed study and practical experimentation is essential. Without it, the designer risks unpleasant visual and aesthetic consequences.

Color contrasts may be helpful or harmful, and they are always present in the environment in one form or another. (See Figure C-53.) Here are some general hints:

1. Hues similar in saturation and value can unify a room and make a space seem larger. However, be sure to avoid monotony.

2. Contrast between walls and furnishings will make the furnishings more prominent.

3. Hue, value, and saturation contrast emphasize contours.

4. Visual spaciousness increases when similar colors are carried from one room to another.

Successive Contrast

If your eye becomes adapted to a particular hue by staring at it for some time, and then you shift your gaze to a white (or gray) surface, the complementary color will appear upon that surface. A white surface will look pale green, for example, after your eye has first adapted to a red-purple stimulus. This is referred to as the *afterimage phenomenon.*

The afterimages are understood as a fatigue effect. As the cones in the retina adapt to a particular color, let us say red, the red-sensitive photoreceptors will be temporarily fatigued and as the red stimulus is replaced by white, they respond less strongly to all the light rays reflected from the white surface. Only those sensitive to the complementary color (in this case, blue-green) will function fully.

The effect is not permanent, but the color patch that seems to float in front of the eyes can be disturbing. This is especially true when performing tasks that require continuous focus on objects of the same color. To illustrate this point, let's review a case history involving a pharmaceutical factory.

Production line workers who were assigned to check purple pills complained of migraines and of seeing green spots in front of their eyes. The problem was eliminated by surrounding the employees with green screens, against which the spots did not show. Company management had realized that green was the afterimage of purple-red, and therefore the green spots were the afterimage of the color of the pills.

To illustrate the point further, we can go back to the days when operating rooms in hospitals were white, as were the cover sheets and surgical gowns. Surgeons working at a strongly illuminated operating table were disturbed by the afterimages of blood and tissue that appeared when they would look temporarily at the white walls, cover sheet, or the white gowns of their colleagues. Most gowns, cover sheets, and walls are now green or blue-green, and the problem has been nearly eliminated.

The physiological reality is that the eye requires any given color to be balanced by its complementary, and will generate it if it is not present. Complementary colors also provide the psychological balance of warmth and coolness of color. There is a strong tendency for people to unconsciously seek warm and cool hues in the same space.

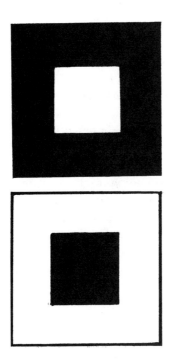

Afterimage is the complementary of a color that appear when the eye has been fatigued by that color. These complements are seen lighter or paler and never in their full chromaticity.

Color consultant and author Louis Cheskin tells of an experiment with three rooms in green. One was treated in a single shade of green, which elicited negative reactions due to monotony. The second room, in three values of green, was considered neither favorable nor unfavorable. The third room was also in three values of green but included the complementary color of one of the values of green (wine red), and reactions were 94-percent favorable.

The physiological phenomenon of afterimage is often used as proof that complementary colors are the basis of harmonious design. Also, when complementary colors are placed next to each other, the effect is both stimulating and pleasing because the afterimage of one enhances the other. A predominantly orange room, for instance, should have spots of complementary blue.

The concept of complementary hues is based on the color wheel; those colors placed directly opposite are considered complementary. In practical color application for architectural spaces it is impossible to seek technically exact complementaries, nor is it necessary. First of all, it's almost impossible to make an exact match among the standard wall paints, wall coverings, and upholstery fabrics that a designer has to work with. Second, exact matches would limit overall color design considerations. The often-quoted maxim that true complementaries must mix or spin to gray may be filed away under things that are good to know, but in environmental design hard to do.

Simultaneous Contrast

Rarely is a color seen in isolation; in the visual field, different colors usually are seen simultaneously. This creates an optical effect closely related to successive contrast (afterimage). The eye will generate the complement of the hue that it is seeing and project it toward the color adjacent to or superimposed upon it. The French chemist M. Chevreul, director of the Gobelins tapestry firm during the 19th century, called this effect *simultaneous contrast,* experimented extensively with it, and applied his findings to the weaving of tapestries.

The effect can be demonstrated by a simple experiment. Place a neutral gray on a surrounding red background, and notice that the gray is tinged with blue-green (the complementary of red—using the Munsell ten-hue color wheel of color notation). Simultaneous contrast occurs not only between gray and a strong colored background, but also between any two hues (as long as they are complementary). Each of the two hues tends to shift the other toward its own complement. Achromatic simultaneous contrast will make a gray appear dark against a light background, yet light against a dark background.

The effect of simultaneous contrast is more pronounced when the background is saturated and when it completely surrounds the surface being contrasted. Other observations show that closely related hues will lose some of their brightness, while complementary colors adjoining each other become intensified.

Color Harmonies and Combinations

Colors were once chosen in terms of definite harmonious color schemes. Today many designers reject rigid rules in favor of innovative artistic choices. Both camps have been able to argue their cases effectively. I, however, am more concerned with the psychological and physiological effects of colors in the environment than with personal artistic statements. In environments in which work must be performed, people's welfare must be considered, and learning must occur, the role of color is more than merely to entertain the senses.

The functional role of color must nonetheless include beauty. It can never be assumed that beauty is unnecessary for mental well-being. Beauty or pleasantness might be an elusive element; what one person may consider beautiful, another may question. But there are color schemes that are pleasant and satisfying, just as there are unpleasant or discordant ones. In general, people react favorably to harmonious surroundings, and few people are completely oblivious to discord.

Awareness of traditional color harmonies is useful in understanding why certain colors work together and why some do not. The fact that they are considered too rigid by some colorists is surprising; it would be quite a task to exhaust all their possibilities. Color harmonies fall into two broad categories: related and contrasting. Related harmonies are subdivided into monochromatic and analogous. Contrasting color harmonies unite hues that are separated on the color wheel. The most common of these harmonies is the complementary color scheme.

Monochromatic harmonies are based on one hue varied in value and saturation—for example, pale green with pure green and dark green. With regard to interior design, there is real danger of monotony in such an arrangement. Used as a background for brighter tones of other colors, this scheme may serve a good purpose, but the overall color arrangement then ceases to be a true monochromatic harmony.

Analogues, or related harmonies combine usually no more than three colors next to each other on the color wheel. The three hues are unified because of a shared color—for instance, red, yellow-red, and yellow; green, blue-green, and blue. Analogous color schemes offer more variety than monochromatic ones, but neither type will satisfy the problem of the afterimage phenomenon described earlier.

Complementary schemes are based on hues directly opposite each other on the color wheel. Examples are red and blue-green; yellow-red (orange) and blue; purple-blue and yellow. These harmonies offer more contrast and introduce both warm and cool colors into the environment. Careful handling of value and intensity, as with all contrasting schemes, is a prerequisite to ensure the success of these combinations.

Analogous-complementary is a term that could be used to describe a modification of the complementary scheme. This harmony is achieved by choosing two colors next to each other and combining them with the complementary of one of the two; for example, yellow-red and yellow combined with blue, the complementary of yellow-red.

Split-complementary harmony consists of one color and the two tones adjoining its complementary color. For instance, the complementary of red is blue-green, which is bordered by blue and green. The arrangement would comprise red, blue, and green.

Double-complementary schemes recommend the use of two closely related hues and their complements. One example would be yellow-red and yellow with blue and purple-blue.

Other systematic variations of color relationships that are considered harmonious are triads and tetrads. Triads use three colors as equally spaced as possible on the color wheel, while tetrads are any four hues equidistant from each other.

According to the traditional school of colorists, complementary colors produce harmony and balance. According to the modern school of colorists, noncomplementary colors produce asymmetry and tension. Asymmetric harmony is based on two or more colors from one side of the color wheel without any shared hue. As with any asymmetric pattern, this creates tension. In some interior design, there is nothing incorrect about tension—as long as there is also relief from it. Then there is the eclectic approach, which uses neither of these two orientations. Here the selection of color is not based on complementary or noncomplementary color systems, or any rules, but rather on the colorist's personal interpretation of what may be appropriate for a given setting.

It is difficult to pass judgment on the asymmetric or eclectic approach without examining actual combinations. This holds true for any of the color harmony systems, since so much depends on their area (amount), value, and intensity relationships. The use of the complementary harmony system in architectural design doesn't exactly mean we can paint two walls in a room red and the other two blue-green. That would produce no harmony at all. It could mean, however, that we can paint all walls blue-green and the doors red, as long as there is a balance in value and intensity. But be aware of one caveat that should not be overlooked by practitioners of the asymmetric/eclectic school: When it comes to interior spaces discussed in this book, the uses of these two methods are limited. This should be very obvious from the word *tension*, which creates environmental conditions that are contrary to many of the psychophysiological principles I discuss.

A Word About Color Systems

Anyone working seriously with color will find it necessary to understand and use some kind of color classification system. Color systems are an aid to composition. They bring order into the confusion of the color range. Colors are presented in sequence and in their relationship to each other, and they are neatly listed by hue, saturation, lightness, and interval.

Unfortunately, no international system has yet been established. Almost every major industrial nation has its own color standards, and most industries in which color is important have developed their own systems—none of which are interchangeable. The Commission Internationale de l'Eclairage (CIE) has devised a color system based on spectrophotometric measurements of a color sample. It's the last word in accuracy, but for everyday practical use, it is not as convenient as those systems composed of color chips or patches with which a sample can be matched visually. CIE specifications are presented in mathematical form, so it is necessary to refer to color samples built up from coordinates.

Most color systems classify color in terms of hue, lightness, and saturation. Some systems describe colors by their content, referring to the proportions of white, black, or full color contained in a particular hue. (A full color is one considered to be highly saturated and at the same time as light as possible.)

Munsell System (Munsell Book of Color)

One of the most widely used methods of color notation is the American Munsell system, which is explained here in some detail. There are many other systems available, each claiming to be the most efficient. I do not attempt to pass judgment on them all or analyze which system is better than another. Munsell is the one I have chosen to explain because many of my notations describing colors and their relationships are based on the Munsell Color Wheel, as illustrated on page 84. My early academic training in the language of color was based on that wheel, which incorporates three elementary color criteria: how a specific color stands in relation to others; how it will look when modified in lightness or darkness; and how it will look when changed in strength or weakness (pureness).

Munsell colors are identified in terms of three attributes: hue, value (lightness), and chroma (saturation). Chosen so that the colors appear equally spaced, Munsell uses five principal and five intermediary hues. Arranged clockwise on the color wheel by name (abbreviated by initials), they are: red (R), yellow-red (YR), yellow (Y), green-yellow (GY), green (G), blue-green (BG), blue (B), purple-blue (PB), purple (P), and red-purple (RP). Each named hue is subdivided further into four sections and designated 2.5, 5, 7.5, and 10, followed by its hue initial 2.5R, 5R, 7.5R, 10R. These are shown at the inner circle of the color wheel and may be used for rough identification of hue. Each named color is also divided into ten sections denoted by the numerals 1 to 100 and shown on the outer circle of the color wheel.

The second dimension of the Munsell system is value notation— the degree of lightness or darkness of a color in relation to a neutral scale. The scale extends from absolute black (value symbol 0) to absolute white (value symbol 10). The symbol 5 designates the middle value for gray and all chromatic colors that appear halfway in value between black and white. For example, a green with the notation 9 would be a light green; with the notation 3, a dark green.

Chroma, or saturation, indicating strength or purity of color, is the third classification. Chroma notation is given from /0 for a neutral gray to /10, /14, or /16, depending on the saturation of a particular color.

Through this method, a color is identified by its three attributes (hue, value, chroma) instead of by ambiguous names indicating vague identity, such as sky blue, primrose yellow, or mint green. Munsell notation for a chromatic color is therefore written in symbols showing its hue, value, and chroma position. For instance, a pink of moderate strength might be indicated as 5R 8/4 (5R = hue position, 8 = value, 4 = chroma).

The three Munsell color dimensions can be visualized in terms of a color space. The central vertical axis is the neutral-value gray scale, graded in equal visual steps from black to white. The hue scale, also equal in visual steps, is positioned around the neutral gray axis. Chroma scales radiate in equal visual steps outward from the neutral axis to the periphery of the color space.

Paint Color Systems

Almost every designer and architect works with one or more paint systems in specifying interior or exterior colors. All paint manufacturers have their own color systems related to their stock or custom-mixed colors. Most of these are adequate for their purposes; some are more elaborate than others. They should not be confused, however, with the color specification systems discussed previously. In many cases written identification is made for hue, and colors usually are presented in some order in regard to chroma and value. But no written or symbolic notation is given for a color's saturation and lightness, so visual judgments must be made. This is adequate, as long as the colors selected for a particular project come from the same paint manufacturer.

One system's superiority over another depends on the variety and amount of colors available, how the system is organized to facilitate design work, and the designer's individual preference.

Chapter Seven

Vision and Light

Vision, the richest human sense, provides us with a wealth of information we would not receive without light—the basic stimulus for vision. Both have a decisive influence on our reactions, ability to concentrate, efficiency, fatigue, and general well-being. The ability of the eyes to function on an optimal level is in direct relationship to light. Therefore, light and the environment where it is to be installed have to adapt themselves to the physiological laws of vision.

The Optical System

Since the eyes and light work directly together, environmental design applications demand a fundamental knowledge of the human optical system. A brief review follows.

The Structure of the Eye

Basically, the eye consists of the cornea, the iris, the lens, and the retina. The cornea, which serves as a preliminary lens helping to focus light, is the transparent covering in front of the eye. Incoming light enters the cornea and passes through the pupil, the opening in the center of the eye. The amount of light admitted through the pupil is controlled by a ring of muscles called the iris (whose pigmentation determines the eye's color). The path continues through the lens, which modifies its curvature to focus the light so that it produces a clear image on the retina.

The retina, the inner surface of the eye, is an intricate network of receptor cells and neurons where light is converted into neural impulses that are forwarded to the brain. The retina contains two types of photoreceptor cells: rods and cones. In dim light, the rods (about 120 million in one eye) react to brightness but not to color. Rods contain rhodopsin, a photopigment that is much more light-sensitive than are photopigments in the cones. Thus, rods can operate in dim light when cones become useless. The cones (about six million in one eye) operate in increased light and are responsible for detailed vision and color perception. Rods predominate in the peripheral regions of the retina, whereas cones are concentrated in the central region of the retina. Cones are the only receptors in the very center of the retinal area that lies almost directly opposite the pupil—the fovea. The fovea is the region of most distinct or detailed vision.

After photochemically registering the presence of light, the rods and cones pass their electrical potential through bipolar cells to ganglion cells. The axons of ganglion cells form the optic nerve, which relays visual information to the brain. When the brain responds to these impulses and analyzes the message it has received, we begin to see.

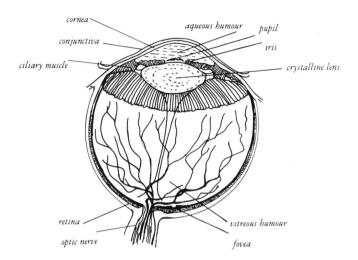

cornea
aqueous humour
pupil
conjunctiva
iris
ciliary muscle
crystalline lens
retina
vitreous humour
optic nerve
fovea

The Eye Muscles

The eye has both internal and external muscles. The external muscles direct the eyes to a point of interest, and they work together to keep both eyes centered upon it. Internal muscles control focusing and pupil size.

The process by which the eye changes focus from one distance to another is called *accommodation*. To change focus, the shape of the lens must change, which involves the ciliary muscle. This muscle is connected to an elastic ring of suspensory ligaments (zonula) around the lens of the eye. In its resting state, the eye is set for distant vision, the ciliary muscle is relaxed, and the suspensory ligaments are tense. When a near object is to be viewed, the ciliary muscle contracts to reduce the tension on the suspensory ligaments thereby changing the curvature of the lens. The ciliary muscle must exert a continuous contracting force to maintain focus on a near object.

Adaptation is the immediate reaction of the eye to changes in the degree of illumination or brightness. The widening or narrowing of the pupil size is accomplished by the tiny muscles in the iris.

Color Vision

Color exists only in our brain. Color is actually the result of different wavelengths of light stimulating certain parts of the brain. The experience of color depends on the intensity of light, the way it is reflected from a surface, and the color surrounding objects.

Many aspects of color vision are still not well understood. Among the several theories proposed are the opponent-process theory and the trichromatic theory, these being the two major ones. Many investigators believe that perhaps elements of both theories are at work.

The trichromatic is perhaps the major one. First advanced in the 19th century by Thomas Young and elaborated by Hermann von Helmholtz, it proposes that color vision is based on three types of cones, each type most sensitive to wavelengths of red, green, or blue respectively. All colors are seen through combinations of them.

Color Blindness

Color blindness is an inherited condition, and it is mostly men who are affected. The gene linked to color vision is the X chromosome; men have only one X chromosome, women have two. This means that both X chromosomes in women would have to carry the defect, which happens rarely.

Color blindness is thought to be caused by either a lack or reduced number of cones of a given type. The type of cone involved and to what degree determines which colors are affected. The condition of not being able to see any color is rare and would depend on all three types of cones being affected.

The Environment and Agreeable Visual Conditions

The question of how much light is needed for clear and comfortable vision has been belabored for many years by lighting engineers. Too little light will handicap vision and too much will overtax it. The technical engineering of lighting installations usually is out of the hands of the designer, but he or she does have control over the relationship between light and the quality of the visual environment.

In the design of a space, concern must be shown for conditions that will affect visual efficiency and comfort. It is often assumed that eye fatigue is a matter of retinal nerve fatigue; this is not so. The retina seems more or less immune to fatigue and can take much stress. It is the muscles, not eye nerves, that are likely to cause trouble. Just like any muscle subjected to excessive activity, eye muscles will tire. Glare, constant adjustment to extreme brightness differences, prolonged fixation of the eyes, and constant shifts in accommodation will tire eyes quickly, causing headaches, tension, nausea, and other disturbances.

Control of extreme contrasts in darkness and light is essential. If these contrasts are not regulated, the iris muscles experience undue stress because the pupil is forced to undergo constant adjustment. E. Grandjean of the Institute for Industrial Hygiene and Work Physiology in Zurich reports on a study where properly controlled brightness contrasts in a work environment significantly increased performance and decreased physiological fatigue.

Vision should be held at midtones, an ideal light-to-reflection ratio being three to one. This means controlling the light-reflection ratios of walls, furniture, and floors. Recommended reflectances for surfaces are 20 percent for floors; 25–40 percent for furniture; 40–60 percent for walls (which can be stretched to 70 percent depending on lighting conditions); and 80–90 percent for ceilings. These percentages may be raised somewhat as long as the three-to-one ratio is respected. Insufficient or feeble contrasts are also emotionally unsatisfying and should be avoided, just as strong contrasts, besides being bothering to the eyes, add to the complexity of a space. (See Figures C-18 and C-19.)

Glare also puts debilitating strain on the eyes. Direct glare results from insufficiently shielded light sources, the extreme being bare bulbs. Unshaded windows can also cause direct glare. Individuals should be situated so that they do not face windows. Window walls should always be light in color to eliminate strong brightness contrasts between dark walls and the entering sunlight. Reflected glare results from specular reflections of high luminances on polished surfaces. This is one of the reasons that matte work surfaces and walls are highly recommended.

Light sources, whether of high or low intensity, always should be properly baffled with louvers or lenses. For work tasks demanding a great deal of light, a localized light source may be introduced, but this should never be done in an otherwise dark room.

Light's Effect on Color

Careful control of color is as important for an agreeable environment as are brightness controls. On a practical basis, this means one of two things: Either color is adjusted to an environment's existing lights (which is less desirable, since they might be changed); or color and lights are specified simultaneously. Depending on a light's spectral distribution in the visible region, color shifts do occur, and some lights render colors better than others. What is also involved is the color of the light itself. For example, is it a warm light (orange glow) or a cool one (bluish glow)?

Observations made by A. A. Kruithof in 1941 are worth noting here. He found that people prefer a cool color temperature when illumination is intense and a warmer color temperature when illumination is low. He also reported that objects and surfaces will have a normal color appearance under warm light at low intensity and under cool light at high intensity.

It is crucial to understand the spectral quality of artificial light in order to know how it will affect color. A brief explanation follows.

Spectral Power Distribution

The amount of power from a light source in each color band or spectral region is called spectral power distribution (SPD). For instance, the energy output of the standard cool-white fluorescent lamp is concentrated in the yellow-green region of the spectrum where the eye is more sensitive to brightness. This was designed to maximize achromatic visibility, thus making it quite different from natural light, which has a more even distribution. Other features can be determined from the SPD.

Color Rendering Index

The color rendering index (CRI) was developed to describe how well colors (including the appearances of people) are rendered by artificial light sources compared with natural light. It must be emphasized that this is a measure of how a light source compares with natural light at a specific *correlated color temperature*. High-CRI lamps provide illumination that affects the color of objects in the same way that natural light does. Phases of natural light vary according to such factors as season, time of day, and weather; these different phases result in color temperatures measured by degrees Kelvin (K). Any source can give a cool cast to colors if its correlated color temperature is high, or a warm cast if it is low. Therefore, the CRI should never be used without relating it to the correlated color temperature.

The CRI measure for natural outdoor light is 100. The higher the CRI of a lamp (also taking into account the color of the light source itself), the more it renders colors in the environment as "true." In other words, spectral distribution of the visible light region is less distorted. Full-spectrum light sources, for instance, have a CRI of over 90; cool white, 68; warm white, 56; and some other types fall below 50.

Color Temperature

The term *color temperature* was devised to describe the color of light emitted by a natural source. The term refers to the temperature in degrees Kelvin at which a blackbody (a theoretically perfect radiator) would have to be heated to match the perceived color of the light source. To simplify, when the old-time blacksmith heated a piece of iron, the iron started to glow a deep red. As it got hotter, its color changed gradually until it finally became "white hot." The easiest way to describe the color of glowing metal is to give its temperature.

Color temperature applies only to natural sources (sun, sky, incandescent metal sources). When referring to light sources, such as fluorescent, mercury, and other arc lamps, the proper term is *correlated color temperature*. A warm-white fluorescent may have a correlated color temperature of 3,000 degrees Kelvin, giving it the appearance of a warm light (orange glow). Daylight fluorescent at 6,500 degrees Kelvin will cast a cooler light (bluish glow).

A Note on Perception

The field of perception has become a major subdivision of psychology and neurophysiology in the last two decades. In this chapter we have discussed "vision," which is the mechanism for "visual perception" and it is nothing more than a reconstruction of reality inside of our mind. Regarded this way, we could say everything is an illusion were it not for our power of perceptual organization. The brain expects certain things from reality. Since infancy we constantly add information or knowledge to the innate knowledge we have inherited. Using both of these "knowledges," the brain analyzes received images to achieve reality.

When sensory information is incomplete, the brain fills in missing details (one of the reasons why authors are appreciative of editors, who have the unusual ability to pick out errors, such as missing words, because the context of an entire passage influences one's perception of a sentence as a whole). This organization has been explained in various ways. One of these is Gestalt (from the German—meaning form or shape) psychology, which proposes that pieces of information are organized into meaningful patterns by the brain. According to this theory, when we look at a scene our minds grasp its full significance intuitively—grouping the array of stimuli to achieve simplicity. The brain also organizes sensations by dividing information into regions that represent objects (figure) and the spaces between figures (ground).

Illusions are not necessarily a mistake by the brain, which in most cases processes information as it is supposed to. But when visual cues are conflicting, making sense out of something depends on what we are looking for.

In practical color application, "figure" and "ground" are of importance, especially in the workplace. Recognizing objects is made much easier when the color of the object is set off from its background.

Chapter Eight

Biological Effects of Light

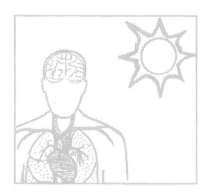

The lighting industry adhered for years to the belief that the only significant role light plays is to provide adequate illumination as an aid in
seeing. Although lamps were developed with efficient light emission,
they left great gaps in the full spectrum found in sunlight.

During the last thirty years it has become increasingly clear that
sunlight (natural global solar radiation) has a profound effect on the
human organism. As Rikard Küller, a Professor of Architectural Psychology at Lund University, stated:

> *The reason for this is firstly that solar radiation was important for the*
> *genesis of life itself; actually without light there would be no life. The*
> *second reason is that the development of higher life and man to this day*
> *occurred under the constant influence of solar radiation affecting living*
> *tissue from the single cell of the skin to the specially adapted light-*
> *sensitive eye. Thus the amount of light, the quality of light, the*
> *distribution of light, and the variation of light between day and night*
> *and winter and summer are closely tied to the genesis of man, and we are*
> *gaining better understanding of some of these ties. (Küller 1981, p. 9)*

In 1984, the New York Academy of Sciences presented a conference on medical and biological effects of light. The conference an-
nouncement explained their goals:

> *Environmental light produces numerous biological effects related to*
> *health beyond simply affecting vision and cutaneous pigmentation. Some*
> *of these involve direct responses of circulating or cutaneous chemicals to*
> *light waves; others are mediated by the brain and neuroendocrine organs.*
> *The sufficient excellent work that now exists warrants a conference that*
> *focuses on recent advances in the understanding of these effects—effects*
> *that may be important for the design of interior environments that*
> *optimize health.*

Many researchers hold the view that light only affects the growth
of plants and has no effect on animals and humans. They further believe that the color of light does not affect the health and well-being of
people, and that most studies claiming it to be otherwise are based on
anecdotal observations and improperly controlled studies. In short,
they believe there is no difference between artificial light and natural
light.

This belief stands in direct contradiction to the declaration made
in 1977 by Hollwich, Diekhues, and Schrameyer in their research article discussing the effects of natural and artificial light via the eye on
hormone and metabolic balance of humans; that it is inappropriate
from the medical point of view to believe that artificial light is the

Research on biological effects has raised questions regarding artificial lighting in our interior environments. (Photo: Frank H. Mahnke)

same as natural light and can fully replace it. It seems pretty obvious that a basic controversy exists among researchers as to the biological effects of light.

Certainly, science has made substantial progress understanding our reaction to light. However, from a practical standpoint this progress has had little value or application in lighting installations in our buildings, especially regarding the use full-spectrum lighting—an artificial light source that simulates natural light (more on that later). Findings from one group of researchers are still being questioned by the opposing group holding a different viewpoint. As long as this division exists, how can we expect to establish lighting standards that consider biological findings?

The question is which group do we, as architects, designers, and consultants, but not as scientific researchers, believe? In our work we can have some influence on lighting conditions and make a difference in the quality of light that is installed. But may we adopt our own opinion when even researchers disagree? We have two choices: Either we shrug it off and wait for the so-called ultimate proof; or we evaluate some of the biological findings and become a little more aware that light isn't just an aid in seeing and that perhaps we should "be more careful about using all kinds of artificial light sources as freely as we do." (Küller 1981, p. 239)

Any objective overview of this field tells us that light affects humans in a variety of ways. In this chapter we concern ourselves with its biological effects and the resultant variety of reaction to light. Then we can explore certain interrelationships from which we may draw some conclusions that will at least help us to recognize negative lighting from the standpoint of biology.

Overview of the Effects of Ultraviolet, Visible Light, and Infrared Radiation

For practical purposes, we will not concern ourselves here with the full extent of electromagnetic energy, but rather with visible light and the adjacent infrared and ultraviolet regions. These three components of solar radiation will affect the human organism in two ways: through radiation on the skin and light entering the eye. Besides stimulating vision, some of these effects are summarized here (details follow later in this chapter).

Ultraviolet Radiation

1. Actinic effects on the skin   *Actinic effects means the way ultraviolet, X ray, and other radiations produce chemical changes.*

2. Erythema   *Reddening of the skin.*

3. Vitamin D production

4. Physiological effects of a general nature

Visible Light Radiation

1. Activation of the pineal organ   *The pineal gland is a small light-sensitive, cone-shaped structure behind the midbrain from which the pituitary gland emerges. It secretes the hormone melatonin.*

2. Endocrine and autonomic effects   *The endocrine glands manufacture hormones and secretes them directly into the bloodstream. These are carried to different parts of the body whose function they regulate and control.*

3. Entrainment of circardian rhythms   *The circardian system is a network of behavioral and physiological (metabolic, glandular, sleep) rhythms usually synchronized by sunlight in order to function in time with each 24-hour cycle.*

4. Effects on performance and fatigue

5. Cognitive, behavioral, and emotional correlates

Infrared Radiation

1. Heating action on the skin

2. Vasodilation   *Increase in the diameter of blood vessels, especially arteries.*

3. Influence on body temperature

4. Influence on physical and mental performance *(Through body temperature)*

5. Cold, heat, and pain sensation

Chronobiology

Without light there would not be oxygen, water, food, plants, animals, or humans—in short, there would be no life on earth. Light controls all of life's processes. Our life is regulated by the relationship of the earth to the sun and moon, our natural light sources. Countless aspects of our physical and mental well-being are influenced by the rhythms of natural light. The earth rotates on its axis every 24 hours and within these 24 hours light changes its color and intensity.

The earth completes its revolution around the sun every 365.25 days, which determines the yearly pattern of light and darkness. The reason for seasonal changes is that the axis of the earth tilts. From March to September the North Pole tilts toward the sun, thereby giving the Northern Hemisphere more sunlight than the Southern Hemisphere. From September to March the North Pole is tilted away from the sun, and the Southern Hemisphere receives more sunlight.

The closer we live toward the North Pole or South Pole, the more extreme the relationship between the hours of darkness or light becomes. In the polar regions, either daylight or darkness is constant around the time of the two solstices (the time when the sun is farthest north or farthest south of the equator).

In the regions above or below the equator, the hours of light and darkness are only equal during the spring (May 21) and fall (September 22) equinoxes—the time when the sun crosses the equator making day and night of equal length in all parts of the earth. At the equator there is no seasonal change in daylight hours; it is always light for 12 hours and dark for 12 hours. All of these various rhythms and cycles of light means that human beings have adjusted physically and mentally to fixed times of daily, monthly, and yearly cycles.

Circadian Rhythm

We humans have developed within us a biological clock that keeps its own approximate 24-hour timetable called the circadian rhythm. The system is a network of inner biological clocks that coordinate our bodily functions within a 24-hour cycle.

Esoteric biorhythm programs claim that humans are subject to three rigid cycles that determine our daily mental and physical well-

Light effects the circadian rhythm of cell function, which in turn determines the circadian rhythm of each fluid or organ in our body.

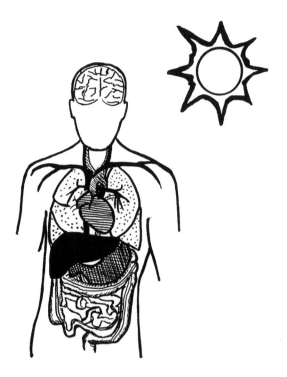

being. From birth on this trio of cycles supposedly functions according to fixed patterns until the end of one's life. Chronobiologists, however, utilizing modern sensor technology, have discovered hundreds of body rhythms that control body functions independent of the hours of birth. They include body temperature, concentration, potency, fertility, dexterity, hearing capability, and many other functions, which vary with the time of day.

Chronobiology pioneer Professor Jürgen Aschoff explained 20 years ago that every living thing ticks in time with cosmic bioclocks. All of a human's functions are subject to rhythms coordinated with the timetables of his environment. The most important of these for humans is the sunrise-sunset cycle—which means light or the absence of light.

Circadian rhythm prepares us for the beginning of the day. For example, before it becomes light and before we awaken, the heart rate, blood pressure, and body temperature rise. Around five or six o'clock in the morning the organism sets its gear into action. It starts to increase the stress hormone cortisol that recharges our inner battery. This is a genetic remainder of our ancestors' hunting behavior. They had to be alert and fit early in the morning to face the challenges and dangers of the strenuous search for food.

These body rhythms continue to regulate our body throughout the day. At about nine in the morning melatonin falls and noradrenaline, a hormone similar to adrenaline, rises. The sympathetic nervous system increases its activity until noon. A division of the autonomic nervous system, the sympathetic nervous system regulates our internal environment by controlling our blood vessels, heart, intestines, and glands. The sympathetic portion dominates in stressful situations or emergencies. It responds in ways that promote energy expenditure—increasing blood-sugar levels, heart rate, blood pressure, and halting digestion. The parasympathetic nervous system dominates in relaxed situations; it conserves energy. Around noon our body temperature continues to rise and at three o'clock blood pressure reaches its highest point. In the evening at about ten our blood pressure and heart rate fall; melatonin has been on the rise since five in the afternoon.

Chronobiologists have found a number of fascinating facts concerning our "inner clock." For example, at eight in the morning most sex hormones are released (when most of us are on the way to work); between nine and ten hand strength reaches its peak; the brain is at its most active stage between ten and noon; at one o'clock the highest amount of gastric acid is produced, whether we have eaten or not; the senses of taste, smell, and hearing are at their most acute between five and seven in the evening; the liver breaks down alcohol between the hours of six and eight; and the skin is more porous at that time, therefore making it more susceptible to the active ingredients of facial cosmetics.

These rhythms also affect our performance of various tasks during the day. From ten o'clock until noon our immediate memory is at its best, and is therefore a positive factor in schoolwork, concentration, and debate; whereas the hours from six in the evening to midnight are favorable for studying since our long-term memory is at its best. Night-shift workers are most clumsy in performing their skills during the hours of three to four in the morning.

Influence on Physical Well-Being

If you're having a routine checkup at your doctor's office, keep in mind that you are not the same person in the morning as you are in the afternoon, nor the same in winter as in summer. Since body rhythms are coordinated to the sunlight-nightfall cycle, so are body substances (blood, hormones, etc.) and tissues in a state of constant cyclic flux.

Every cell in the body has numerous parts, and each part fulfills a daily task. Most cells reproduce themselves by means of division. As the cell divides itself, the mother cell passes on to the daughter cell what it will be and what function it will have to carry out, and thus the generations of cells continue. Every cell function has its circadian rhythm, and every cell is a part of the network of cells that helps to determine the circadian rhythm of each fluid or organ.

At any given time of day cells in different parts of our body are in different stages of their function, depending on the organs to which they belong. Blood pressure, for example, fluctuates with the time of the day (but is also affected by other factors, such as a person's emotional state when blood pressure is taken and so forth). In general, however, blood pressure is higher in the afternoon and evening than in the morning.

Just as we do not have the same degree of concentration throughout the day, our resistance to infection and disease also fluctuates. The body has daily, monthly, and seasonal rhythms in its degree of susceptibility and tolerance to illness.

Many illnesses and health problems have a rhythmic effect. In other words, normal function and pain coincide. For example, breathing difficulties in asthma are much more common at night and upon awakening in early morning than at other times of day. The lungs and air passages are rhythmically predisposed toward breathing difficulties in hours of darkness. The lungs are also adversely affected by lying prone.

The normal rhythms of heart rate, blood pressure, and functions of the arteries coincide with rhythms in heart pain (angina pectoris) and heart attacks. This "timing" is partly due to the circadian rhythms in blood pressure, heart rate, certain hormones, and oxygen consumption. Some people with angina pectoris suffer at night or in early morning, when the arteries are less flexible than, for example, in late afternoon.

Research in chronobiology has had a revolutionary effect on pharmacology. Our bodies react quite differently to medicines at different times of day. To lessen headache pain three headache pills are needed in the morning, yet only one at night to produce the same effect. When lesser doses of medication are needed if taken at the right time, side effects are also lessened. Pharmaceutical companies are now investing millions in bio-timing research.

The Important Hormone Melatonin

Professor Rütger Wever, of the Max Planck Institute in Germany, placed volunteers in a windowless dungeon underneath the earth. The test subjects were isolated from their environment, the daily phases of the sun, and had no watches or clocks. But their body rhythms still more or less swung within day/night timing. The subjects ate and slept in accordance with their usual routines, yet measurements taken weeks later showed that their original 24-hour rhythm had extended to 25 hours. This means that after 24 days their "inner" timing was off by one day. Then how, under normal circumstances, does the organism stay synchronized with the shorter 24-hour day?

The most obvious relationship between man and light is the light/dark (wakefulness/sleep) cycle of day and night and its complex physiological and biochemical variations. The timing of diurnal (day-time) and nocturnal (nighttime) rhythms and the functional variations related to them depends on internal processes, which can be referred to as the biological clock. There must be a synchronizer to keep time with sunrise and sunset. Richard Wurtman and his associates have proposed the melatonin theory of pineal function. Melatonin is a hormone produced by the pineal body (also known as the epiphysis) that regulates the activity of certain glands. It seems that the synthesis of melatonin in the pineal gland holds a central position in producing the effects of light received through the eyes.

Wurtman wrote: "The role of the pineal cells appears to be to convert a neural input controlled by an exogeneous factor (light) to an endogenous glandular output (its hormone)." (Wurtman 1969, p. 32) In short, light signals that are transferred by the eye and the nerves to the pineal body regulate the amount of melatonin that is secreted into the blood. During darkness more melatonin is secreted; under sunlight it is reduced. It is widely believed that environmental illumination controls the rate of melatonin synthesis.

It is also thought that melatonin affects the regulation of behavior changes in animals, but this has not been shown clearly in humans. In one study, drug-size doses of melatonin given to volunteers produced a sedating effect; alertness, vigilance, and reaction time declined. In both animals and people, melatonin is turned off during the day and released at night. But animals respond to lower levels of light in melatonin suppression, while humans are unresponsive to even bright indoor lights.

It may be possible for chronobiological research to make man respect his natural bio-timing. The German periodical *Stern* states: "In the working place a chrono-revolution is starting to take place: in all the factory plants of the chemical manufacturer Bayer, for example, all 13,600 night-shift workers' polarity is being chronobiologically reversed." Their work schedules are being adapted to their natural bio-rhythms. Instead of working six consecutive night shifts, employees are now required to work only three night shifts consecutively. Industrial scientist Peter Knauth ascertained that's as long a time that the body will tolerate abuses against the sleep needs set by our inner clock.

SAD—Seasonal Affective Disorder (Winter Depression)

Nowadays, winter depression is considered a genuine illness. In 1982, Dr. Alfred Lewy and associates demonstrated that very bright light in the morning and evening could grant relief to a manic-depressive patient suffering from winter-long depression. Meanwhile, "the efficacy of phototherapy with bright, fluorescent, full-spectrum light for treatment of seasonal affective disorders (SAD) has been widely demonstrated in controlled studies." (S. Kasper, T.A. Wehr, N.E. Rosenthal, 1988, p. 200)

Patients with this illness show symptoms of decreased physical activity, irritability, decreased energy levels, sleeping problems, and an increase in carbohydrate craving. The accompanying craving for something "sweet" may be due to the fact that carbohydrate in sugar makes the body produce more of the hormone serotonin. This hormone activates and makes people feel more energetic; thereby, serotonin is the antithesis of melatonin. Scientists believe that melatonin may be the key chemical messenger responsible for seasonal affective disorder because not enough light is taken in by the patient to stop or curb the production of melatonin.

Some of the symptoms that might point toward SAD are:

1. As early as summer the individual has apprehensions about the coming, dreary, winter days.

2. Seasonal Affective Disorder may stir up an unusual craving for sweets during the months of October through March.

3. People with SAD need longer sleeping hours in autumn and winter without waking up in the morning and having the feeling of having had enough sleep.

4. Sufferers find it becomes harder to concentrate on a task.

5. More irritability is experienced in winter than at other times of the year.

6. The feeling of uselessness and depression is present.

7. Moodiness is experienced especially in late afternoon.

Norman Rosenthal and associates (1984) using 2,500 lux (which seems to be the norm) of full-spectrum light, also found that artificial extension of the day, three hours before dawn and three hours after dusk, had an antidepressant effect on patients. However, light acts as a drug on patients with SAD. As with any drug, it must be carefully monitored. Prescribing that very bright lights (as 2,500 lux are) be installed in every artificially lit environment in winter to prevent the possibility of SAD would be ridiculous. Bright artificial light can also have negative effects, from the standpoint of visual ergonomics alone. Some SAD patients discontinued their therapy because they became unusually and nervously active, irritable, and experienced eyestrain, headaches, nausea, or insomnia.

Ultraviolet Radiation

The Controversy

Ultraviolet (UV) radiation is considered to be in the wavelength range of 100–400 nanometers. The system most frequently used by photobiologists subdivides UV radiation into three bands:

UV-A (315–400 nm): penetrates deeper into the skin (the dermis) than UV-B; activates pigmentation (tanning).

UV-B (280–315 nm): produces erythema (reddening of the skin) and Vitamin D.

UV-C (100–280 nm): has a strong germicidal effect.

The position on ultraviolet radiation and its effects on health has split into two camps. One school of thought warns of health risks, which leads some people to protect themselves from any trace amounts of UV (eyeglasses that won't let UV pass, sunscreens, sunglasses with UV protection). Within this camp are also those who believe that there does not exist sufficient reason for the inclusion of balanced UV radiation in artificial light.

The contrary school of thought believes that overexposure to UV radiation is harmful, as is anything received in excess, but that moderate amounts of this radiation may be essential for the healthy growth and development of plants and animals; also that it is essential to human welfare. By completely protecting ourselves from any trace amounts, we risk creating a deficiency in this life-supporting energy. This group also believes that balanced trace amounts of ultraviolet radiation in artificial light are necessary, especially for those people who spend most of their time indoors.

How damaging to one's health is ultraviolet radiation? Studies have shown that UV-B and UV-A (in wavelengths under 340 nm) will further the risk of cataracts. Sunglasses that block UV will protect against this risk. UV-B may also temporarily damage the cornea. Such damage is generally caused by sunbathing on a sandy beach or skiing without wearing sunglasses. The UV radiation reflected by sand or snow leads to a more powerful dose. Studies suggest that UV might contribute to the onset of eye cancer. People with blue eyes are the most vulnerable; those with brown eyes are the least at risk.

It is generally known that UV radiation may cause damage to skin in the form of sunburn, photoallergies, skin cancer, and premature aging of skin. For example, repeated sunburns will add up and damage the skin for life. Especially the wavelengths under 340 nm, UV-B, and UV-A[2] further the risk of skin cancer. The experts' warning is: People who double their exposure to the sun's radiation quadruple their risk of skin cancer. The skin forgets nothing. All sins against it will add up through the years, then at some future time skin cancer will erupt. In Germany, which has a pretty moderate number of sunny days through the year, 120,000 people a year develop skin cancer; 800–1,600 die of it. These high numbers more than likely include people from northern countries who venture south in summer to "fry" themselves in Spain or Italy. However, in view of all the health risks associated with UV, it's understandable why some people believe that UV radiation should be avoided by completely shielding oneself from it.

There is no doubt that overexposure to UV radiation is harmful, but the question is: What type of exposure and for how long? Personally, I don't believe that health risks posed by UV radiation can be ignored, nor do I believe in the extreme of totally shielding people from it. While new products are being designed to protect us from the harmful effects of UV, other products have been developed to let through the natural UV in sunlight, including artificial light sources that add ultraviolet.

People are often influenced by news headlines that sensationalize a negative finding in a scientific study, without getting to the small print of the report for further edification. John Ott cites an example of this in a 1985 article about the effect of light and color on plants, animals, and people. He cites the example of an article that had appeared in the March 1982 issue of the *American Journal of Ophthalmology* entitled "Action Spectrum for Retinal Injury from Near-Ultraviolet Radiation in the Aphakic Monkey." The report was meant to show that the retina of monkeys was damaged by ultraviolet radiation in the range of 300–380 nm. The animals were tranquilized, their pupils dilated wide open; a special device held the eyelids open and frequent applications of a saline solution prevented drying of the cornea. The radiation beam came from a 2,500-watt xenon lamp, which is an extremely intense light source containing high levels of UV radiation, equipped with quartz optics. The time of exposure was 1,000 seconds, a little more than 16 minutes. The result was irreparable damage to rod and cone photoreceptors.

Ott commented that it was "a totally abnormal and unrealistic condition and might be compared to somebody thrusting his hand directly into the fire of a furnace for a little more than 16 minutes and then jumping to the conclusion that we must live at absolute zero temperature if this procedure produced any blisters or burns on his fingers." (Ott 1985, p. 3)

In a German magazine (*Bunte*, Heft 41, 1990) column called "The Critical Patient," Peter Schmiedsberger commented on skin cancer through ultraviolet radiation in the article "How Dangerous Is the Sun Really?" One of the comments by Dr. Schmiedsberger was:

Six university dermatology clinics found that there is no evidence of damage from sunlight. In this study, UV exposure during leisure time was not found to be a risk factor for the development of malignant skin cancer—so stated by the medical journal Der Hautarzt.

Professor F. Schröpfl, of the German Clinic for Diagnostics, warns against "unreasonable UV exposure." He makes it clear that one should avoid the strongest radiation around midday as one should avoid any type of sunburn. He gives this advice not because of the dreaded malignant melanoma, but as a precaution against developing less dangerous skin cancers. He points out that for melanoma to develop it takes 120,000 hours of sunlight, or 240,000 hours in a solarium.

A provocative though baffling study on the incidence of skin cancer among Australians appeared in the August 7, 1982, medical journal *The Lancet*. Research conducted in England by the Department of Medical Statistics and Epidemiology, London, School of Hygiene and Tropical Medicine, and in Australia by the University of Sydney and Melanoma Clinic, Sidney Hospital, found that "exposure to fluorescent light at work was associated with a doubling of melanoma risk." This risk grew with the increasing duration of exposure to fluorescent light and was higher in women who had worked mainly in offices than in women whose main place of work was not in offices yet still indoors. The report also mentioned that melanoma rates in Britain and Australia are higher among professionals and office workers and are lower in people working outdoors.

Faced with the results of these studies it seems that we are back to point zero. How can it be that skin cancer is found to be higher in people working in environments without UV radiation? The small amount of UV radiation that is emitted from fluorescent lights usually is absorbed by the fixtures on which they are mounted. Also it cannot be a matter of the sunlight that falls through a window; ordinary window glass will absorb essentially all UV-B radiation. Ultraviolet of the A range passes through most types of glass but produces virtually no erythema, unless the skin has been subjected to the action of drugs that makes it abnormally light-sensitive. If only one thing can be proven conclusively from these controversial studies, then it seems to be the need for further research.

Positive Health Effects of Ultraviolet Radiation

Several processes that go on in the skin depend on the photochemical (actinic) effect of UV radiation. One of these is the synthesis of calciferol, or vitamin D_2. Vitamin D, which promotes the metabolism of phosphorus and calcium in the body, is produced by UV radiation in the B range, which also has an erythemal effect on human skin. Deficiency might result in rickets or dental caries in children, or brittle bones in the aged. It is commonly held that only small amounts of ultraviolet radiation are needed to help develop calciferol. Rickets, for example, can be cured by repeated exposure to one-tenth the dose of UV required to obtain reddening of the skin. R. M. Neer pointed out that the amount of radiation involved is roughly the equivalent of exposure to UV radiation that a Washington, D.C. resident might receive during a fifteen-minute midsummer lunchtime stroll.

Some American scientists now suspect that a gene might be the risk factor in the development of osteoporosis, a gene that makes the absorption of vitamin D more difficult. Scientists say that bone density is 75-percent hereditary and 25-percent dependent on environmental factors. Children, who might be prone to osteoporosis in later life, can protect themselves by a higher intake of calcium and vitamin D.

Vitamin D deficiency among the elderly tends to be a matter of concern. Elderly people who often stay indoors, especially during the winter months, or who are institutionalized and eat poorly, may run the risk of simultaneous reduction in both cutaneous and dietary vitamin D. A 1979 study by Lawson and colleagues concludes that the vitamin D condition of the elderly may reach levels associated with osteomalacia (soft bones) in winter.

R. M. Neer and associates conducted a study among elderly residents of the Chelsea (Massachusetts) Soldiers' Home during two consecutive winters. It was found that intestinal calcium absorption increased among subjects exposed to a fluorescent lamp designed to duplicate daylight as best as possible—these are known as full-spectrum lights. True full-spectrum lights simulate the balanced ultraviolet and full visible spectrum of natural daylight. In the control group exposed to conventional cool-white fluorescent, intestinal calcium absorption decreased. Even after dairy products were fortified with vitamin D, the same results were obtained.

Although definite conclusions cannot be drawn from the few studies conducted, it is possible that vitamin D deficiency may also cause an increase in dental caries. In 1974, R. P. Feller and associate investigators exposed rats to three different light sources: incandescent, conventional cool-white fluorescent, and full-spectrum fluorescent. They found that the incidence of caries was significantly higher in those rats housed under cool-white fluorescent than those under the other two light sources. I. M. Sharon and two colleagues found that golden hamsters exposed to light simulating the visible spectrum and UV spectra of natural light had one-fifth as many caries as those exposed to standard fluorescent illumination.

L. W. Mayron et al. studied schoolchildren in two classrooms, one lighted by cool-white fluorescent, the other by full-spectrum lamps. The incidence and extent of caries among the cool-white group were significantly higher than among the full-spectrum group.

Research suggests that UV radiation might also have general physiological effects, such as decrease in pulse rate; a drop in blood pressure; changes in skin temperature and metabolic rate; a reduction in reaction time; an improvement in health conditions; and resistance to certain types of infections. Studies by E. F. Ellinger (using a bicycle ergometer) have indicated that exposure of human subjects to erythema-producing doses of UV radiation resulted in an improved work output due to decreased fatigability and increased efficiency. (Ellinger, quoted in Birren 1982) M. A. Zamkova and E. I. Krivitskaya were able to show in their experiments that subjects irradiated with UV had a shorter reaction time to light and sound, a lower fatigability of the visual receptors, and an improvement in working capacity. During these experiments, which were conducted with schoolchildren, the investigators found that the subjects' academic standing also improved, probably due to these favorable shifts.

The Russian Academy of Medical Sciences compiled extensive clinical data on the effects of ultraviolet radiation. These data point out that lack of exposure to sunlight, in addition to vitamin D deficiency and demineralization of bones and teeth, will result in a weakening of the body's immunological defenses and an increase in stress and fatigue. Research undertaken by MIT, NASA, Harvard, and others confirms these findings.

At the 16th meeting of the International Commission on Illumination, held in Washington, D.C., in 1967, N. M. Dantsig and two associates from Russia reported positive clinical and physiological changes, a reduction in the incidences of diseases, and an increase in overall immunological responsiveness in children irradiated with UV. They also noted that the majority of nonirradiated children showed a reduction in body defenses. Similarly, a study of children in a Swedish day-care center showed a clear-cut relationship between the duration of outdoor activity (therefore UV exposure) and resistance to respiratory infections. The three Russian scientists also stated: "The Institute of General and Community Hygiene under the USSR Academy of Medical Sciences has taken a positive view of the effectiveness of utilizing erythemal lamps in the system of artificial lighting." (Dantzig, Lazarev, and Sokolov 1968, p. 227)

With regard to the Russian literature, Luke Thorington remarked:

It is noteworthy that all of these reported effects are achieved through suberythemal dosages of ultraviolet dosages delivered over an eight-hour

*day that are only one-tenth to about one-half of that required to produce
the least perceptible skin reddening. (Thorington 1973, p. 8)*

There is also some evidence that UV radiation might affect muscle tone and strength. According to a report sent to John Ott from the National Institutes of Health in 1978, modest amounts of near-UV light increased shoulder muscle tone and improved short-term strength. Specific exclusion of near-UV light reduced muscle tone and strength (only shoulder muscles were tested). Some studies by other investigators have also demonstrated increase of muscle strength when subjects are exposed to ultraviolet radiation.

Some of the studies that I have discussed are almost 30 years old, and still the positive aspects of balanced UV radiation are disregarded when it comes to the installation of lighting systems—even though full-spectrum lights with a balanced amount of UV radiation have been in existence for years.

Personally, I plead for the inclusion of balanced UV in artificial lights, mainly because of the reasons I have presented so far. Humans need sunlight, which has nothing to do with "sunbathing." Millions of people work in buildings with windows that can't be opened, or with no windows at all. Ordinary window glass absorbs essentially all of the "biologically active" ultraviolet spectra, and standard indoor incandescent and fluorescent lamps do not emit significant amounts of ultraviolet. Furthermore, many people travel (especially in winter) to and from work in closed vehicles and venture outdoors only in early morning or the evening, when UV radiation is minimal. I think it's logical to use artificial lights that include a modest amount of UV. From a good-health standpoint I think it's justified, if not actually necessary.

Let us not forget that despite their dark and enclosed housing, cavemen were much more exposed to the sun than we are. Our bodies are still adjusted to the timing of the sun, our biological clock depends on it, and our bodies are used to the positive effects of UV radiation. But how many people in our industrialized nations still feel the sun in their face? Even in sunny California it is estimated that young people, on the average, are outdoors only an hour and a half a day. In middle Europe, for example in Germany, most people spend 90 percent of their work and leisure time indoors.

To make my position perfectly clear, I will state it once more: I warn against the health risks of UV radiation. Surely, no reader will throw away his sunglasses and bask in the sun without proper protection. But I also believe that blocking ourselves completely from this radiation might also have harmful effects. At least some studies support this speculation.

C-1: *Horton Plaza Shopping Center, San Diego, California*
Photo: Frank H. Mahnke

For the purposes of showing an overstimulated environment, this shopping center is an example. An abundance of visual noise, i.e., various architectural forms, is supported by a variety of color in a dense space. However, in this case especially, the color design visually supports the feeling of activity and movement, invites exploration, and sets an exuberant and "fun" mood. In this particular situation, where the expression of festivity is allowed to reign, the color design is appropriate.

C-2: *San Diego, California*
Photo: Frank H. Mahnke

Strong color and unusual combinations are fine if utilized in small doses. However, as the overall appearance of a townscape, this use of color would be overstimulating, aesthetically inappropriate, and tiring.

C-3: *Shopping center, San Diego, California*
Photo: Frank H. Mahnke

Color choice has reached the limit of chromaticity. The space does not allow for this much color without being over-stimulating and overpowering. Strong color closes in a space—does not open it up.

C-4: *Housing complex, Geneva, Switzerland*
Photo: Jeffrey Westman
Perfect example of overstimulation due to pattern and color.

C-5: *Apartment complex, La Jolla, California*
Photo: Frank H. Mahnke
The severity of form and monochromatic color understimulates this environment, leading to sterility and a lack of emotional satisfaction.

C-6: *Office building, Geneva, Switzerland*
Photo: Frank H. Mahnke
Architectural style and supporting color express to the highest degree aloofness and power.

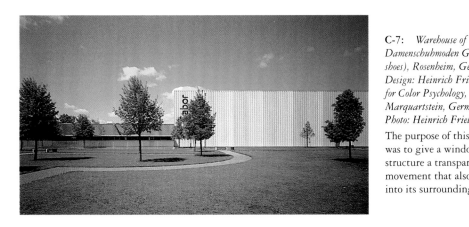

C-7: *Warehouse of Damenschuhmoden GABOR (ladies' shoes), Rosenheim, Germany Color Design: Heinrich Frieling, Institute for Color Psychology, Marquartstein, Germany*
Photo: Heinrich Frieling
The purpose of this color design was to give a windowless, static structure a transparency and movement that also blends well into its surroundings.

C-8: *Row housing in Obergösgen, Switzerland
Color Design: Barbara Fleischmann, Architect
and IACC Color Consultant, Aarau,
Switzerland
Photo: Jiri Vurma*

Yellow was chosen for the facade for a light,
friendly appearance. It differs from the
surrounding green of nature, while still
harmonizing with it. The soft, harmonizing
accent colors of light blue and light
turquoise distinguish each housing group.

C-9: *Row housing in Öbergösgen, Switzerland
Color Design: Barbara Fleischmann, Architect and IACC Color Consultant, Aarau, Switzerland
Photo: Jiri Vurma*

These accent colors contrast well with the dominant wall colors. The whole ensemble appears friendly and inviting.

C-10: *Building in San Francisco,
California
Color Design: Jill Pilaroscia,
Architectural Color, IACC Color
Consultant, San Francisco, California
Photo: Doug Keister*

Northern exposure allows use of
darker-value exterior colors. By
using a dark body color, the light
trim emphasizes structural
framework and enhances shadow
play and texture.

C-11: *Stanford Park Development, Sacramento, California
Color Design: Jill Pilaroscia, Architectural Color, IACC Color Consultant,
San Francisco, California
Photo: Ed Asmus*

Monotonous roof line and repetitive architectural style are broken by
color rhythm.

C-12: *Nordmende exhibition stand*
Client: Christian Stümpke, Nordmende
Conception: Bernd Kracke, Agency MA Network Communications, Hamburg, Germany
Detail Planning and Construction Supervision: Roland Seger, Interior Architect and IACC Color Consultant,
Frankfurt, Germany
Photo: Dieter Kahl

Nordmende manufactures electronic entertainment equipment. The colors were chosen for their association with outer space, distance, and infinity of time, from the source where wavelengths originate (dark blue), to the power that results from it (red-orange).

C-13: *Main entrance of the Tampere Polytechnic School, Tampere, Finland*
Color Design: Seppo Rihlama, Architect, IACC Color Consultant, Tampere, Finland
Photo: Seppo Rihlama

Structural shapes and materials are clarified through color design. The blue of the wall optically prevents the feel of cutting space, which a massive wall will easily cause. The clearness of the colors creates an appropriate atmosphere.

C-14: *Main staircase of the Tampere Polytechnic School, Tampere Finland*
Color Design: Seppo Rihlama, Architect, IACC Color Consultant, Tampere, Finland
Photo: Seppo Rihlama

The stairs, bannister, and walls are taken as one art unit, which underlines as well the feeling of ascent and structural beauty. The warm yellow and orange emphasize the opposing blue.

C-15: *Church in Mouhijärvi, Finland*
Color Design: Seppo Rihlama, Architect, IACC Color
Consultant, Tampere, Finland
Photo: Seppo Rihlama

Emphasizing the feeling of ascent, the increasing lightness of colors from the benches' quiet dark brown to the ceiling's celestial blue elevates the space to represent reaching toward heaven. White, gold, and blue suggest the ethereal; orange and yellow enliven the peacefulness of green and blue and balance their coolness.

C-16, C-17, C-18, C-19: *Computer color design and photography: Seppo Rihlama*
Example of how color sets the mood although the architectural elements and furnishings are identical.

C-16: The chromaticity of this room is over-powering. Although more or less monochromatic, it leads to overstimulation.

C-17: Example of contrasts that are too harsh.

C-18: Contrasts are too weak and emotionally unsatisfying.

C-19: Contrasts are more satisfying and more in the three-to-one relationship.

C-20: *St. Luke's Regional Medical Center, Boise, Idaho*
Principal Designer: Nancy K. Armstrong, Armstrong Planning and Design, Boise, Idaho
Photo: Farshid Assassi

Colors and finishes selected for the entrance lobby create a comfortable and friendly environment for patients and visitors.

C-21: *St. Luke's Regional Medical Center, Boise, Idaho*
Principal Designer: Nancy K. Armstrong, Armstrong Planning and Design, Boise, Idaho
Photo: Farshid Assassi

Planters terrace up the entry stairway to the lobby.

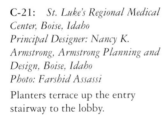

C-22: *St. Luke's Regional Medical Center, Boise, Idaho*
Principal Designer: Nancy K. Armstrong, Armstrong, Planning and Design, Boise, Idaho
Photo: Farshid Assassi

This pediatric room was designed for the child who may feel too old for a playroom. The mural and aquarium spark a child's interest toward the environment.

C-23: *St. Luke's Regional Medical Center, Boise, Idaho*
Principal Designer: Nancy K. Armstrong, Armstrong Planning and Design, Boise, Idaho
Photo: Farshid Assassi

This pediatric-ward playroom displays an abacus in red, yellow, and blue with wood spheres making this child-height unit inviting. In the background are cabinet fronts with village-inspired houses of textured red brick. Accent colors of VCT titles are set into a light background to create a colorful but not confusing floor.

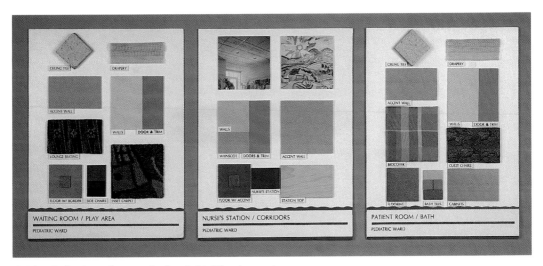

C-24: *Pediatric ward presentation boards, IACC seminar assignment*
Color Concept and Design: Claudia Dawley, Interior Designer, IACC Color Consultant
Photo: Steve Hall of Hedrich Blessing

This hypothetical pediatric ward was designed for location in New Mexico. Its colors and materials help to create a cheerful, friendly, safe, and comforting atmosphere for patients and visitors. Turquoise helps balance the warm yellows and terra cottas and is also a symbolic color for protection as was traditionally used throughout the Southwest. A variety of colors and patterns add interest to elements throughout the space and help focus attention outward, away from a patient's inner trauma.

C-25, C-26, C-27, C-28: *Psychiatric treatment center for children and adolescents, El Cajon, California*
Photos: Frank H. Mahnke

C-25: Typical hallway before renovation. Staff and patients were upset with the sterile and impersonal atmosphere.

C-26: *Color Design: Mahnke & Mahnke Environmental Design, San Diego, California*
Typical hallway after renovation. The atmosphere is friendlier and invites social contact. Only the wall colors were changed.

C-27: Typical patient room before renovation.

C-28: *Color Design: Mahnke & Mahnke Environmental Design, San Diego, California*
Patient room after renovation. Only wall colors were changed, yet the difference is dramatic.

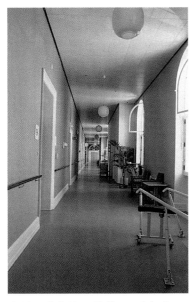 

C-29 and C-30: *Hallways of the Commune Hospital, Copenhagen, Denmark*
Color Design: Erling Friis, Artist and Color Consultant, Humleboek, Denmark
Photos: Anne Friis

Two distinctly different colors chosen for hallways, making them easily distinguishable. The colors are warm, friendly, reassuring, and set a positive mood.

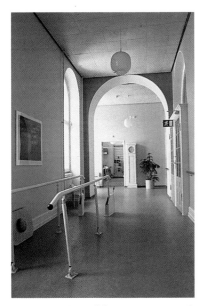

C-31: *Hallway of the Commune Hospital, Copenhagen, Denmark*
Color Design: Erling Friis, Artist and Color Consultant, Humleboek, Denmark
Photo: Anne Friis

In this hallway the color designer introduces a cooler ambience, which sets it off from the other hallways. Orientation and variety are thus served.

C-32: *Canteen interior, "De Gamles By" Retirement Home, Copenhagen, Denmark*
Color Design: Erling Friis, Artist and Color Consultant, Humbleboek, Denmark
Photo: Anne Friis

These colors invite social interaction, a good example of our discussion in Chapter 15, "Food and Foodservice."

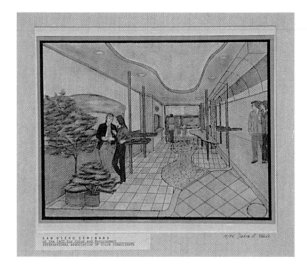

C-33: *Snack bar, IACC seminar assignment*
Original architectural concept and drawing by Prof.
Gerhard Meerwein
Color Design and modifications: Debra Wade,
Creative Designs, IACC Color Consultant, Eugene,
Oregon
Photo: Walt Grodona

Peach reflects warmth and gentle sociability;
lighter-colored walls suggest the outdoor coming
through windows. Blues and greens complement
the peach tones.

C-34: *Snack bar, IACC seminar assignment*
Color Design by Debra Wade, Creative Designs,
IACC Color Consultant, Eugene, Oregon
Photo: Walt Grodona
Material board.

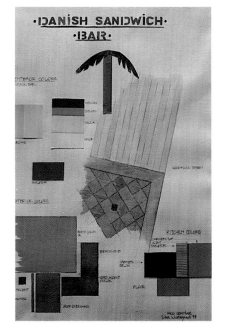

C-35: *Snack bar, IACC Seminar assignment*
Color Design: Vera Westergaard, Architect,
IACC Color Consultant, Harrison Studio, Del
Mar, California
Photo: Vera Westergaard
Material board.

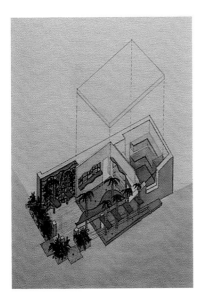

C-36: *Snack bar, IACC seminar assignment*
Original architectural concept and drawing by Prof.
Gerhard Meerwein
Color Design and modification: Vera Westergaard,
Architect, IACC Color Consultant, Harrison
Studio, Del Mar, California

A proposed "Danish Sandwich Bar" for a southern California city. The concept is to create a breathing space in a hot, urban desert, by combining the sun and heat of southern California with the cool, clean design and colors of Scandinavia.

C-37: *PTC Placer Title Co. office building, San Leandro, California*
Color Design: Vera Westergaard, Architect, IACC Color Consultant, Harrison Studio, Del
Mar, California
Photo: Vera Westergaard

This color scheme works with its architectural elements. Colors emphasize the layout and stepping of the building, first by anchoring the corner section in a dark terra cotta, then by using a lighter yellow for the building parts stepping back. Terra cotta is repeated as a base on the yellow parts of the building so that the structure sits solidly on the ground.

C-38: *ABC Cinema, Copenhagen, Denmark—*
model photo
Color Design: Vera Westergaard and Erling Friis
Photo: Vera Westergaard

An elaborate series of zig-zag hallways lead patrons to various cinemas in this complex. The goal was to create a series of visually stimulating, yet elegant, hallways. The framing of the wall pieces create an interesting folding-screen look with a perspective feeling, making some sections of the hallway seem wider and others narrower. The colors create a series of color events along the hallways, making it an interesting and uplifting experience to find each cinema along the way.

C-39: *Central heating installation, Hoje Gladsaxe,*
Denmark
Color Design: Erling Friis, Artist and Color Consultant,
Humleboek, Denmark
Photo: Anne Friis

In this example color serves to bring order and
identification to the setting.

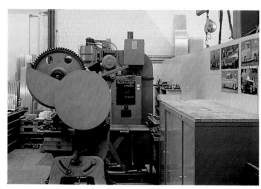

C-40 and C-41: *Brönnimann AG Metalbau (metal construction) Oberengstringen, Zurich, Switzerland*
Courtesy of CRB Schweizerische Zentrale für Baurationalisierung, Zurich, Switzerland
Color Design: Rose-Marie Spoerli, Designer and IACC Color Consultant, Winterthur, Switzerland
Photo: Christine Seiler

This color design is based on color's psychological and visual ergonomic principles. Decorative wall elements supply
interest and diversion.

C-42 and C-43: *Window frame factory, Tryba S. A., Gundershoffen, France*
Color Design: Hans-Urich Baer, IACC Color Consultant, Plancolor, Zofingen, Switzerland
Photo: Hans-Ulrich Baer

Walls and ceiling were colored to achieve a visual aesthetic unit, all components (including window frames) create
an ideal form-figure contrast, thereby making the work material—the window frames—easier and acceptable to the
eye; aiding visual ergonomics and preventing premature fatigue.

C-44: *Entrance of the University of Illinois Sigmund E. Edelstone Medical Student Center, Chicago, Illinois*
Color Design: Claudia Dawley of Mekus Johnson, Designer, IACC Color Consultant, Chicago, Illinois
Photo: Jon Miller of Hedrich Blessing

The center is situated in an almost windowless basement. To transform this area from dreary to uplifting, the entrance is illuminated with glass panels lit from behind with lighting bounced off painted panels that move from yellow through red-violet on the interior.

C-45: *Reception area, Marshall, O'Toole, Gerstein, Murray and Borun law firm, Chicago, Illinois*
Color Design: Claudia Dawley of Mekus Johnson, Designer, IACC Color Consultant, Chicago, Illinois
Photos: Jon Miller of Hedrich Blessing

This client requested an environment that was friendly and pleasant to work in. Wood, a variety of greens in addition to general wall colors of golden straw, offset with terra cotta, amber, and silver pine, abstracted into natural textures and patterns, give an overall effect of "bringing autumn nature" into the interior, thereby creating an appealing and comfortable working environment.

C-46 and C-47: *Underground parking garage "Alter Bahnhof," Baden-Baden, Germany*
Color Design: John F. K. Lübbe, Designer, IACC Color Consultant
Photos: John F. K. Lübbe

Colors separate the different levels and establish a connection to the exterior. Many people are apprehensive about entering an underground parking facility. This overall color scheme reduces tension.

C-48 and C-49: *Ganahl-Objeckt, Feldkirch, Austria*
Color Design: Edda Mally, Color Institute Vienna, IACC Color Consultant, Vienna, Austria
Photo: Edda Mally

The long facade (over one hundred meters) of this 19th-century building is softly broken up in units of light yellow, light brown, and light red. Yet an overall unity is preserved through color harmony and the unifying feature of white trim on windows, doors, and rain gutters.

C-48:   Southern Facade

C-49:   Facade detail

C-50: *Ganahl-Objeckt Parking Garage, Feldkirch, Austria*
Color Design: Edda Mally, Color Institute Vienna, IACC Color Consultant, Vienna, Austria
Photo: Edda Mally

This color design distances itself from the usual concrete or white found in most parking garages. The reason was to counteract *cave anxiety* produced by dark enclosed spaces, and to avoid disorientation. The triangle form produces rhythmic and lively walls.

C-51: *Juvenile Hall Cell, California*
Color Design: Mahnke & Mahnke Environmental Design, San Diego, California
Photo: Jeffrey Westman

Pastel colors open up a small space. Yellow makes space appear friendlier; pastel green is calming and adds visual variety—both colors bring outdoors inside (sun yellow, green foliage).

C-52: *Private residence*
Color Design: Danielle Bontempo, Geneva, Switzerland
Photo: Frank H. Mahnke

Little girls' rooms do not have to be pink. Here blue-green widens a narrow room. The traditional feminine tone is brought in by accent pink.

C-53: *Private residence*
Photo: Frank H. Mahnke

Bedroom with view to hallway and living room. Notice how the blue hallway provides an accent between the two rooms.

C-54: *Private residence*
Photo: Frank H. Mahnke

Blue does not always give a cold impression; much depends on its hue and texture. Blue enhances wood through complementary contrast. Blue was used in this narrow hallway to open up space and also sets an inviting, dignified mood.

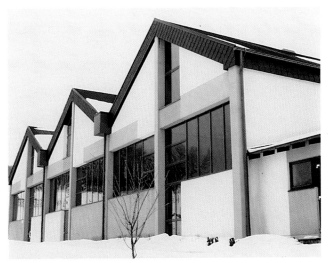

C-55: *Sports and multipurpose hall, Unnau, Germany*
Color Design: Gerhard Meerwein, Architect, Interior Architect and IACC
Color Consultant, Mainz, Germany
Photo: Gerhard Meerwein

The building's structure in conjunction with its cheerful, yet elegant, color scheme is meant to visually reflect the importance it has in the community life of this small village. A community life that is marked by sports, festivities, and play.

C-56: *Housing complex with stores on ground level, Geneva, Switzerland*
Photo: Frank H. Mahnke

A friendly, colorful exterior can be achieved without the use of highly chromatic colors.

C-57 and C-58: *Housing Complex, Carouge, Switzerland*
Photo: Frank H. Mahnke

This is a good example of sensitive architecture and exterior colors attuned to an existing environment. This complex interacts well with much older nearby buildings, thereby visually working with the overall ambience and quality of the community.

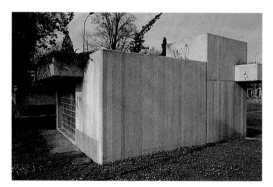

C-59: *Public toilet, Carouge, Switzerland*
Photo: Frank H. Mahnke
A little "color fun" contributes to an otherwise functional building which usually would have simply been left gray concrete.

C-60: *Housing complex, Carouge, Switzerland*
Photo: Frank H. Mahnke

The overall gray and uninviting atmosphere of this complex is not loosened up by introducing a bit of color in the playground. The effect is like hanging an earring on an otherwise gray elephant—it remains gray.

Artificial Light Versus Natural Light (Sunlight)

For nearly a century, the human organism has been subjected to electric light. The spectrum of the incandescent bulb does not differ too much from that of natural light in the visible light region (within its correlated color temperature). Because of its low color temperature, incandescent light is a warm light illumination closely resembling fire, candle, kerosene lamp, and gas mantle light. Nowadays used primarily as residential illumination, it fits into the spectral exposure history of humans: natural light during the daytime and fire (warm light) at night. Some adaptive effects might be evident, at least psychologically, since warm light is associated with relaxation.

Fluorescent light, introduced on a large scale in the late 1940s, is potentially of far greater significance biologically, mainly for two reasons: First, its spectral composition differs markedly from that of natural light; and second, it has replaced natural light during the daytime for a large majority of the population. Artificial light, however, although an efficient optic substitute, cannot replace natural light, in physiological terms.

Today, with more understanding of the effects of natural light (sunlight), the emphasis in artificial light is shifting from vision alone to biological needs. If sunlight is normal, artificial light is subnormal or abnormal, and research indicates that constant exposure to artificial light is unnatural. If sunlight, the balanced light, is essential for the growth and health of living things, including humans, it seems logical to raise questions about the effects that unbalanced (artificial) light may have on life, including the human organism. Answers to these questions have been the goal of many investigators.

One of these is the American John Ott, renowned for his research work on the influence of light and color on plants, animals, and humans. A pioneer in the field of time-lapse photography, Dr. Ott shot sequences of flowers and plants and noticed that the periodicity, intensity, and wavelength distribution of light energy controls plant growth processes. He observed that too much exposure to artificial light had adverse effects, and this raised questions in his mind about the effects of light on animals. Subsequent experiments with rats showed that their growth and health were also affected adversely by excessive exposure to nonnatural light. Included in these findings was the fact that rats developed various aberrant behavior patterns, including hyperactivity.

All this caused Ott to wonder whether light might have effects on the basic physiology of human beings. In 1966, the Environmental

Health and Light Research Institute of Sarasota, Florida, was established under Ott's directorship. During a lifetime of investigation, his multifaceted studies, often substantiated by other scientific research, point to the fact that natural or artificial light has a profound effect on human beings. As Ott pointed out:

> *We know that every chemical, mineral, vitamin, or substance of any kind that we take into our bodies as food has a maximum wavelength absorption characteristic of electromagnetic energy. We also know that this wavelength energy penetrates the skin and interacts directly at the molecular level with the chemicals and minerals in the blood supply. (Ott, 1985, p. 21)*

This conclusion may be exemplified by the medical use of light radiation for curative purposes in infant jaundice (hyperbilirubinemia). In hyperbilirubinemia, there is a high concentration of bilirubin in the blood. Bilirubin, formed from the hemoglobin of red blood cells during their normal breakdown, is excreted after undergoing chemical changes in the liver. In the first days of an infant's life, especially a premature infant, the liver may not be fully functional in this respect. If high levels of bilirubin are allowed to persist, the result is kernicterus (brain staining), which leads to various degrees of mental and motor retardation, and even death.

In 1958, Dr. R. Cremer noted that infants placed near windows showed less jaundice than those located away from incoming natural light. This led to experiments with artificial light that showed bilirubinemia declines under the influence of visible blue light. To date it has been found that the best spectral emission in the treatment of infant jaundice is 445–450 nm (blue light).

The Energetic Portion of the Visual Pathway

Physiological effects of light are not confined to radiation on the skin, nor is light entering the eye confined to the stimulation of vision. This we know, since earlier in this chapter we discussed how the hormon melatonin is diminished by light and activated by the lack of light. But how does light stimulate the endocrine system to trigger the production and release of hormones?

This occurs via a pathway independent of the visual process that F. Hollwich has described as the "energetic portion" of the visual pathway. The preface to his book about the effects of light on metabolism introduced this idea:

> *In experiments performed over a period of almost three decades (1948–1975), the author {Dr. Hollwich} and co-workers were the first to*

demonstrate conclusively that the eye is the channel for light's stimu-
latory effect. In order to elucidate this effect and separate it clearly from
the visual process, in 1948 the author {Dr. Hollwich} designated the
neural pathway conducting the photostimulus to the pituitary gland
(hypophysis) as the "energetic portion" of the optic pathway. Vision it-
self proceeds independently via the "optic portion" of the optic pathway.
(Hollwich 1980)

This neural pathway seems to involve the hypothalamus, which
monitors changes in the body's internal environment. It sends signals
to the autonomic nervous system to respond to environmental changes,
and it affects the production of hormones through the endocrine system by influencing the pituitary gland. Also affected by light is the
pineal gland, involved in the synthesis and secretion of melatonin. The
pineal and pituitary glands are the master glands that control the entire endocrine system.

Ott commented on this:

This then seem to me to be a carry-over of the basic principles of photo-
synthesis in plants—sometimes referred to as a conversion of light energy
to chemical energy—to animal life, a phenomenon not heretofore recog-
nized. Thus the wavelengths that are missing in various types of
artificial light or that filtered from the spectrum of natural light by
window glass, windshields, eyeglasses (particularly tinted contact
lenses or deeper shades of sunglasses), smog, and even suntan lotions,
are causing a condition of malillumination, similar to malnutrition
that occurs when there is a lack of a proper nutritional diet. (Ott 1981,
p. 25)

Is Artificial Light the Same as Natural Light in its Biological Effect?

Standard fluorescent lamps emit a white light that does not contain the same spectral composition of natural light, because the eye
cannot differentiate the single colors but only perceives the sum of the
spectral composition of light—which is white.

The eye perceives brightness best in the yellow-green region. But
in addition to the necessary brightness it is important for the eye to see
and experience color correctly. Hollwich pointed out that compared
with sunlight, where colors of the spectrum are fairly equal in proportion, fluorescent light has peaks in some areas and deficits in others.

Hollwich and colleagues studied the effect of strong artificial light
with considerable deviation from the spectral composition, and on the
other hand, minimal deviation in healthy persons. In those persons

subjected to light with greater deviation, they found stresslike levels of ACTH (a hormone synthesized and stored in the anterior pituitary gland, large amounts of which are released in response to any form of stress) and the stress hormone cortisol. Hollwich concluded that this explains the agitated mental and physical behavior of children who stay in school the whole day and are subjected to artificial illumination that deviates strongly from daylight.

Mayron and colleagues demonstrated in 1974 that full-spectrum fluorescent lighting decreased the hyperactive behavior of students in two first-grade classrooms. The comparison was made between full-spectrum light and standard cool-white fluorescent.

Hollwich and his associates reported in 1977 that increasing the intensity of artificial light with fluorescent tubes leads to "light stress." Proof of this was again established by increased hormone production, especially cortisol.

Researchers in the United States and Australia believe that standard fluorescent lights activate the production of melatonin even during the day. At the same time, when artificial light is bright it also produces ACTH and increases cortisol. This constant alternating of the body's own tranquilizer and stimulant leads to dangerous constant stress. However, I do not have the details of this study, and since we know that bright light reduces or stops the production of melatonin, I have a problem with this study's premise. Perhaps in this case there exists a very fine difference in brightness levels.

The lighting industry energetically opposes the findings of these studies and the conclusions that can be drawn from them. They state that the increased hormones are still within the framework of what are considered normal levels.

However, symptoms such as sleep disorders, weakening of the immune system, depression, neuroses, high blood pressure, heart and circulatory problems, muscle and joint problems, obesity, and so forth, manifested themselves among the sailors and officers who served on the Polaris submarines and did not see sunlight for six months.

Consequently, the Duro-Test company developed a fluorescent light called Vita-Lite, and in Europe True-Lite. It is a true full-spectrum light because it simulates as exactly as possible the full spectrum found in sunlight, with the addition of balanced UV radiation (at a certain correlated color temperature). Dr. John Ott also developed a full-spectrum light marketed under the name Ott-Lite.

I have great concerns about the spectral composition found in the interior of buildings with tinted windows or entire exterior walls of tinted glass. Different colors of glass absorb and transmit different portions of the color spectrum, but all of them act as filters. Green window glass, for instance, transmits no red wavelengths. If we add to this artificial interior lighting of poor spectral quality, the result must be a

Tinted glass acts as a filter, absorbing certain colors and transmitting into the interior a spectral composition that differs from natural light coming from the outside. (Photo: Frank H. Mahnke)

cocktail of different wavelengths that can't possibly be close to natural light.

Hollwich believed that light not only affects efficiency but also health, and in the end health determines efficiency. That is why it is false to believe that the only criteria for maximum lighting efficiency are sufficient amount of light and adherence to basic principles of visual ergonomics (contrast, glare etc.).

Professor R. Blackwell, a vision expert at Ohio State University, simulated typical working conditions under different lighting in a 1984 experiment. He found that under full-spectrum lights general performance increased by 12 percent and that full-spectrum lights greatly improved visual performance.

A study conducted in 1974 by Douglas Kleiber and associates at Cornell University demonstrated that Vita-Lite increased visual acuity and decreased general fatigue over a four-hour study period.

I hope I have been able to make it clear that for humans light is not only important for seeing. Scientists argue among themselves over many aspects of light and its impact on us. Some are for full-spectrum light; others see no necessity for it. One school talks about light stress and increased hormone levels; the other contends that it's all within accepted normal levels. Ultraviolet opponents warn us to protect ourselves from its radiation; the other group feels that reasonable levels are important for health. Arguments will continue over details; there will always be pros and cons.

Until the time arrives (if ever) that scientists are in agreement with at least some basic, usable findings, and until the long-term effects of artificial lighting have been researched to a fuller extent, it seems to me that full-spectrum lighting has a more positive effect on the well-being of humans. Therefore, I see no reason not to utilize it in those environments where it would be of benefit.

Artificial Sunlight—When and Where?

Should full-spectrum lighting be recommended for every environment? A clear "yes" cannot be given without first knowing:

1. *What type of environment is it (will it be)?*

2. *What will its function be?*

3. *Who will inhabit it, for how long, doing what tasks?*

There are lighting situations in which full-spectrum light may be introduced, and in others where it may be left out. To illustrate the point: In schools, full-spectrum should definitely be installed in classrooms, libraries, gymnasiums, and administrative offices, but it is not needed in corridors and in the cafeteria. Traffic areas in hospitals do not need to be lit with full-spectrum, and under no circumstances should it be used in the nursery (see Chapter 11, "Health Care Facilities").

If the inclusion of UV—as found in full-spectrum lights—is a matter of concern for some individuals, I suggest the use of lights with a high CRI (Color Rendering Index). The index was developed to describe how well colors are rendered by artificial light sources as compared with natural light. But for biological purposes it also gives us an indication of how close to the natural spectrum the light is.

Hughes and Neer pointed out in 1981 that a number of researchers have examined the significance of using high-CRI lights, as opposed to standard cool-white sources, for illuminating work areas. It should be stressed that high-CRI lamps produce a subjective visual clarity much higher than that achieved by standard cool-white lamps. Based on visual clarity studies, lighting engineers in Europe recommend a minimum of CRI 85.

Some lighting applications do not require simulated sunlight. These may be where lights of a lower color temperature (warmer) are desired to induce various psychological effects, including relaxation. Examples would be employees' lounges, cafeterias, restaurants, hotel lobbies, hotel rooms, and so forth.

Chapter Nine

Analysis
and Establishment
of Design Goals

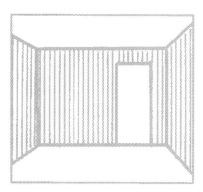

This chapter and those following offer practical advice on the use of color in a variety of architectural spaces. Although I do not believe at all in giving color "recipes," because every architectural space must be analyzed in terms of its own particular situation, function, and needs, I will give some *suggestions* for selecting the predominant color in various kinds of spaces. By *predominant* I mean the color that is important to establish the overall mood or ambience of a place.

The previous chapters should give the reader a sufficient foundation for making necessary color choices. I cannot overstress how important color is in setting the background for our "experience of a space." Color is the decisive factor in determining how a particular space appears to us. As color specifiers, we create a set of visual conditions that will affect the user psychologically and under certain circumstances physiologically.

Not only color influences the appearance and feeling of a space, but also its size, shape, materials, light distribution, furnishings, and so forth. Still it is *color* that has the greatest influence on the overall ambience of a space. If we compare architecturally *identical spaces,* each furnished and arranged in identical fashion, except for the predominant color, the appearance will change dramatically even though all elements other than color are the same. The experience of a white room is different from a blue one, a red one, yellow, green, and so forth. (See Figures C-16, C-17, C-18, and C-19)

The Polarity Profile

Designing an ideal ambience demands careful analysis. Ask yourself these two basic questions:

1. *What are my major design goals for this environment?*

2. *How do I meet these goals with some measure of predictable accuracy?*

An efficient tool that eliminates guesswork by bringing order to the many factors to be considered is the *semantic differential chart,* or *polarity profile.* The polarity profile pairs descriptive adjectives with their antonyms. These polarities provide a range of "feelings" about a space. For example:

unpleasant—pleasant

exciting—calming

contemporary—traditional

meaningless—symbolic

elegant—unadorned

The polarity profile is used after some primary identification about a project has been made:

1. Type of building or space it is (school, hospital, patient room, office space, manufacturing plant, etc.).

2. What function the space serves, for example:
   a. Office requiring high amount of concentration
   b. Reception area giving first impression of a company
   c. Assembly line for quantity and quality output
   d. Meeting space conducive to group therapy

It is self-evident that different criteria and design objectives exist for various environments. Naturally, the design of a school and a family restaurant, and the supporting ambience for each is vastly different. Sections within a given structure are also treated very differently. A classroom, school corridor, library, auditorium, and gymnasium all serve different functions.

The polarity profile can aid in establishing some of the necessary criteria. To illustrate with a family restaurant, wouldn't you agree that it should reflect the following visual qualities?

friendly not unfriendly

stimulating not sterile

warm not cold

familiar not unfamiliar

good value (for the money) not expensive

informal not formal

comfortable not uncomfortable

appetizing not unappetizing

In comparison, although both serve the same function, an elegant restaurant will have different criteria from the family restaurant, because representation and expectation are different. In the case of the noble restaurant the following mood would be appropriate:

elegant not modest

formal not informal

dignified not common

IMPRESSIONS POLARITY PROFILE

	3	2	1	0	1	2	3	
Variable								*Monotonous*
Interesting								*Boring*
Dynamic								*Static*
Imaginative								*Unimaginative*
Complex								*Simple*
Uniform								*Motley*
Arousing								*Calming*
Protecting								*Uneasy*
Friendly								*Unfriendly*
Warm								*Cold*
Soft								*Hard*
Modern								*Timeless*
Powerful								*Weak*
Harmonious								*Disharmonious*
Silly								*Serious*
Expensive								*Cheap*
Heavy								*Light*
Meaningless								*Symbolic*
Clean								*Dirty*
Elegant								*Common*

Yet, the moods that both restaurants would have in common would be:

friendly not unfriendly (one being a casual friendliness; the other more formal—both giving an inviting impression)

stimulating not sterile (but less so for the noble restaurant)

comfortable not uncomfortable

appetizing not unappetizing

Your color design, most of all the predominant color (walls), but also the total ensemble (color in incidental areas, carpeting, furnishings, etc.), may now be specified in accordance with the desired impression. For example, choices for the family restaurant should be friendly, stimulating, warm, appetizing colors, whereas the noble restaurant should have elegant, formal, dignified, inviting, and appetizing colors. (For "appetizing" colors, see Chapter 15, "Food and Foodservice".) This leads us right back to the section in Chapter 4, "Hue Effect, Impressions or Associations— Character": the psychological aspects of color.

The polarity profile may also be reviewed with the client or user. To find out their concerns, what is important for them in their environment, will help you greatly in establishing design goals, and it will make the user feel involved. The polarity profile may also be used to analyze existing environments and their problems that must be cor-

COLOR ANALYSIS POLARITY PROFILE

3   2   1   0   1   2   3

Hue Attributes

Light (Value)	*Dark (Value)*
Strong (Chroma)	*Weak (Chroma)*
Clear	*Muddy*
Warm	*Cold*

Impression or Effect

Calming	*Arousing*
Quiet	*Loud*
Stimulating	*Boring*
Refined	*Unrefined*
Encouraging	*Discouraging*
Friendly	*Hostile*
Receding	*Advancing*
Harmonious	*Disharmonious*

Functional

Appropriate	*Inappropriate*
Vision (Ergonomics)	*Vision (Ergonomics)*
Task Supporting	*Task Opposing*
Problem Compensating	*Problem Supporting*

Copyright © Frank H. Mahnke 1990

rected. Some designers pin down public reaction to an environment through use of the polarity profile.

In my design work I have devised three different polarity profiles, not just one; each has its own purpose and function to supply me with the necessary information for realizing my design goals.

The Impressions Polarity Profile

This profile helps to plot the design goals for a particular space. The example shown on the previous page is not a rigid set of adjective polarities. As a matter of fact, you will have to devise your own polarity profile to suit your needs, and one that adapts itself to the space in question. The impressions profile is also the one to be used to test public reaction to a space, or to identify mood problems within an existing environment that is to be redesigned.

Color Analysis Polarity Profile

This profile, illustrated above, I use to analyze the dominant and subdominant colors inherent in an existing space, or to recheck my color design specifications. The profile is separated into three different areas:

1. Hue attributes: Are the colors dark, light, weak, strong, clear, muddy, and so forth?

2. Impression or effect: What impressions do the individual colors produce—regardless of the entire ensemble of the space? What needs changing? Are the colors appropriate to satisfy the goals established by the "impressions profile"?

3. Functional: Indicates whether or not the colors are appropriate from the standpoint of visual ergonomics. Are they task-supporting or hindering? Do they support or eliminate certain problems?

Special Environmental Problems Polarity Profile

Color may support, or be in agreement with, a given situation; therefore, it has a consonant action. When it counteracts specific environmental problems, it may be said to have a compensatory action. For example, the problem of heat in an environment will be supported by a warm color such as orange and counteracted by the subjective coolness of blue-green. Orange has adopted the consonant role and blue-green the compensatory one.

This polarity profile, as shown on the following page, identifies special environmental problems. Its use may not be necessary in all environments, but it is of aid in certain industrial and manufacturing plants. Spatial effects may also pose certain problems (in all spaces), being either too high, low, small, wide, etc.

All polarity profiles have an evaluation scale to indicate the degree of importance of each given polarity. This scale may be changed as wished. For my purposes, and I have found it more suitable not to be too complex in degree of evaluation, I have broken the scale down into four degrees:

0 = Does not apply

1 = To a low degree (or somewhat)

2 = Middle value (midway)

3 = Highest Value (most important, or most extreme impression)

To clarify these degrees with the "impressions profile," and in conjunction with the establishing of design goals (not as an analysis of an existing environment), I might want an environment to be "highly imaginative," therefore I would assign degree three (3); yet it should be somewhat complex—degree one (1); it doesn't need to be highly arousing, but arousal should be of importance—degree two (2); heavy or light is of no consequence—degree zero (0).

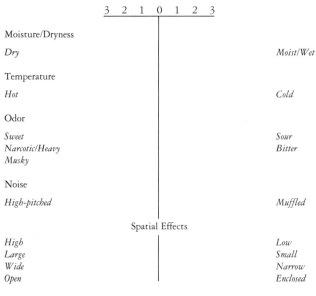

SPECIAL ENVIRONMENTAL PROBLEMS POLARITY PROFILE
(SUBJECTIVE COMPENSATION/CONSONANCE-MOSTLY
INDUSTRIAL)

	3	2	1	0	1	2	3	

Moisture/Dryness

Dry   *Moist/Wet*

Temperature

Hot   *Cold*

Odor

Sweet   *Sour*
Narcotic/Heavy   *Bitter*
Musky

Noise

High-pitched   *Muffled*

Spatial Effects

High   *Low*
Large   *Small*
Wide   *Narrow*
Open   *Enclosed*

Copyright © Frank H. Mahnke 1990

Polarity profiles may be designed to be complex or simple, but no serious color designer can afford not to utilize a polarity profile. The environment, its design goals, and particular problems must always be analyzed to ensure purposeful design.

Design Considerations

Whatever the ultimate design goal is for a particular architectural space, there are some fundamental rules and considerations that must be adhered to. These are:

1. The need to consider psychological and physiological effects in design for the well-being of the user must be explained to the client. He must be made aware that "personal taste" is not the major criterion.

2. The balance between unity and complexity, color variety within reason, must be respected. This balance depends on the visual information rate within a space produced in majority by dominant (walls), subdominant (incidental surface areas, such as end walls, also flooring and ceiling), and accent color (furnishings—including decorative items), and color contrasts.

3. Visual ergonomics (agreeable seeing conditions) depend on the colors used and on contrast. Rules must be respected especially in the workplace, health facilities, industry, schools.

4. Satisfying the mood or atmosphere desired depends on the specification of colors based on their psychological content (effects, impression, association, synesthetic aspects).

Color is the major factor in establishing a desired room experience. It contributes heavily to the "emotional loading" a space exhibits. However, your first consideration must be the question: Which ambience is desired for which function?

To illustrate, a post-surgery recovery room in a hospital should be calming. The first that comes to mind would be a cool, restrained, peaceful, dominant color choice; a low-key, subdued stimulus environment (not to be confused with monotony). This would be a correct direction. On the other hand, a warm, and somewhat more active environment that picks up the spirits, reminds patients of "living," and appears friendly, is also a solution. Why? Inviting surroundings because of their friendliness are also calming. This does not imply that the cooler, low-stimulus environments are necessarily unfriendly. Both solutions (with the exception of intensive care for the latter) are acceptable.

Color in itself is a tool for the ambience we wish to choose. First, we must be sure which ambience is the ideal. We are not choosing color first; we analyze the goal of the "room experience" and *then* we choose its appropriate color. Color is the alphabet; with this alphabet we form the words; but the words, the statement, must be appropriate.

The major misconception made regarding color psychology is the simple fact I have stated above. It reminds me of the words of a well-known architect who said: "I will never use the services of a color psychologist. If I design a school, for example, he [the color psychologist] will just advise green to calm the kids down." This reveals a basic misconception. Just because green is considered calming, doesn't mean it is the only solution.

A color specialist trained in applied psychology would certainly have been able to create a calm school environment without necessarily using green. An expert would have analyzed first what constitutes a calming environment, then would have known that single color applications, regardless of color, are not calming because of the unity and complexity balance. This color specialist would have known that environments may induce emotions, and that this emotional content may affect other emotions, such as the example with the "friendly" post-surgery room.

Color design that serves a purpose has only three major rules to adhere to:

1. It supports the function of a building, and the tasks that are being carried out in it.

2. It avoids overstimulation and understimulation.

3. It does not create negative emotional and physiological effects.

We can summarize it very simply by saying: Not every architectural space a color, but every architectural space *its* color. An architectural space should not just have a color (for color's sake), but rather its appropriate color that fits the purpose of the building or space.

Offices and VDT Computer Workstations

General Guidelines

More and more business managers recognize that employee efficiency and the work environment are directly connected. In the past personal comfort was rarely an issue. If a decision had to be made between employee comfort and cost control, cost control won. The first reason for providing the employee with a safe and comfortable workplace should be the employer's concern for his employee. Management's awareness of human factors in the office environment usually comes from enlightened self-interest: the realization that better conditions lead to higher efficiency, hence more productivity.

There are consultants in the "human factors" field whose excellent advice is essential in creating the optimum office environment. They will concern themselves with all the ergonomic factors: efficient space planning, lighting, noise and temperature control, and their advice should be followed. But what is missing in most cases is any reference to color. Therefore, the human factors expert and the color expert, who set the mood and image of a space, must work in hand to create the optimum office environment.

Good office design is more than just pastel colors and plants. Primary concerns must be:

    1. Correct lighting: preferably not the standard overhead rows of uniform fluorescents; also concern for the quality of the light in terms of its biological effects on human beings.

    2. Strict adherence to the rules of safeguarding vision (short review to follow).

    3. Ergonomic furniture: Chairs, desks, and equipment designed and arranged so that people and things interact most efficiently and safely.

    4. Psychological factors: design choices that consider interactions among employees, for example.

    5. Image: how the environment reflects the company.

Correct Lighting

Correct lighting levels and placement are the task of the lighting engineer. However, the interplay of light and color in regard to visual ergonomics falls within the sphere of the color designer. Concern should also be shown for the *quality* of light and its biological effect. For good visual acuity and positive physiological effect lamps should be full spectrum or with a high color rendering index (CRI) rating (for details see Chapter 7, "Vision and Light," and Chapter 8, "Biological Effects of Light").

Agreeable Visual Conditions

The question of how much light is needed for clear and comfortable vision has been belabored for many years by lighting engineers. The subject of too much versus too little light is a matter of constant debate. Too little light will handicap vision and too much will overtax it.

In the design of the interior environmental space, visual efficiency and comfort are foremost. Although I discussed agreeable visual conditions in the previous chapter "Vision and Light," I will take the liberty of repeating these to emphasize their importance.

It is often assumed that eye fatigue is a matter of retinal nerve fatigue; this is not so. It is muscles, not eye nerves, that are likely to cause trouble. Just like any muscle subjected to excessive activity, eye muscles also tire. Glare, constant adjustment to extreme brightness differences, prolonged fixations of the eyes, and constant shifts in accommodation will tire eyes quickly, causing headaches, tension, nausea, and other disturbances. It is essential to control extreme contrast in light and dark, otherwise the iris muscles experience undue stress because the pupil is forced to undergo constant adjustment.

Vision should be held at midtones, an ideal light-to-reflection ratio being three to one. This means controlling the light reflection of walls, furniture, desks, and floors. Recommended reflectance for surfaces are: 20 percent for floors, 25–40 percent for furniture, 40–60 percent for walls (which can be stretched to 70 percent depending on lighting conditions), and 80–90 percent for ceilings. These percentages may be raised somewhat as long as the three-to-one ratio is repected. Insufficient or feeble contrasts are emotionally unsatisfying and should be avoided.

Working surfaces (desktops) should be a warm gray (30 percent light reflection). The color is neutral and nondistracting, and it strikes a good brightness balance between white and black, keeping the eyes at a uniform and comfortable level of adjustment. Wood desktops are also acceptable since the pattern helps to diffuse reflection. Desktops should never be too dark or too light—especially black or white tops should never be specified. The desk's body may be darker than the top.

Glare also puts debilitating strain on the eyes. Direct glare results from insufficiently shielded light sources and unshaded windows. Individuals should be situated so that they do not face windows. Window walls should always be light in color to eliminate strong brightness contrasts between dark walls and the entering sunlight. Reflected glare results from specular reflection of high luminances on polished surfaces. This is one of the reasons that matte work surfaces and walls are highly recommended.

Light sources, whether of high or low intensity, should always be properly baffled with louvers or lenses. For work tasks demanding a great deal of light, a localized light source may be introduced.

Psychological Factors—From the Standpoint of the Employee

Elimination of drab, employee-unfriendly and emotionally unsatisfying office surroundings does not mean that "humanization" of the work environment demands developing recreational or living areas. The objective should be to eliminate influences that interfere with tasks—be they visual, physiological, or psychological. Office workers are meant to get things done, not to be entertained. The design criteria must be based on objective guidelines and look upon the office as being a tool for the employees to aid them in their tasks.

1. Drab offices are counterproductive. Off-white, buff, and gray surroundings offer little inspiration. Employers must reflect an image of caring for their employees, and this involves providing environments that will raise spirits, not suppress them.

2. Satisfaction with the environment is closely associated with job performance.

3. Office workers spend half of their waking hours on the job. A pleasant setting will positively reinforce their efforts to represent the company's interests.

4. Orderly environments inspire orderliness; chaotic surroundings may breed chaotic thinking.

Image

Corporate image is big business these days. It includes not only the image of corporate offices, but also logo, stationery, etc. Unfortunately, many new corporate office buildings are so concerned with corporate image that a style or fashion approach supersedes good practical sense. Too great an effort often is made to create an atmosphere that is associated mentally with the product or service the business sells.

Certainly a connection between product and design can be achieved in various ways. One way would be to carry certain logo colors to incidental areas. But corporate offices are better served by creating an image that stands less for the product and more for the company-client relationship. This relationship should reflect trustworthiness, dependability, and stability, all key words that can be carried over visually into the design of corporate offices. All efforts should be made to convey an impression that reflects a people-oriented, therefore client-oriented, image.

A very popular but totally incorrect ambience is the high-tech image. Heavy emphasis is placed on sterility created by grays, white, and black, with occasional hues in upholstery. (See Figure C-6.) One case history involves an office suite with white walls, black desks, and deep-purple carpets. The whole impression can be summed up with the word *impersonal*—not to mention the total disregard of visual ergonomics. White walls reflect 80 percent of light and black about 5 percent; the brightness contrast ratio is 16:1. This is outrageous.

Modern offices too often start out as giant dark-tinted glass or gray cement cubes on the exterior. That exterior gloom and aloofness is then carried to the interior. The impression of "corporate power," and in the case of government buildings "bureaucratic power," must be avoided. Just as a receptionist is required to greet the public in a friendly and personable manner, so should the environment reflect goodwill.

Lobbies and reception areas especially should be accessible and friendly. They should make people feel at ease, relaxed, and reflect an attitude of business on a neighborly basis. (See Figure C-45.) It is very hard to get this impression standing on dark shiny tile surrounded by gray walls. Color means life and the living; achromatic is associated with inanimate objects such as machines, and corporate offices are not machines. The office worker is not to be reduced to a cog in such a mechanism.

Open Offices

Most offices today have adopted the open-office system. The idea behind such design is better communication—no endless corridors to travel and doors to open. The introduction of small movable cubicles affords more privacy than the large open office with its rows of desks, seen in earlier years. But it is still an inadequate substitute for privacy. And it is difficult for managers to operate in this environment, since they often need to discuss sensitive information with employees. The ability to concentrate is also impaired, especially with the problem of high noise levels with phones constantly ringing and voices constantly talking. Often no allowance is made for distant seeing, which is a requirement to relax the eyes. Of course, one advantage of the movable partition system is its adaptability to changing space requirements.

It is important that a variety of sensory information be included in the design. The office worker should be able to gaze in different directions and have varying visual experiences. Departments within the same open office space could receive different partition colors; this would also aid in orientation (especially for clients) and give the office worker more of a sense of individuality. Multisensory experiences

Open office partitions should be varied in color to achieve differing desired effects and safeguard against visual blandness. (Photo: Frank H. Mahnke)

should also be introduced: textures such as rough stone walls in incidental areas; spots with plants and even fountains. The cubicles in the center of the open office could be darker in color than the surroundings sections. Workers in the center would then not feel "squeezed" into the middle, but be the center radiating outward.

Color Specifications

In color specification, first come those that should *not* be used as dominant (wall) colors: no purple, violet, vivid yellow, yellow-green, bright red, and please—no white or gray. Beyond that, the choice of hues, guided by good judgment, is fairly broad. Remember that in offices where intense concentration is required, attention should be directed inward with cool hues. In general office areas, the choice of warm or cool hues depends on preference. Soft yellow, sandstone, pale gold, pale orange, pale green, and blue-green are always appropriate.

Video Display Terminals

An office without some type of computer equipment that uses a video display terminal (VDT) is almost nonexistent today. Despite the advantages offered by such equipment, operators of VDTs have been the largest single source of health complaints registered with the National Institute of Occupational Safety and Health. According to a survey conducted by the Data Entry Management Association, over 66 per-

Reflective glare on VDT screens must be avoided under all circumstances. (Photo: Frank H. Mahnke)

cent of the respondents reported they had experienced eye strain, back pain, fatigue, and neck and shoulder pain. More than 33 percent had burning eyes from looking at computer screens and felt general irritability. Headaches and loss of visual acuity were also common complaints.

The Suffolk County (New York) Legislature enacted a local law in 1988 providing employee protection against VDT problems. The legislature found and determined "that it is in the public interest to provide public and private sectors employees who operate video display terminals within Suffolk County with a safe and healthy work environment." The law sets down a number of requirements having to do with vision examinations, employee education and training, work breaks, and workstation standards.

A big difference exists between general office work and work being performed utilizing VDTs. Work undertaken on a flat horizontal surface, such as reading, handwriting, typing, and filing is done with the employee's line of sight usually directed downward. Work on the VDT, because of the terminals screen's upright position, requires employees to raise their line of sight higher than they would when looking at a horizontal surface.

When looking at a computer screen, mirror images of overhead lighting fixtures are seen reflected. Off-white walls that veil the screens and bright clothing also reflect back into the eyes. In numerous cases the illumination is too high causing a decrease in display contrast which reduces the visibility of the characters displayed on the screen.

Potential sources of glare.

General Illumination Level

There is some controversy in regard to appropriate light levels for VDT workplaces. However, an excellent paper by William Cushman of Eastern Kodak suggests 15–35 foot-candles for tasks not involving paper documents, with a bit more light, 35–50 foot-candles, for tasks involving transfer of information from paper documents to VDT. There are other experts whose recommendations fall within the general scope of Cushman's specifications, which tends to confirm these illumination values.

There is no question that light levels in VDT rooms should be lower than those of general offices. It would be wholly appropriate to let workers decide efficiency and comfort levels for themselves by equipping illumination in computer rooms with dimmers.

Close Distance and Frequent Eye Movements

By far, most health complaints experienced by VDT operators are associated with eyes and vision. Human eyes were made for most efficient seeing at far distances. VDT use, on the other hand, calls for intense concentration at a close distance. Long periods of fixation on the screen at such close range often causes visual fatigue. External eye muscles work together to keep both eyes centered at the same character and from one character or word to another. Internal muscles, in this case the ring of ciliary muscles, contract to compress the lens of the eye. This steady effort, as is true for any static muscle exertion, may cause the eye's muscular system to tire.

Optical relaxation is achieved by occasionally looking into the distance. Hence, allowance must be made for distant seeing of at least 15 feet. This pertains not only to VDT operators but to office workers who have their vision confined to near distance only. The eyes must be given a chance to relax.

Work involving reference material requires the eyes to shift constantly between the material, keyboard, and screen—a frequent change from horizontal to vertical and back. Each time the eye must change and accommodate its focus, which may prove tiring and be aggravated further if there are big differences in the luminous density of the reference material, the keyboard, and the screen. The American Optometric Society, along with others, suggests placing the reference material as close to the screen as possible to avoid large eye and head movements, and at the same distance from eyes as the VDT screen—thereby also avoiding frequent change in focus.

Controlling Glare and Brightness Contrast

A great amount of discomfort is caused by glare and extreme differences between light and dark. The result of undue stress put on the tiny muscles (iris) that control the amount of light entering the eye readily causes visual discomfort, headaches, nausea, general fatigue, and true pain.

Reflected glare or specular images on the VDT screen from the operator's own bright clothing, light walls, luminaires or other objects above or behind the VDT must be avoided at all cost. These reflections make it difficult to see the characters on the screen because the display contrast is reduced. Some characters may even be partially or totally obscured. Attempts by the operator to read obscured characters or minimize glare by contorting body posture may result in neck and back pain.

How can glare be reduced or eliminated? The first consideration is the direction of light. Most offices have direct lighting systems with overhead troffer fixtures and plastic lenses. These should be modified or changed. If it is not possible to remove the fixtures entirely and replace them with better luminaires positioned to eliminate glare, then in some instances fixture lenses can be replaced with louvered parabolic "egg crates." Lighting can remain directed from above, but neither lamps nor images will be reflected on the screen.

You may also consider indirect lighting from special fixtures, or perhaps attached to partitions or other stationary objects. Light levels must be kept on the low side. Be careful that an illuminated ceiling does not cause the VDT screens to have a veil spread over them.

There are instances where changes in or to lighting systems may not be allowed. The alternative is to relocate the VDT equipment so that light sources do not reflect upon the screen. The ideal would be to position VDTs so that the viewing direction, windows, and row of luminaires are parallel to one another; i.e., there should be no windows or luminaires directly behind or in front of the operator. To clarify further, workstations must be placed between the rows of overhead light fixtures and not underneath them.

Extreme contrast in light and dark must be controlled in all areas: equipment, furniture, walls, and floors. Vision must be held at a uniform level by midtones, avoiding extremes in dark and light. The ideal ratio is three to one, meaning that optimum visual comfort is maintained when task luminance is not greater than three times the luminances in the immediate vicinity of the task.

The term *luminances* does not apply only to the light source but to the surfaces reflecting light as well. Walls in computer rooms should reflect 50–60 percent, 20–30 percent for floors, and 30–50 percent for furniture. The ratio of the low 20 percent and the high 60 percent would be three to one.

Shades, venetian blinds, or opaque drapes should be installed on windows to block out excess daylight, since it can be a source of glare. If daylight cannot be blocked out completely, then the light level of the row of luminaires parallel to the windows should be adjustable (dimmers). Then during the day the illumination level can be lowered to compensate for the entering daylight; at night it can be raised, since some light will be lost through the windows.

To eliminate reflection from walls use a matte or flat finish— *never* semigloss or gloss paint. Wallcoverings in fabric, wallpaper, or wood paneling is preferred. The reflection ratios advised for walls should be respected, so this rules out white and off-white walls. In rooms strictly used for VDT work, the color of the walls is optional since attention is focused on the screen and light levels are low. Dr. Heinrich Frieling has suggested color specifications that compensate VDT characters in green. He advises that the bothersome light-purplish-pink afterimages created by the green characters may be intercepted by purple-brownish (grayed) coloration on the walls (green phosphor has a dominant wavelength of approximately 500 nm; the color for walls was calculated from that). Of course only a panel of the complementary color to the hue of the screen characters (whatever they may be) will suffice.

The color of the workstation should be olive-gray, which will gray the afterimage. Interestingly enough, some time ago an item in the *Chicago Tribune* mentioned the color distortion VDT operators can suffer. In the wake of VDT safety studies operators reported noticing pink edges on white paper and walls after prolonged periods of VDT use.

Single or Low Number of VDT Installations

Many general offices have few VDTs, from one station to perhaps no more than five. Where there are more than five I recommend that, if possible, a room be set aside for VDT installation that adheres to guidelines given so far.

Limited installations (especially the single VDT station) are usually installed in a general office with a ceiling full of bright fluorescent lights. In such cases VDTs should be placed in a subdued corner where the ambient lighting is fairly low. The VDT screen should be positioned facing a nonglossy wall (the operator faces away from the wall) or any other vertical surface that does not reflect light. Luminaires should not be in the operator's immediate field of view, or behind the operator as to reflect on the screen. Often room dividers, bookcases, or filing cabinets may be used to obstruct direct glare from luminaires.

Chapter Eleven

Health Care Facilities

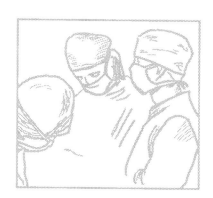

The "temples of healing" designed by the finest architects in ancient Greece were elaborate buildings with gardens, libraries, and theaters. The philosophy was to honor the suffering, not to punish them. Beauty was to be a natural right not only of the strong and healthy, but also of the weak and sick. Caring emotionally for the patient seems to have been a part of the healing method. It is our task, as designers, to express this type of care visually in the hospitals of today.

For hundreds of years hospitals were associated exclusively with suffering, pain, and death. No one is ever happy over the prospect of having to enter a hospital, even when the patient knows it will be of great benefit to do so. For many people, especially the novice patient, going to the hospital is a frightening event.

Most people entering a hospital for the first time feel as though they are in a foreign country. This new strange region has its own customs, food, clothing, and language that is incomprehensible to them, and with seemingly arbitrary rules that govern every action. They do not know why something is happening, what it is intended to accomplish, or how they should react to it. If determined enough, one can ask questions, but the busy, depersonalized hospital atmosphere discourages questions. The patient may well feel uncertain, apprehensive, and worst of all, ignored.

Indeed, having placed themselves in the hands of others, most patients feel stripped of the power they have over themselves. They might also harbor subconscious fears or consciously recall past unpleasant experiences connected with medical treatment and health-care facilities. All this adds further to the feeling of being institutionalized—in the negative sense of the word.

In 1978, the U.S. Department of Commerce—National Bureau of Standards issued reports of a special workshop entitled "Color in the Health Care Environment." The publication states that "medical facilities represent perhaps the most critical category of buildings in need of proper criteria." Dr. Thomas Sisson, who headed the workshop, noted that "the use of color in hospitals is often inconsistent and potentially detrimental to the feeling of well-being by the patient." (Sisson, quoted in NBS Special Publication 516 1978, III)

Health care facilities can aid the healing process by establishing an environment that contributes to the psychological and physiological well-being of the patient. Psychosomatic medicine has verified the strong ties between physical response to surgical and medical care and the emotional attitude of the patient.

The ill person is in disharmony; not only is the harmony of his body disturbed through his illness, but also the harmony between his body and his soul. His emotional makeup and needs are not the same as when he is not sick. Patients need to feel that they are being cared for—not just medically, but emotionally as well. The best of medical

Hospitals are the most important buildings in need of proper color design goals. For patients entering a hospital, especially for the first time, the experience may be frightening. (Photo: Frank H. Mahnke)

care and nursing attention should be found in hospitals. Patients and visitors have a right to be critical and apprehensive. The "image" of the hospital depends on the user's confidence in that facility's efficiency, and its level of care and caring. Such a desirable impression comes to us first through the appearance of the hospital.

General Design Objectives

Hospitals are highly complicated buildings. At their best they are efficient, functional, and technically perfect. However, these qualities should not be presented through design; otherwise the impression of a "hospital factory" is quickly reflected. Patients are not medical material on an assembly line. The most important design objective must be to *minimize* the institutional look as much as possible.

Due to its departmental structuring, the health care facility is also a complex set of different environments, each demanding a supportive visual milieu of its own—yet all interrelated to preserve the facility's overall unity.

The general appearance must not be coldly formal, aloof, and inaccessible. Even the most wonderful bedside manner of physicians and nurses will be of little value if the environment does not reinforce them. On the other hand, a too-casual look might stimulate skepticism as to the level of professional services offered. Exaggerated charm or too much colorfulness in an attempt to express friendliness is quickly unmasked as being cosmetic and without professional substance. A friendly appearance is not synonymous with a merry or jovial one. Too many strong colors and patterns increase visual noise, interfere dangerously with the performance of the nurse's or doctor's task, and in the long run will not lessen the patient's apprehension or anxiety.

In areas where surgeons, nurses, medical, and administrative staff perform their duties (i.e., operating rooms, intensive care, X ray, therapy, laboratories, etc.) the environment must not tax vision, lead to undue fatigue, or induce emotional monotony. Especially in these areas there must be a judicious use of color and light based on functional and practical necessity. The well-being not only of the patient is important, but also that of hospital personnel. The daily task of caring for the ill and the constant confrontation with suffering requires a lot of strength and patience. Incorrect environmental conditions will put further burden on personnel, and perhaps affect their efficiency and how they relate to their patients.

The general design objectives that constitute proper color and light design are as follows:

1. The facility must retain a dignified and respectful appearance, yet be attractive as well.

2. Color specifications must play a psychological and aesthetic role thereby:

a. promoting the healing process by guarding the physiological and psychological well-being of the patient;

b. being an aid in accurate visual medical diagnosis, surgical performance, and therapeutic and rehabilitation services;

c. enhancing light, visual ergonomics, supporting orientation, supplying information, defining specific areas, and improving working conditions through visual means.

3. Lighting must be chosen with respect to function, psychological reinforcement, visual appeal, color rendition, and biological concerns.

Development of a Color Plan

In existing facilities that need renovation, an analysis of conditions must be conducted. Use a polarity profile to elicit the following information.

1. Identification of existing environmental problems with regard to the ambience (monotony, overstimulation, incorrect color from a color-psychological standpoint, insufficient orientation, too many sensory or conflicting signals, etc.).

2. Analysis of lighting conditions (too bright, too dark, bothersome glare, too much light and dark contrast—includes color) and the type and quality of light (warm, cold, color rendering index).

3. Familiarization with the functions of each area of the facility (surgical, intensive care, maternity, long-term or short-term patient areas, therapy rooms, etc.). Valuable information can also be gained by asking the nursing staff about their concerns, tasks, and activities. Spend enough time in each section to get an impression of its heart, soul, and character. You must collect enough data and impressions to be thoroughly familiar with the facility.

4. Discuss design objectives with the client.

For newly planned institutions, a prerequisite is an understanding of the architectural drawings and proposed light. As in existing facilities, an understanding of the function of each area of the hospital is essential.

All data can now be compiled into three major categories:

1. Atmosphere (ambience): patient rooms, corridors, waiting rooms, reception, lounges, general office areas, staff and/or visitors' cafeteria or dining room.

2. Specific-task sections: X ray, EEG-EKG rooms, radiation therapy, examining and treatment rooms, intensive care and recovery rooms, operating rooms, laboratories and work rooms, etc.

3. Functional areas: utility, equipment, storage areas.

The foregoing information should provide an excellent basis for commencing color selection.

Recommendations for Specific Hospital Areas

Entrance Lobby and Patient Reception

The entrance lobby and patient reception, with the exception of the exterior of the building, is the most important first impression patient and visitors receive of the facility. (See Figures C-20 and C-21.) From a color-psychological viewpoint and in connection with a decorative approach the appearance should transmit a sense of friendliness, human warmth, and the promise of care and emotional security. A hotel-lobby look would be more appropriate than an expected "hospital look."

However, the designer must be careful that the appearance of the lobby is in general agreement with the rest of the facility, not especially in its use of color, but in regard to the quality of the environment. From a psychological viewpoint it would be detrimental if the lobby promises an environmental quality and raises hopes that the rest of the facility does not keep. This was the case in an Alzheimer treatment center I once visited. The entrance lobby, reception, and administrative areas were richly decorated, but the patient areas were stark-white, impersonal cubicles. The first impression of a health-care facility must never be misleading.

Corridors

Corridors are not only functional traffic areas; they also make up a large part of the surface area within a hospital and therefore contribute significantly to an overall impression. The mood of a ward depends on the color used in its corridor. (See Figures C-29, C-30, and C-31.)

That the corridors in the surgical ward should reflect an ambience different from that of the pediatric ward, for example, is self-evident. Corridor design should indicate the function of the section they are located in, which also aids in traffic orientation. If hospital administration wishes to keep all corridors in the same color (out of the mistaken belief of easier maintenance), then certain architectural elements and doors may take over the task of unit identification and orientation. The often-used system of wall stripes for orientation is fine for factories and parking garages, but they have no place in hospitals because they are too typically institutional.

Whether the mood should be warm or cool depends in some cases on the function of the unit itself. For maternity and pediatric sections, warm colors are a good choice. Intensive-care units and surgery corridors can be in cool colors, such as blue-green or green to reflect a functional and more serious atmosphere. These greens should not be too dark and weak, since such tones are often associated with "institutional" green.

In any case, all corridors should be attractive and reflect an atmosphere of calm. *Calm*, of course, does not depend solely on the use of a cool color; the effect can be transmitted just as well by warm hues. Chroma, value, pattern, and amount of hue variation are the principles in establishing either an exciting or calming effect. For example, a pale orange or peach will appear calmer than a bright, intense green.

With large areas, such as corridors, a common mistake is choosing color and pattern for an empty space. Let us assume a hypothetical situation.

A designer is asked to design a hospital corridor. Since not much can be done in terms of accessories, a logical step would be to add interest with imaginative decorative designs or patterns on the wall. Maybe different-colored wall sections running horizontally in attention-producing hues would add decoration. More interest is added from patterns in the carpet or a carryover of the wall designs to the carpet.

This plan certainly would have impact and perhaps be aesthetically pleasing when the proposal is presented. But now let us add people to that corridor—nurses busily going about their tasks, carts and equipment being pulled from one area to another, unsteady patients trying to navigate a path. The once-empty corridor on the presentation board abounds in pattern, activity, and excessive visual information. Will this be a calm setting to reduce anxiety?

On the other hand, the designer could lessen the information rate by keeping the walls neutral, with color added in incidental areas. The absence of color creates emotional sterility and may not be calming (or attractive).

Long corridors may be color sequenced. In long corridors the end wall should always be color differentiated. For example, the sides could be peach and the end wall a medium blue. If the two-color effect is used, then careful attention must be paid that the brightness ratios of the two hues on the side of each wall are similar. This will minimize contrast and establish a uniform field of view. There should never be one dark side and one light side. The color of the floor, and the side of the door that faces the corridor, should be either related to the dominant hue or complementary. Under no circumstances should there be too many radically different colors in the major areas of the corridor.

Patient Rooms

Medical doctors and psychologists are in agreement that a patient's room should be comfortable, cheerful, optimistic, and tranquil. Of course, with limited exceptions, patient rooms cannot be tailored to the specific illness of the patient. Were it so, we could eliminate those colors that patients reject due to their specific ailment, as for example yellow that is rejected by patients suffering from liver disorders. Susan Castelluccio, who works with children suffering from cancer, wrote that these patients selected red, blue, black, and purple as being indicative of their illness. When asked about their preferences for environmental colors they expressed choices that specifically did not include red, blue, purple, and black.

Because patients are often supine, the ceiling may be tinted. However, caution must be taken with green since this may cast an unfavorable reflection on the skin. Ceiling colors should always be light so that they do not appear disturbing and heavy.

For reasons of visual diagnosis the wall located at headboard end of the patient's bed should not carry highly saturated hues. These may alter the patient's skin color (reflection and simultaneous contrast). The wall the patient faces may serve as a different colored end wall to add interest and color change to the room.

A warm room could be pale orange on three sides with the fourth wall slightly darker but not brighter. A cool room, for example, might have sandstone on three walls and pale green on the end wall. If a single color is used on all walls, suitable choices are peach, soft yellow, pale gold, and light green; interest and color change must be added in accessories or incidental areas.

Fairly soft tones are better than sharp ones. For reasons of refinement, and because strong colors may be unduly unsettling or grow monotonous to a patient confined for a long term, caution must be exercised in purity of color.

The designer must use good judgment and some psychological insight in color selection. There is good reason to consider comfort of vision as a primary concern, as is the case with any environment, but psychological factors are also of great importance. Some rooms can also be suited to their function, as for example patient rooms in intensive care, recovery, maternity, and pediatric. Since cool colors in general may be more conducive to relaxation and quiet, chronically ill patients should feel more at ease in light green or aqua.

Never create a total unit environment in only warm or only cool hues (this applies to all areas of a health facility). One atmosphere may predominate, depending on the section in question, but always introduce hues of the opposite color temperature somewhere in incidental areas or accessories.

Intensive Care

Reduced light levels are usual in intensive-care units, which need a restful and psychologically cool atmosphere. Aqua and lower chroma greens are appropriate. However, be careful that it does not result in monotony. The introduction of accents in small areas in warmer colors may eliminate this problem.

Operating Rooms

Optimum visual is the priority in operating rooms. Appropriate brightness proportions must exist between the visual task zone, its surrounding area, and the room perimeter.

For years green and bluish-green have been used for gowns, caps, masks, and covers in surgery. This color reduces glare under intense light. It is the complementary of the red color of blood, thereby, neutralizing the afterimage produced by prolonged concentration on a wound. If the wound were surrounded by white, surgeons would see a disturbing afterimage whenever they looked up. The 8–10-percent light reflection of the covers is approximately the same as the wound, thereby keeping the brightness contrast level.

Brightness contrasts must be controlled, which means that the

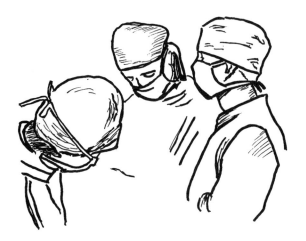

Color is an aid in designing optimum seeing conditions in operating rooms.

walls of the operating room should not exceed 40-percent light reflection (ideal is 30–35 percent); the floor should be 15 percent and the ceiling 80 percent. The wall color can be similar in hue (not brightness) to the color of the gowns and surgical sheets.

Recovery Rooms

Recovery rooms can be lighter blue-greens, pale green, or aqua, but don't need to be. As stated before, quiet, relaxing surroundings can be achieved in many ways. Perhaps even a slightly warm color may pick up the spirits of the patient who has just undergone surgery.

Laboratories

Areas such as these, including sterilizing rooms, can be in tan, pale green, gold, or aqua. Where color discrimination is critical in the work performed, walls must remain neutral—gray is advised. The danger of environmental monotony may be eliminated somewhat by introducing color on doors, tables (not the working surface), chairs, and so forth.

Pediatric Units

Where children are patients, every effort must be made to create appealing, caring, and anxiety-reducing surroundings without becoming too clichéd. Primarily clear and light colors, warm, friendly, and varied are called for—but without appearing too confusing. Wall decorations should show a normal world and not dominantly a fantasy world, which does not mean some playfullness cannot be included. But crying clowns or scary dinosaurs will not help children, especially younger ones, to cope with the reality of receiving medical treatment in a strange environment they have difficulty understanding. Carefully chosen art can be used as a form of communication to lessen anxiety, and to convey a sense of caring, gentleness, and reassurance. (See Figures C-23 and C-24.)

Maternity Units

Corridors in the maternity section should set themselves apart from other areas of the facility. The spirit of the anticipated happy event may find expression through visual means—or color's associative power.

The labor room should not exhibit strong colors, but perhaps also not too warm tones as the dominant choice. The room has to be relaxing and ease tension. Colors should not appear "blocking" (very opaque) and heavy, but rather "relieving" or "releasing" (give way—not block), which supports the act of labor as leading finally to release—to birth. My concept of the ideal color for the labor room is a light blue-green. It should be used as the dominant hue with subdued red-orange accents, or at least blue-green should be on the wall the patient is facing. Strong red-orange might carry an association of blood, therefore the red-orange must be subdued, but not to a point where it appears dirty. Support for my recommendation comes from the Institute for Color Psychology in Germany, where Heinrich Frieling tested subjects and found that blue-green was preferred. Dr. Frieling also remarks that the effects of the color combination blue-green and orange-red is "tension releasing and the gathering of motoric actions (as for example the process of giving birth)."

Specification of color in the hospital nursery should take into consideration the nurses' tasks in visual diagnosis and observation of babies. Pink or blue walls, which might delight parents, will not help nurses in their job of observation. A fact not known by many designers is that the skin of infants is highly reflective and is affected by the color around it. The function of the physician and nurse must come first, and charm must yield to practical necessity. Skin tones may be altered by yellow, pink, blue, green, and gray. A blue wall may make an infant look cyanotic; yellow or green walls may give a jaundiced look. Pink walls, by giving a false healthy look, may obscure the early tint of jaundice or obscure the real pallor of anemia. Light hues, weak in chroma and toward the neutral side, such as pale beige or sand, are acceptable as long as adequate attention is paid to light-reflection ratios (not too high).

There is also the problem of general illumination in hospital nurseries. Lamps with a high color rendering index must be used. Color rendition must be regulated so that, once again, the appearance of the patient is not altered. Full-spectrum lamps may be the best answer, but not those that contain the ultraviolet element. As Dr. T. R. C. Sisson,

Professor of Pediatrics and Director of Neo-Natal Research at Newark Beth Medical Center, remarked in a letter to the author dated February 3, 1986:

There is no doubt in my mind that general lighting which would add significant output in the UV-A spectrum can be hazardous. Although the cornea does not absorb UV-A, the lens does. It is not known how much UV the developing (i.e., neonatal) eye can safely absorb, nor what is a safe dermal exposure in such infants—safe enough that UV damage to the relatively thin skin of the newborn will not occur, or that the exposure (whose depth is increased above that of visible light because of the short wavelength) could not exceed the capacity of inherent repair mechanisms.

In my inquiry to Dr. Sisson regarding the possibility of full-spectrum lighting which includes the UV element being perhaps an effective general light source for the prevention of infant jaundice, he replied:

Reliance upon a general nursery light source of broad spectrum including UV-A to prevent hyperbilirubinemia would be misplaced: it would have little or no discernible effect in either prevention or treatment.

This, then, would indicate that the photic energies necessary to handle infant jaundice far exceed the environmental lighting of nurseries. In short, it is doubtful that general lighting, including full-spectrum light, is an aid in the prevention of hyperbilirubinemia.

In the latter part of 1985, the press reported on the hazards to vision from high levels of illumination in hospital nurseries. This was based on a study by Penny Glass and associates that appeared in the *New England Journal of Medicine* in August of the same year. The study stated:

In summary, this study suggests that the levels of light common in the hospital nursery may contribute to the incidence of oxygen-induced retinopathy of prematurity, especially in infants weighing less than 1000 grams at birth.

To explain further, I quote Dr. Sisson from his editorial that appeared in the same issue of the journal regarding intensive-care nurseries:

The impact on the newborn of the crisis atmosphere of the intensive care unit—its bustle, noise, and perhaps more important, its unremittingly brilliant illumination—has scant regard compared with the attention paid to space requirements for the machinery of intensive care, visualization of monitors and skin color, pumps, tubing, access to the patients,

*and so on. The report by Glass and her associates in this issue of the
journal draws attention to this by showing a relation between the light
environment imposed on newborns and the incidence of retinopathy. Glass
et al. observed that the incidence of retinopathy of prematurity in two
infant intensive-care nurseries was greater among infants exposed to high
illumination (60 ftc) {footcandles} than among infants kept under
reduced lighting (25 ftc).*

What recommendations can be made for "general" nursery lighting? Beyond the suggestion made earlier regarding the use of a high
CRI light source, illumination should be muted, but not to such an extent as to interfere with the procedures of care for the newborn or to
cause visual deprivation. Local light sources can be installed to make it
possible to see one infant without exposing others to high illumination
levels at the time of observation.

The study by Glass et al. points out that some evidence indicates
that cycled lighting may protect against damage caused by light. Constant or uninterrupted lighting is inappropriate, and, as Dr. Sisson
points out, "may disrupt fundamental physiological and metabolic
processes in the newborn." A workable solution may be to install dimmers that control each row of overhead luminaires separately. That
way, nurses can control light levels and raise the levels as needed in
particular areas.

Nurses' Stations

The nurses' station is a key traffic spot and should stand apart visually. Regardless of the adjacent wall color, the back area of the station
should be so color designed as to contrast with the other surroundings.
This may be achieved through hue, chroma, or value contrast.

EKG and EEG Rooms

These rooms must not be arousing or exciting. Low-intensity blues
or greens may be an effective aid in achieving this goal. However, this
is a generality and the choice of tone is very important so that it does
not result in monotony. We know from research that a monotonous
surrounding influences heart rate and brain-wave activity (as does overstimulation).

Very often the design error of monotony manifests itself in rooms
where an attempt was made to create a relaxing and arousal-free space.
In the monotonous environment, because there is nothing to look at,
the patient may turn to inner thoughts, which will influence his physiological state. Not only is color an important factor, but all design elements in the room are to be considered. A "quietly" designed room

may, for example, exhibit an interesting wall decoration—an abstract painting, for example—that the patient can explore while measurements are taken. This may do more for a patient's state of calm than only low-stimulus colors.

Examination Rooms

It is important that colors in examination rooms do not interfere with visual diagnosis. In general, a friendly milieu would be more appropriate than a stark, sterile one. Being examined isn't usually a pleasurable experience; some people even feel it to be an intrusion of their privacy and feel quite uncomfortable about it.

Therapy and Treatment Rooms

To give color specifications for these rooms, the designer must first find out just what goes on in them. Most helpful is asking how patients feel when they undergo treatment—for example, radiation therapy. In treatment rooms pale green or aqua are good choices for cardiac, cystoscopy, orthopedic, and urology procedures; pale coral or peach are suggested for dermatology, obstetrics, and gynecology. These specifications are general; your design goals should be set through analysis of each given situation.

For physical therapy, aqua is an excellent selection. It is cool, clean, reduces muscular tension, and gives a pleasing glow to the complexion. However, depending on circumstances, a yellow might be advised for its motoric effect, as would murals with designs that show gentle motion. Where patients are in therapy to regain the ability to walk, floors might be divided into sections of different colors. This device stimulates patients and shows their daily progress. The first section could be red—the first steps are usually the hardest, followed in sequence by orange, yellow, green, or blue. Blue or green represent the final release of the difficult learning process. The association of the sequence would be appropriate; red being tension and blue or green being release.

Waiting Rooms

The waiting room must be anxiety-reducing and also seem to make time go faster. How? By assuring that the room is not boring, and that it has enough visual interest to focus occupants toward the environment and not to inner thoughts. This, of course, is not done by loading a table with old magazines in an otherwise sterile room. Lively effects can be created through decorative accessories. An aquarium holds a sitter's interest for quite some time. (See Figure C-22.) Seating should be arranged to encourage conversation in small groups. It would be ideal if every waiting room in a medical facility had an outside view, preferably of a landscaped area.

Waiting rooms in pediatric sections must contain a play area for children. There is nothing worse than having a child sit unoccupied on a chair or parent's lap while awaiting medical consultation, treatment, or hospital admission. What better way for children to occupy themselves than with toys, gadgets, and books they can explore by themselves or with their parent?

Staff Lounges

Staff lounges should never contain design features or furnishings, color, and lighting fixtures that are reminiscent of other parts of the facility. Warm light should be used and if possible no overhead fluorescents—only incandescent. Wallcoverings are preferable to paint; textiles, woods, and comfortable seating should be incorporated. These rooms must provide a relaxing ambience to refresh and revitalize staff energy.

Cafeteria

Cafeteria light and color design must also be different from other parts of the hospital. It is quite appropriate to design a complete "restaurant atmosphere" (see Chapter 15, "Food and Foodservice") even though it's located in a medical facility.

A Note About Flooring

Exercise caution in the selection of flooring, whether it be carpeting or vinyl composition title (VCT). It is wiser to keep it simple and have a uniform field of view than to use too much pattern. Floors should be appear "steady"—there is nothing worse than having patients, who might already be unsteady on their feet, walk on a light, highly polished, glaring, ice-skating-reminiscent floor, which also looks coldly institutional. The floor should always be darker than the walls.

Lighting

In view of research conducted on the biological implications of artificial light, I advise that hospitals not use lighting that deviates considerably in its spectral composition from that found in natural light.

In addition, as pointed out, lamps that emit a balanced spectrum are particularly important for visual diagnosis. Unbalanced light sources are also unfavorable to the appearance of the patient's skin. Visitors may find it difficult to give proper encouragement to a patient if undue concern is shown for a sickly pallor. Lighting with a slightly warm quality rather than cool will enhance the complexion more. The Illuminating Engineering Society strongly recommends color-improved lights, such as deluxe lamps (those with a higher CRI rating) in health-care facilities.

Artificial full-spectrum lights may also be used in many areas of the hospital (except the nursery), especially for patients who are required to be indoors for a long time.

Chapter Twelve

Mental Health Centers and Psychiatric Hospitals

Staff members in mental health facilities ceased wearing uniforms years ago, and for good reason: It helped foster less formal relationships between patients and staff, thereby breaking down barriers of mistrust and hostility—the uniform being so symbolic of institutionalization.

This philosophy should now be carried over into the patient's total environment. The design objective in mental health centers and psychiatric hospitals should be to eliminate their institutional appearance as much as possible. But unfortunately, many facilities for the mentally ill are still drab, monotonous, and depressing.

The mental health facility often becomes a long-term home for its patients. The average time spent there is greater than that spent in medical facilities. Therefore, the designer must create a climate that will decrease anxiety and reflect an overall milieu of concern for the individuals undergoing treatment there. A treatment program and its environment must complement each other.

A Case History

The positive impact of a good environment can be quite dramatic. In 1978, my colleague and I were asked to develop a color plan for a mental health center treating emotionally disturbed children and adolescents. This facility was subjected to much more destructive behavior than that produced by the normal exuberance of young children and teenagers. For example, emotionally disturbed patients often are particularly prone to deface walls.

We were somewhat restricted in our design decision because the facility's lighting system could not be changed. Color and wall decorations were the only tools we were at liberty to renew. A new color scheme was selected, using principles established by research into the psychophysiological effects of color. An environment was created in each ward that would be beneficial and relevant to the particular age, function, and activities of its occupants.

The plan made use of a variety of colors. Most were pastel orange, yellow, peach, light green, blue-green, and blue (in incidental areas). In the children's corridor, yellow and orange contrasted with cooler colors for accents such as doors and door frames. One side of the adolescent-unit corridor was tan, the other, pale green. Both colors were set off by tangerine, again on doors and their frames. The adolescent patient rooms alternately had cool and warm tones so that staff members could try to assign introverted or extroverted personality types to the surroundings that suited them best. As one reporter wrote: "The net effect looks cozy but at the same time sophisticated."

Careful attention was given to the selection of paintings and wall decorations. In the children's section, themes reflected a sense of caring, gentleness, and reassurance. The objective was to establish a form of communication and aid cognitive learning. In adolescent units, the artwork ranged from Impressionism and Post-impressionism to contemporary styles of various types.

Remodeling started in early 1979, one unit at a time. As each unit was completed, the vandalism there diminished. By the conclusion of the project, the destruction had declined to almost nothing. The patients' deliberate, angry destruction of property simply had ended.

The project received a good amount of newspaper, radio, and television coverage. The magazine *Health Care Horizons* headlined its story, HEALTH CENTER FINDS COLOR THERAPEUTIC. Indeed, color and sensory variety can go far as definite psychotherapeutic agents.

The facility was monitored for almost six years. The patient population had changed many times over, and there was no report of significant destructive behavior toward hospital property. Questionnaires produced one year after the completion of the new environment showed that, in addition to an immediate positive effect on patient behavior, staff morale also had improved.

Skeptics began to suggest that vandalism had subsided because a new and fresh environment had been created, and the occupants—remembering the old surroundings—were unwilling to live in an abused environment again. The contention was that *any* redecoration would have produced the same effect. However, that was not the case, since the facility had been redecorated before. If "any" new environment would have produced the same result, why had it failed to do so after previous refurbishings?

Sensory Stimulation

Mental hospitals are highly dependent on environmental influences on the well-being and recovery of their patients. Light and color, in particular, may affect behavior and social interaction. Therefore, they must serve as psychological aids to recovery, or at the very least be instrumental in the development and maintenance of well-being.

The balance between unity and complexity is an extremely important design consideration. Patients housed in mental hospitals are prone to experience hallucinations. Their environment must not generate, or be supportive of, the continuation of hallucinations.

A monotonous environment, one that is low in stimulus, may well produce hallucinations. Sterile and uninteresting surroundings deprived of sensory stimulation and offering few opportunities for human interaction fail to stimulate conscious brain activity in the patient. In the absence of stimulation, the mind tends to seek some source, any source, of stimulus. Subsequently, it begins to seek greater meaning in the flow of thoughts and inner images. During the hallucinogenic process, the patient may get so locked up in his or her inner world that it becomes difficult to participate in what is considered reality.

On the other hand, too much information also will be supportive of hallucinations. Too many signals, or signals that conflict with one another, produce a kind of sensory chaos that the disassociating patient has difficulty sorting out, separating, and assigning to relevant categories. The manic and the schizophrenic have particular difficulty in filtering, selecting, and editing sensory experiences.

In their most vulnerable phases of illness, patients may find that rooms with strong colors overwhelm their sensory systems. The presence of strong color can bring forth associations or prod the patient to relive incidents. In some cases, the color stimulus may be carried over into other sensory channels, and the patient might experience synesthesia—hearing, feeling, or tasting colors.

Visual Deceptions

Another circumstance that may stimulate hallucination is that of visual deception. The environment should be perceptually honest, not deceptive. Mirror reflections of faces in glass partitions, glass doors, or other shiny surfaces may convince the patient that he is "seeing things."

Patterns, especially on flooring, such as checkerboard, lines, grids, etc., must be avoided. These tend to generate optical and kinesthetic illusions. The environment always gives "signals," and these must be clear and give accurate information, not visual noise that might be confusing and difficult to interpret. There are countless such situations that the designer must learn to recognize and attempt to correct.

General Recommendations

1. Color specifications for mental facility corridors, patients' rooms, and examination rooms should follow the guidelines presented for other medical facilities in general. However, the emphasis must be on eliminating the "institutional look" even to a greater degree than in other medical facilities. The designer should strive to create a more "ideal-home" atmosphere. (See Figures C-25, C-26, C-27, and C-28.)

2. Recreation areas, lounges, and occupational therapy rooms should be in cheerful, stimulating colors selected specifically to serve the function of each area. Some imagination should guide design choices in recreation areas—especially for children and adolescents.

3. Quiet or seclusion rooms should not look like punitive environments. If a patient is to be isolated, he or she should be in a cozy, inviting, sparsely and safely furnished space. This does not mean it should be barren—just simple and uncluttered. The room should give an impression of refuge, protection, and recuperation—not punishment. Sensory overload should be avoided and relaxation furthered by cool colors. Choose your colors carefully, so that they won't look institutional. Lighting should be on the warm side. Avoid lighting that is too uniform, that doesn't produce shadows. Shadows are a natural experience in the environment and help define the three-dimensionality of items. On the other hand, shadows should not be too extreme as to create effects that might be perturbing.

Mental Disorders and Color Preferences

A number of studies shed light on mentally ill patients and their relationship to color. However, these are primarily of statistical value; hard-and-fast facts cannot be derived from them (especially in connection with the environmental design). Also bear in mind that color preferences depend on individual personalities of the persons tested. Just because a person has a favorite color does not mean he wants to be surrounded by it. There is a difference between favoring a particular tone when shown color chips and living with it on all four walls.

We must beware of drawing erroneous conclusions. Perhaps a study tells us that schizophrenic patients love green. In practical situations it doesn't mean that a mental facility should now be painted green, or a schizophrenic patient's room should have green walls. Perhaps tomorrow a manic-depressive will occupy that space. Then what? That is not to say that if nonconflicting research points to a group profile, those findings should not be incorporated into the design scheme. Under special circumstances, with careful analysis and possible color modification such findings may be a useful guide.

Manic-Depressive Psychosis

This is a severe mental illness causing repeated episodes of depression and of mania. *Mania* refers to an elation of mood where the subject feels unusually overactive, overtalkative, and cheerful, then sinks back into a depressive period.

Birren reports manic-depressives seem particularly pleased with color. Schaie reports that they tend to favor purple, brown, and gray, with lower preferences for red, yellow, and orange. Though not indicated, it would be relevant to know in which phase the individuals were tested.

Schizophrenia

Schizophrenia is categorized into five groups:

1. Disorganized schizophrenia: *Behavior is almost unpredictable and speech may be unintelligible. The individual lives in his own world dominated by delusions, hallucinations, and fantasy.*

2. Catatonic schizophrenia: *Individuals show either a mute, unmoving, and stuperous state, or they show excessive motor activity which at times can be violent. Some schizophrenics of this type alternate between these two states, but in most cases one or the other behavior predominates.*

3. Paranoid schizophrenia: *Individuals trust no one and are constantly watchful and convinced that others are plotting against them. Illusions of grandeur may also be present.*

4. Undifferentiated schizophrenia: *The individual is schizophrenic but does not meet the above criteria, or shows symptoms of several subtypes.*

5. Residual schizophrenia: *Patients show residual symptoms but are not in an active phase of schizophrenia.*

In one reference Birren (1978, p. 90) states: "Schizophrenics favor green, followed by purple, brown, white and gray." In the same reference he mentions that Swiss psychiatrist Hermann Rorschach discovered that schizophrenics may resist color altogether. In another reference Birren (1963, p. 188) echoes this: "Schizophrenic types tend to reject color, seeing it as something which might prove 'catastrophic' by breaking in upon their inner world." Some investigations with the pyramid test found that white was used 76.6 percent of the time by schizophrenic patients, 9 percent by nonschizophrenic patients.

Deborah Sharpe made the following observation about schizophrenic individuals:

> *Schizophrenic adults of severe and mild autism (an escape from reality into either need or wish-fulfilling fantasies) often respond differentially to high-and low-saturated colors. For example, the presentation of high-saturated colors interferes with cognitive functioning for both groups more than does the presentation of low-saturated colors. Interference was greater for patients with severe autism than for those with mild autism, both of whom responded similarly to low-saturated cards. There appears to be a direct relationship between the severity of the illness and the intensity of the response to the degree of saturation. (Sharpe 1974, P. 73)*

Sharpe (1974) also reports that a study done in Taiwan comparing differences between schizophrenics and normal people in a color-usage task showed schizophrenics used fewer colors, but more deep green and black, than the non-patient group. These results parallel those obtained in tests conducted in America. This suggests that there are not many cultural differences in this type of pathology.

Frieling (1990), who had done extensive testing with the mentally disturbed, stated that the claim of researcher Szondi that schizophrenics prefer yellow; manics, red; hysterics, green; and paranoids, brown; he could not confirm in such simple form generalities. Frieling's research showed cases suffering from episodic dimming of consciousness were marked just as often by their choice of yellow and white as those suffering from schizophrenia. And he found that although yellow does in fact play a role in pictures executed by schizophrenics, it is not all that dominant.

In private conversation with me, Frieling did mention that when he asked schizophrenics to choose the warmest and the coolest color samples in the "Frieling Test" (a psychodiagnostic test), white was chosen as the warmest and red as the coolest.

Epilepsy

An epileptic attack is characterized by an abnormal and uncontrolled discharge of energy from the cells of the brain.

Minor epilepsy, called *petit mal* is a mild seizure with loss of consciousness lasting a few seconds. In *grand mal* (major seizure) the person falls to the ground unconscious with his muscles in a state of spasm; the temporary stoppage of breathing causes blueness in the face. This phase is then replaced by convulsive movements. At the end of an attack the patient may rouse confused with a severe headache, or he may fall asleep.

Many epileptics keep their intellectual capacity unimpaired. In others who suffer from frequent attacks, mental deterioration may occur. This deterioration shows itself first in memory defects followed by concentration and attention difficulties. Every degree of mental impairment may occur. Apart from medical treatment by means of drugs that act as sedatives, epileptics are cautioned to avoid emotional disturbances and excitements.

D. Sharpe (1974) reports that although epileptics give fewer responses than do normal people taking the Rorschach test, their answers are unbalanced in favor of CF (color form); that responses first emphasize color and then form, indicating these patients are motivated solely by color—form having no bearing at all. Sharpe concludes that this suggests epileptics have limited emotional communication with the environment. The communication that does exist is diffuse, undifferentiated, and coarse. This conclusion should be analyzed and investigated more in depth. Why would a color preference, which is perceived before form, indicate limited emotional communication with the environment, when color exhibits emotional communication? It may be a difference of intellectually grasping the environment, or of "feeling" the environment.

Birren (1978, p. 90) writes: "Epileptics have a high preference to green and low preference for yellow." W. Köhler (reported in Frieling 1990) investigated the color choices of epileptics and came to the conclusion that the patients, with little difference as to sex or age, chose red over blue, and blue over green—these making up the most chosen colors. Low chromatics or achromatics were rejected for the most part. It was also very noticeable that patients undergoing character or personality changes rejected yellow. Köhler's study seems to point out that the demented person often chooses only red because he is not capable of any better performance.

Frieling (1990) reports on the investigations of Kyr Pohl who, using the Frieling Test, found a remarkable absence of yellows being chosen by epileptic children. Frieling, who did extensive testing with three hundred severe epileptic patients, found for the most part there was a pronounced resistance against the test and against those who were giving the test. Of the required seven phases (layings) most were able to only complete the first two or three. Red tones overwhelmed all other choices (the aggressivity was evident). Frieling also mentions that epileptics are very sensitive to yellow and other loud colors as also flickering (shimmering) color contrasts. Even television can become the source of an attack.

It is interesting to note that if epileptics are sensitive to loud colors—which would include red—why did they choose overwhelmingly red during Frieling's investigation? We know that the patients were upset about taking the test; therefore, the choice of red was a momentary expression of their aggression.

Chapter Thirteen

Industrial Work Environments

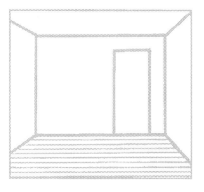

Studies, including those conducted in the field of industrial psychology, point out that an inappropriate working environment may lead to monotony and boredom, resulting in job weariness, lack of motivation, and negative interaction—all of which affects the overall work climate. In addition, the tasks performed in various types of industries may be physically demanding, tedious, repetitive, monotonous; may expose workers to unusual levels of heat, noise, or odor; and may place great demands on vision. All of these factors will negatively affect psychological and physiological well-being, thereby further undermining worker morale. It is evident that a negative industrial milieu will ultimately also affect the quality and quantity of production.

To give written advice with fairly specific color recommendations is more difficult for industrial surroundings than for other environments. Manufacturing-oriented businesses are as diverse as the products they produce. Attempting to cover all types of industries with a standard set of color recommendations would be too simplistic. Too much depends on knowing the nature of the work performed, the kind of equipment being used, lighting conditions, dimensions of the plant area, and so forth.

However, certain principles having to do with vision as well as functional uses of color and safety are common denominators for all industrial environments. Before I suggest some basic guidelines, let us first understand what the correct use of color can accomplish. (See Figures C-39, C-40, C-41, C-42, and C-43.)

1. Correct color improves perception, protects the eyes and general physiological well-being, and is an aid against frustration and stress.

2. Increased efficiency and fewer errors result from correct color usage, which reduces monotony, irritation, and premature fatigue.

3. Appropriate colors increase morale through the creation of better working conditions.

4. Increased safety, better orientation, and tighter order all result from correct use of color in industrial settings.

Eye Fatigue

The tempo of modern production is much faster than ever before, requires greater accuracy and precision, and thus places an ever-increasing demand on workers' eyes. Although vision has been discussed in previous chapters, let me emphasize again that the causes of visual fatigue and distress are the result of improper illumination (either too high or

A correct use of color in industrial environments will improve perception, aid efficiency, and increase morale and safety. (Photo: Frank H. Mahnke)

too low), glare, extreme changes from light to dark (also on surfaces), and prolonged fixation of the eye without suitable areas and distances for visual relaxation. Some additional guidelines that must be followed to minimize eye fatigue:

1. Insufficient contrast between the work surface and the items being assembled or inspected may prove as uncomfortable as too much contrast. For example, it is tiring to assemble a green object on a green work surface because of the extra effort required to differentiate between the two. A neutral (gray) work surface with about 30-percent reflectance is best. In those instances where products being assembled are consistently the same color, the work surface should be the complement of that color, but with the proper reflectance and saturation (grayish). This also will aid in eliminating the menace of afterimage.

2. Background shields may also be used for delicate visual tasks. Such shields reflect light and provide contrast with materials, hold eye adjustments at a relatively stable level, confine vision to the task at hand, and cancel out background movement by providing a sense of isolation.

3. Work surfaces—and walls when possible—should have matte or dull surfaces to avoid reflected glare. For walls, there are paints that are durable and washable without being high-gloss.

4. If machines are positioned so that a wall is constantly in the immediate field of vision, it is important to control brightness contrast by establishing approximately the same brightness and using colors that rest the eyes. A dark wall and a light machine, or vice versa, demand unnecessary eye adjustments when vision is directed from the machine to the wall and back again.

5. Surrounding surfaces, which may include walls, must be provided to rest the eyes; if possible, they should be similar in brightness to the work surface. These may be in pleasing colors with a reflectance of 30–55 percent.

6. In general, walls should reflect 50–60 percent if floor and equipment are dark, and 60–70 if most surfaces and areas are light. Machines, equipment, tables, and desks should have a reflectance ratio between 25 and 40 percent.

7. Walls containing windows must have a light color. Dark walls adjacent to sunlight shining through windows will result in unnecessary brightness contrasts.

Color Consonance and Compensation

Color may support, conform, or be in agreement with a given situation; therefore it has consonant action. When it counteracts specific environmental problems, it may be said to have compensatory action. For example, the problem of heat in an environment will be supported by a warm color such as orange and counteracted by the subjective coolness of blue-green. Orange has adopted the consonant role and blue-green the compensatory one.

Particularly in industrial surroundings, environmental conditions may become so bothersome as to be a real burden for the worker. In some industries (such as perfume and food processing), smells can be so penetrating that workers almost taste them. Irritating, repetitive noise from machines and equipment may be increased subjectively by the color of the surroundings and become even more disturbing. These and other problems can be minimized by the compensatory action of color. This "color action" can serve as a measurement or guideline for the choice of a dominant color within the environment.

The colors listed below can supply action in either a consonant (increasing) or compensatory (decreasing) role for a variety of problems often encountered in industry. However, not all of them qualify for dominant wall colors; they may be used for incidental areas or machinery. The designation *maximum level* refers to those colors with which maximum consonant or complementary action is achieved, although other colors may work. Green, for instance, is conducive to the impression of coolness, but blue-green creates the impression to a greater extent.

Temperature

Heat   is supported by red through orange and compensated for by light blue, blue-green, light green, and white.

Cold   is supported by a blue-green and white (maximum level) and compensated for by red-orange, orange, and brown.

Noise

High-pitched sounds   are supported by yellow and compensated for by olive-green.

Muffled sounds   are supported by dark colors and compensated for by light colors.

Odor

Sweet odors   are supported by red and pink and compensated for by green and blue.

Narcotic and heavy odors   are supported by brown-red and violet and compensated for by yellow-green and orange-yellow.

Bitter odors   are supported by brown/violet and compensated for by orange/pink.

Sour odors   are supported by yellow/yellow-green and compensated for by red-purple (maximum level).

Musky odors   are supported by greenish brown and compensated for by light blue.

Moisture/Dampness and Dryness

Moist or damp conditions   are supported by green-blue (maximum level) and compensated for by yellow-tan (sand).

Dry conditions   are supported by yellow-tan (sand) (maximum level) and compensated for by blue-green (maximum level).

Smog/Haze

Smoggy, hazy conditions   are supported by gray-blue and compensated for by clear orange.

Muscular Effort and Speed

Tasks involving a high degree of muscular effort and speed are supported by lively colors and compensated for by relaxing colors.

Machinery

Machines and equipment are meant to serve man, not vice versa. Therefore, they must have colors that serve the functional process by improving the perception of critical or operating parts of the machine. Machines also need not be separate intrusive components on the visual landscape of a factory interior; they can be integrated to become part of an overall pleasing whole setting (safety permitting). Below are some considerations in the coloring of machines and equipment:

1. *Focal colors (any color that commands attention through its brightness or contrasts to surrounding colors) direct the eye to the critical or operating parts of a machine. Eyes are attracted to the brightest or the most contrasting area in the field of vision. Focal color on machinery discourages eye travel and also supports quick location of parts needed to operate the machine. For instance, a green machine may have light-beige working parts and red off-buttons or handles.*

2. *Bases for machinery or equipment should be painted darker than the body color. This makes them appear steadier and more solid.*

3. *Gray machines demand a colored background.*

4. *There should be sufficient contrast between the machine and the material being fabricated to establish an easy-to-see line of division; otherwise, the operator is constantly straining to see where the material ends and the machine begins. For instance, where brass is the dominant material on the assembly line, blue-green would provide good contrast; orange would not.*

5. *Large, numerous, and closely spaced machines should not be highly saturated or too dark in color. Too many objects in a space will add to complexity and present a spotty effect. Therefore, they should be colored so that they appear to recede (less saturated or lighter colors).*

Basic Safety Colors

1. Red *identifies fire-protection equipment, containers holding dangerous contents, and buttons or switches on machinery. In pipeline identification, red is used for fire-protection materials.*

2. Orange *designates danger and is used for machine parts that may crush, cut, shock, or injure in some way. It is also used on exposed edges (pulleys, gears, rollers, or other moving parts) and on starting buttons. In pipeline identification it is used to identify dangerous materials (steam, high pressures, etc.).*

3. Yellow *suggests caution and identifies physical hazards (obstructions, low beams, pillars, posts). Materials-handling equipment such as cranes*

and hoists are painted yellow. Yellow signals easily ignited and explosive materials (gas, acids) in pipelines.

4. Green *is the basic color for safety. It is used to identify first-aid stations and kits. In pipeline identification, green (along with white, gray, or black) indicates safe materials that pose no hazards to life or property.*

5. Blue *identifies electrical controls and special repair areas.*

6. White *is the housekeeping color used for the location of trash cans, trash receptacles, drinking fountains.*

Basic Recommendations

As mentioned earlier, it is not possible to set up recommendations that cover all types of industrial environments. But in general we may say that factories fall into two categories, based on the nature of the work performed:

1. Precise and very delicate work *requires colors that encourage concentration and quiet. Strong colors and patterns will interfere with workers' concentration,*

2. Monotonous assembly-line procedures *that repeat themselves in rapid order but otherwise do not require excessive concentration call for color that counteracts monotony by putting some interest into the environment.*

Locker Rooms

These areas greet employees as they begin their working day. Long, boring rows of gray lockers and bad lighting let motivation and morale slip quickly. Good lighting and colored lockers arranged in tonal harmony will set a more positive mood to start the day.

Restrooms/Washrooms

Color choices here must reflect a feeling of cleanliness and hygiene. Dark colors should be avoided, since some have a tendency to look dirty.

Lunchrooms and Lounge Areas

It is important that color and lighting in these sections contrast with the rest of the shop floor, to foster an ambience of relaxation during work breaks. (Also see Chapter 15, "Food and Foodservice".)

Corridors and Stairwells

To neglect these areas because they serve no particular function would be an oversight; they contribute to the total look of an industrial facility. Corridors and stairwells should not be too dark, but rather on the cheerful side. Color may be important as an aid in orienting traffic.

General Guidelines for Specific Industries

Heavy Industry—Large-Scale Assembly

1. The ceilings should always be white or a very light color, essential for efficiency in combination with natural and artificial light.

2. Since work is often performed in large spaces, a rhythmic color arrangement on columns may produce variety.

3. Where noise levels are high, compensation comes from the use of green tones as the dominant color. For subdominant surfaces, ochre may be introduced.

4. A lack of light in dark spaces may be compensated for by yellow.

5. Control tasks require full concentration. Disturbing visual background influences may be eliminated by screens.

6. The body color of cranes and other equipment that is moving should be yellow, since yellow is highly visible and suggests caution.

7. Area divisions, important for retaining some order, are often designated by painted lines on the floor; these should be white or yellow (or a combination of the two).

Foundries

1. Compensation for heat must be made by the choice of blue-green or green/blue-green for all major surfaces.

2. Light orange-yellow in incidental areas, such as columns and smaller wall areas, should be used to offset the predominant bluish greens of the major surfaces.

Wood Processing

1. The smell of wood is generally considered pleasant; compensation need not be made.

2. Room colors may be green or olive tones (the natural look), with red-

orange or orange accents. Avoid brown and tan or colors closely resembling that of wood itself, which could create a monotonous visual arrangement.

3. Warm light is more suitable than cold to enhance the inherent colors of wood.

Leather Industry

1. The dominant color of the work area should contrast with the color of the product.

2. The heavy odor of leather may be compensated for by light, airy colors, such as light green or light yellow on major walls and light blue on incidental areas.

3. The color of the work surface for the leather-cutting process is important. For brownish leather, a light-green work surface is ideal.

Chemical and Pharmaceutical Industries

1. The desired impression of hygiene and cleanliness must not lead to the use of white (usually the machines already are white or off-white). The same impression may be conveyed by using green or blue-green.

2. The dominant cool-colored atmosphere may be broken up by warm-colored chairs, doors, and laboratory smocks.

3. A warm and stimulating atmosphere in corridors and work-break areas should be provided to give employees a change from the normally cool atmosphere of work areas.

4. Where accurate color discrimination is important to the work at hand, surfaces must be in neutral gray, as should background shields, screens, and walls (in the immediate area) to avoid color reflection. Monotony can be prevented by using accent tones and colors in incidental areas.

Chapter Fourteen

Schools

School administrators and facility planners are faced with a dilemma. The taxpaying community demands an increase in efficiency, quality, and security of their schools and simultaneously wishes to cut costs. This directly affects the choice of color used in the schools. For budget reasons, professional counsel rarely is sought, leaving the interior planning often to the notions of the administrators, teachers, or maintenance department. The last-mentioned are most concerned with ease of maintenance—the less color, the better—and administrators and teachers choose color on a subjective basis, not on scientific principles.

Even professionals often do not plan color from the onset, or color at all. Often their approach is not based on sound knowledge of psychophysiological factors. As one has stated: "In the past, it was believed that schools must be colorful, but that is over. Children bring enough life into the rooms. A discreet light gray in a concrete-tone, so to speak, is therefore the right choice for school buildings." What is forgotten here is that the more impersonal the schoolroom, the more it will encourage liveliness as a compensation. An impersonal environment brings about a reaction. In this case, the room devoid of visual pleasure or a sense of caring channels the childrens' feelings toward irritability, fidgeting, etc.

Another well-known professional declared openly, at a seminar I attended, that his next preschool was going to be built in natural materials whose basic color is black (interior and exterior). As the audience showed its concern about that choice, he simply stated: "If the kids want color they can always hang their drawings on the walls." What questionable professional knowledge both these statements show. Yet, their designs will influence thousands of children throughout the years.

"Colorful," of course, is not the solution. Color for the sake of color accomplishes little that is constructive, just as bleak environments accomplish nothing constructive either. Education leaders must recognize this fact. They must also understand that the school's physical plant is a vital psychophysiological contribution to the study situation. Appropriate colors are important in protecting eyesight, creating surroundings that are conducive to study, and in promoting physical and mental health. Many cases of nervousness, irritability, lack of interest, and behavioral problems can be attributed directly to incorrect environmental conditions involving poorly planned light and color.

One architect, known for his love of white, was asked how he would design a school. Upon some reflection he replied: "I would ask myself first, 'What does the child need?'" This answer is the main question to be considered when it comes to the design of an effective school environment.

What do children need? The bottom line is that they need security—the feeling that develops within children when they are surrounded by understanding and nurturance. The ideal school conveys

*Schools have the
responsibility of reflecting
a supportive environment.
(Photo: Frank H.
Mahnke)*

the feeling that it is a place that cares about students as individuals. (See Figure C-13.) It paves the way toward responsible adulthood. Education prepares children to function in society. Providing a good education is more than just drumming in facts and figures; it requires setting up a positive social climate within the school, a sense of caring and guidance that must take place in a positive environmental setting. (See Figure C-44.)

We adults do not wish to work in a dreary, emotionally depressing environment, so we can hardly expect our children to enjoy doing their work, which is learning, under unfavorable conditions. Both young children who enter school for the first time away from the security of home, and teenagers, who are soon faced with the challenges of adulthood, will need the support that only a positive school ambience can give.

Frieling Color Tests

Of course pupils are not all the same; a first-grader's needs differ greatly from a tenth-grader's. Psychological color tests on children have shown that the acceptance and rejection of certain colors are a mirror of their development to adulthood.

Heinrich Frieling of the Institute of Color Psychology tested ten thousand children in all corners of the world. His findings indicate which colors might be best suited for different age groups in the school environment.

Frieling's statistics are for ages 5–19, wherein he reads the psychological development stages of each age group as reflected by their color choices. It is not my intention to discuss these lengthy statistics and resulting analyses. I have taken only some highlights as they pertain to the color design of schools, and only for ages 5–14.

In general, Frieling found that black, white, gray, and dark brown were rejected by children between the ages of five and eight; red, orange, yellow, and violet were preferred. At ages nine and ten, gray, dark brown, black, pastel green, and blue were rejected. Preferred were red, red-orange, and green-blue. The 11–12-year-olds rejected achromatics (black, white, gray), olive, violet, and lilac. Preferences of the 13–14-year age group were blue, ultramarine, and orange.

Frieling is the first one to point out the difficulty of using actual preference colors, as shown in the tests, as wall colors. They are not always suitable as wall paints and must be modified together with other factors, such as visual ergonomics to be considered. However, I believe it is possible to implement the basic direction indicated by Frieling's tests.

Wohlfarth Study

Several significant studies were performed by Dr. Harry Wohlfarth of Canada on the effects of color and light in the school setting. One of these, entitled "Effects of Color and Light on the Development of Elementary School Pupils," investigated the impact of a psychodynamically designed color environment on mental performance, scholastic performance, and physiological reactions of elementary school students from September 1982 to June 1983.

Four elementary schools were included in the study, (which cost several million dollars). One school was selected as the control school and had no changes made to it. In the second school color and light (light was changed to full-spectrum) were changed; the third school received only lighting changes; and the fourth, only color.

In those schools where the color was changed, a warm light yellow was used on three walls the students faced, while a light blue was used for the wall and vertical surfaces of the student desks the teachers were facing. All "blackboard" colors were changed from green to blue. All carpets in classrooms and offices were in a warm golden-gray.

The control school, which had no changes made to it, exhibited dark brown, gray, off-white, putty, and orange. Unfortunately, no mention is made in the study which colors were applied to what surfaces.

Some of the results of the study were as follows:

1. Blood pressure tests, taken over almost a year, showed that the "least stressed" students were in the school that received the light and color changes.

2. Psychodynamically chosen colors were shown to significantly reduce the average reported incidents of destructive behavior, aggressiveness, and habitual disruptiveness.

3. Light and color showed the largest percentage improvement of the four schools in regard to academic performance and I.Q. test scores—the control school showed the lowest.

Grangaard Study

In her doctoral dissertation and thesis for an IACC diploma, Dr. Ellen Grangaard conducted research similar to the Wohlfarth study, "The Effects of Color and Light on Selected Elementary School Students."

She changed the color of the classrooms, originally mostly white, to blue; removed much of the visual noise; and installed full-spectrum lighting with UV content. The results concluded that off-task behavior declined and academic standing improved.

By citing both these reliable and excellent studies, I do not wish to give the impression that only yellow or blue should be used in the classroom. This would be too recipelike. I believe the positive results were due to the elimination of colors that held little positive psychophysiological effects; the change of lighting to full-spectrum; and also, as in Dr. Grangaard's case, the elimination of visual noise.

Recommendations

Aside from the studies quoted above, I offer the following recommendations based on additional research and my own experiences and observations:

Preschool and Elementary Grades

Children of kindergarten through elementary-school ages are mostly extroverted by nature. A warm, bright color scheme complements this tendency, thereby reducing tension, nervousness, and anxiety. Color may be light salmon, soft, warm yellow, pale yellow-orange, coral, and peach. Colors of opposite temperature should also be introduced as accents. Under no circumstances should it be believed that by pinning drawings, cartoons or the like on the wall, the child's need for change in hue, color intensity, and lightness, is satisfied, or that it will reduce a monotonous room experience.

Color design in classrooms must adhere to principles of visual ergonomics, and consider the needs of various age groups. (Photo: Frank H. Mahnke)

Upper Grade and Secondary School Classrooms

Softer surroundings created by subtle and/or cooler hues have centripetal action, which enhances the ability to concentrate. Beige, pale or light green, and blue-green are appropriate, and they permit better concentration by providing a passive effect.

In classrooms where students face one direction, it is particularly useful to make the front wall a different color from the side and back walls. The purpose of this is to relax the students' eyes when they look up from their tasks, thus providing effective contrast with chalkboard, materials displayed, training aids, and the instructor, as well as drawing attention to the front of the room. By adding interest to the classroom through a different appearance from different directions, visual monotony is avoided. Side and back walls may be beige, sandstone, or light tan, while the front wall might be in medium tones of green or blue.

Libraries

Pale or light green creates a passive effect that enhances quietness and concentration.

Domestic Arts and Manual Training

For home economics, luminous hues such as light yellow and light orange are appropriate; tan or pale green are suitable for manual-training workshops.

Corridor colors give a distinctive personality to each section of a school; establish a milieu for each age group; and or aid in orientation and identification of various areas within a school. (Photo: Frank H. Mahnke)

Corridors

More color range is possible in hallways. Color schemes should be attractive and give the school a distinctive personality. In the lower grades hues may be lively; in a multistoried school, each corridor can be treated differently. Complementary color schemes are quite appropriate. For example, light-orange walls offset with blue doors; or a light-green wall with lower-chroma red doors (not the tone of fire doors). (See Figure C-14.)

Administrative Offices—Cafeterias

Follow the guidelines presented in the chapters on offices and on food and foodservice facilities.

Light

Fritz Hollwich concluded that the agitated mental and physical behavior of some children who stay in school the whole day might be caused by artificial illumination that deviates from natural light. Mayron et al. demonstrated that full-spectrum lighting decreased the hyperactive behavior of students in two first-grade classrooms. Comparison was made between full-spectrum fluorescent and standard cool-white fluorescent lights.

A study conducted by Douglas Kleiber and associates at Cornell University demonstrated that Vita-Lite (a full-spectrum light with balanced UV) increased visual acuity and decreased general fatigue.

The vision expert H. R. Blackwell stated that lighting limited to a narrow band of the visible spectrum can diminish productivity; full-spectrum lights greatly improve visual performance. The Wohlfarth and Grangaard studies also point toward the beneficial effects of full-spectrum lighting.

In views of these findings and many others, I strongly recommend full-spectrum lighting at least in classrooms and libraries, if not in all areas of a school facility. Corridors may be excepted.

Vision

It should be quite obvious that causes of visual discomfort (eye-strain and fatigue) may have a great bearing on scholastic performance. Once there is ample light to see clearly, attention must be given to control of glare and brightness. Principles that ensure comfortable conditions for vision have been discussed in previous chapters.

Food and Foodservice

When one is ravenously hungry, it matters little where one eats as long as the body's craving is satisfied. Of course, the immediate gratification of a biological need is not the primary purpose of a foodservice establishment. Restaurants are designed to create a "dining experience" (at the very best) and an "eating experience" (at the very least) as opposed to mere "feeding." Therefore, we must distinguish between hunger and appetite.

Hunger, Appetite, and Color Associations

A person normally has an appetite when he is hungry, but there is a difference between appetite and hunger. *Hunger* is the physical need for food called hunger pangs, accompanied by the contraction of the stomach walls; *appetite,* by contrast, expresses a craving independent of hunger; a person might have a full stomach and still have an appetite.

Foodservice establishments must create a total ambience that stimulates the appetite, through smell, sight, and associated thoughts of food. Odor is a strong appetite stimulator or suppressant. Scent signals are dispatched directly from two small patches of olfactory cells located on the top of each nostril, to the olfactory bulbs which are an extension of the brain's limbic system. The limbic system processes emotions and gut reaction, so that the mere whiff of an agreeable odor (fresh-baked bread for example) will cause an involuntary response such as salivating, or in the case of a disagreeable odor, recoiling—even to the point of the stomach becoming queasy.

In short, odor stirs sensation, emotions, and memories. The odor of mother's delicious Thanksgiving turkey has been stored in your memory; a similar odor will bring to mind not only the turkey, but perhaps a reminiscence of the whole event and circumstances of the meal. It also works in reverse; the odor of a dish that might have once made you ill may turn your stomach queasy.

Color may bring about a subjective association with odor. Pink, lavender, pale yellow, and green hold pleasant associations with smell. Bitter smells are related to certain hues in the brown and violet region; sweet smells with red and pink; sour aromas with yellow and yellow-green; narcotic smells with brown-red and violet; and musky odors with greenish browns. These, of course, are not all directly associated with food.

In the use of color for restaurants the emphasis should be directed more toward color's association with appetite appeal. But we can learn from the odor-color relationship that some colors simply do not work in restaurants.

Appetite also depends on the sense of sight. A roasted turkey's golden-brown crust along with the smell makes up the total association. When it comes to sight, color plays a substantial, if not the ultimate, role in our judgment of the freshness, ripeness, and palatability of food. Deviation from established associations and expectations seldom are accepted or tolerated. Sometimes the natural color of certain food is rejected in favor of what it is "expected" to be. Although people may have different preferences for certain colors of food, by and large there are common denominators.

The food industry is well aware of color conditioning, and processors treat food to retain natural color or apply food coloring where necessary. Packaging, too, plays an important role. Bread, cereal, and nuts are controlled precisely during baking or roasting so that they emerge neither too light nor too dark. Light beers are brewed pale yellow and often sold in green bottles, while strong beers are deep brown and sold in dark-brown bottles. Dairy products, which consumers associate with coolness and hygiene, have blue or white packages. For butter packaging, gold or silver may indicate luxury; yellow and green might suggest countryside. Some meat counters are illuminated with lights whose spectrum is closer to red, making the meat seem redder and more succulent.

Experiments have been done with people's appetites being stimulated by dishes containing the finest of delicacies shown under normal light. The substitution of colored light produced nausea. Dark-gray meat, orchid potatoes, muddy-violet salads, black peas, and blue bread found no takers—even though people knew the food was edible.

The odor and color of food are, therefore, the two ingredients that have much to do with appetite stimulation, but the conditions under which you eat also have a good deal to do with appetite. Not only must food appear appealing, but the total ambience must be inviting enough to approach it with relish. Appetite, through optical-chemical channels, mobilizes digestion; salivating lubricates the food so that it can be swallowed (by the way, taste buds can't detect dry food); and saliva contains the digestive enzyme ptyalin which acts on carbohydrates.

Psychological studies on appetite appeal and color reveal that warm reds (vermillion, flamingo, coral), oranges (peach, pumpkin), warm yellows, light yellow, and clear greens are true appetite colors. Purple-violet, purplish red, orange-yellow, yellow-green, mustard, grayed tones, and gray hold little food appeal. To be more specific, a peak of appetite and agreeable associations exists in the red-orange and orange regions. Pleasure decreases at yellow-orange, increases again at yellow, reaches a low at yellow-green, and is restored at clear green. Blue-greens (aqua, turquoise) although seldom associated with food itself, are well regarded and can be used to advantage as backgrounds for food display.

It is amazing how fast our appetite can be "turned off" or diminished by negative influences. Enjoyment or the anticipation of enjoyment is a mood state dependent on many factors: Noise, bad lighting, impressions of unclean conditions, and sterile and depressive surroundings all play a role. An ambience must be created in surroundings that delight the eye and charm the emotions, thereby helping to make eating a relaxed and pleasurable occasion.

Restaurants

No one factor makes or breaks a business, but a number of combined factors can do so. In the restaurant business, success depends on four conditions: food, service, price, and ambience. As long as the criteria for good food and service are met, the inviting and attractive restaurant will always be the more successful one.

Light is as important a factor as color in the design of an attractive restaurant. The first rule in providing a good lighting ambience is that it be neither too bright nor too dark. Bright lights do not create cozy or intimate surroundings. Although we are aware in a restaurant that many others are present, we need our personal table space to have some degree of privacy.

Personal space comes from the placement of the tables, as well as through light, which should illuminate the table's surface well but not exceed that boundary. Local incandescent light is ideal, with other lighting (such as wall lamps and hanging lamps) strategically placed to illuminate entrances, exits, passages from kitchens, and other areas needed to ensure safety. Bright overhead lighting destroys the feeling of personal space. It may be appropriate for places where mass social interaction is desirable, but it has no place in an intimate dining environment.

Nor should light be too skimpy, as with the ever-popular single candle in a glass container. Guests like to see their food (including its color), and they find it annoying to be faced with a dark mass on a plate. Also, most of us find eye contact to be an important part of social interaction and conversation—to which darkness does not contribute.

A restaurant's decor depends largely on the particular feeling it wishes to evoke—festive, elegant, homey, rustic—which also clearly relates to the type of food it serves. A restaurant serving *haute cuisine* should have elegant furnishings; one serving hot dogs and hamburgers would look ridiculous with a chic decor. Specific color choices cannot be given; however, a general rule is to take into account the hues that appeal to the appetite as discussed above. Understand that modifications may have to be made to fit particular design objectives, but in all cases the polarity profile should be employed.

In general, appetite-appealing hues should be taken into account. In the red range, flamingo or coral is perfect; in the orange range, peach and pumpkin will provide a lively setting. Yellow can create a light, sunny (breakfasty) atmosphere. Exercise caution, however, in regard to the color's saturation; if it is too pure or too grayed down it can appear cheap. Accents may be darker reds, turquoise, or a medium tone of blue. Pale greens are also appropriate in certain instances (be careful that they do not look poisonous), as are clear greens for accents.

Color must be given a value and expression. If the decor is elegant, make sure the colors appear the same; if it is a family restaurant, livelier, clearer colors may be used. Walls, tablecloths, dishes, furniture (if it is not natural wood), and upholstery should harmonize in analogous and complementary tones, and unappetizing hues should be avoided. Complementary accents are appropriate; for example, blue-green carpets or tablecloths with flamingo walls. Among the high-appetite-appeal colors there are enough possible combinations to satisfy the most discriminating taste. Psychological appeal, distinction, and a feeling of harmony and identity are always linked to products that sell well, and that also applies to foodservice establishments.

A few observations are relevant here in regard to complementary colors and food, although they might not always be feasible from a practical standpoint. Green salad may look greener and fresher on cool pink serving dishes; the richness of butter is enhanced by green-blue or bluish white; bread appears best on green or green-blue plates.

Stay away from white and gray as dominant wall colors—they have no emotional appeal. For tablecloths and certain accents and incidental areas, white can be considered; however, for walls, there are better choices. The following case history may illustrate this point.

A newly opened restaurant failed to attract business. Although the owner tried to establish an exquisite and refined atmosphere, his choice of colors came from a misguided concept of elegance. Major walls were light gray, accented with shades of bluish gray; tablecloths and upholstery were snow white. The result would have delighted a penguin, but it left diners cold. Elegance must not be perceived as aloofness; coldness and sterility are uninviting and certainly not relaxing. Gray is not an appetite color. People do not like gray food, so why should they be expected to look at gray walls?

As noted often in these pages, studies have been and are being conducted by experienced professionals who probe people's attitudes, reactions, and subjective feelings toward various settings, including restaurants. Take advantage of these findings. An educated approach based on respected research is always better than intuitive guesswork.

Cafeterias and Coffee Shops

In full-service restaurants, colors should be somewhat refined and subtle. Cafeterias and coffee shops, on the other hand, may be a bit brighter, although colors should not be intense and aggressive. Light red-orange, light orange, pale yellow, warm yellow, apricot, and pale green are good dominant wall colors (yellow should not be too bright); somewhat stronger for accents are blue and blue-green. (See Figures C-32, C-33, C-34, C-35, and C-36.)

Laminated tabletops may be in wood grain or the colors specified as appetite colors. For purposes of cleanliness, floors should not be too dark; texture and pattern may conceal unremovable stains.

To ensure comfort of those who are eating, the serving line should always be separated physically from the seating area. If this is not possible, at least effect separation visually with dividers or large plants. Mahogany tables, reddish brick walls, wrought-iron grillwork, and vines around ceiling supports are great favorites in cafeterias.

Many firms provide cafeterias or coffee-break areas for employees. These are not just lunchroom facilities but are also provided for relaxation and work breaks. A total break from the work routine is important for physical and mental refreshment. Therefore, it is advisable to create surroundings that differ in light and color character from those found in the work environment.

Lighting should be on the soft side, with incandescent hanging lamps placed low enough to illuminate only table surfaces, with supplementary lighting at strategic other spots. Overhead fluorescents are not ideal in cafeterias; if they must be used, illumination levels should be lower than those in work areas. Incandescent standing, table, or wall lamps may be added to low-level fluorescent illumination.

Warm light is imperative in all foodservice establishments. It flatters the complexion, creates coziness, and adds to the effects of warmth, thus inducing the desire to rest. Warm light is always more relaxing, allowing the building up of energy during work and lunch breaks.

Food Display

Food stores should follow the color specifications given so far, avoiding all unappetizing hues. Store shelving doesn't leave much open wall space for color application, but some walls behind shelves may be colored to make packaged items stand out, or to provide orientation through color association: clear green for produce; sea green for seafood; bright yellow for baked goods (an association with golden wheat fields and sunshine); pale yellow for dairy products (suggesting butter and cheeses); dark red-orange for coffee and chocolate (brown, unless it is wood, is not appropriate, especially as paint). Be sure that background colors do not interfere with merchandise colors.

In the meat section, turquoise or sapphire blue on a background wall or fixtures will enhance the color of meat (the meat trays themselves should be white to suggest cleanliness).

Fixtures for refrigerated items should be white or cool hues (light blue or aqua) to convey a feeling of coldness. Food items displayed in refrigerated units colored orange would look out of place.

On a final note, floors should be unobtrusive; eyes should be directed toward the merchandise.

Color for Exteriors

Exterior color is enjoying a renaissance, thanks to Postmodernism. Chromatic facades that would have been unthinkable some years ago are now featured. However, a lot of repetition is seen in color choices. I often wonder whether or not the palette truly adapts itself to a particular environmental situation, or is it simply making its own statement?

Color and architecture go hand in hand. We must realize that form first reaches the human eye by way of color, and that if form and color are characteristic qualities of nature, then they cannot be separated from each other. Color cannot be delegated to second rank, and it should not be thought of solely as cosmetic treatment. The glorification of "form itself" is an illusion, and does not exist in nature. If color is the language of form, it is also the language of emotions. To paraphrase the words of professor Sune Lindstrom, quoted in a previous chapter and repeated here because of their far-reaching significance: It is the spontaneous emotional reaction to each particular architectural product that is of importance to us.

Since specific color recommendations can't be given without full information on a given setting, in this chapter I'll discuss overall general considerations regarding colors the architect should bear in mind. Previous chapters have given sufficient information as to the importance of color, its effects, and human reactions to it. These apply to exterior as well as interior spaces.

The following fundamentals should be considered:

1. *Color can modulate a building and bring it in harmony with its surroundings. (See Figures C-7, C-8, and C-9.)*

2. *It can differentiate elements; it can contain, unite, equalize, accentuate, underline, or draw attention to proportions. (See Figures C-37 and C-55.)*

3. *In their coloration, individual buildings may appear pleasant or oppressive, well proportioned or distorted, stimulating or monotonous (as may be the case with achromatics). (See Figures C-10 and C-11.)*

4. *Buildings that exhibit the same or similar design can be given individuality through color detailing. (See Figures C-48 and C-49.)*

As a designer whose emphasis is on applied color psychology, focusing on the visual impact spaces have on users, and not being concerned with short-lived trends but with long-term acceptance, I consider that architecture's most important goal is *Lebensqualität*—quality of life. Whether it be a city, a neighborhood, an architectural ensemble or a singular building, positive emotional content must always be the guide.

The Public's Attitude

People are very conscious of color and texture in the built environment, and they do favor variation. The capacity to enjoy looking at or living in the purity and severity of colorless, unadorned buildings is limited to those who have the same aesthetic values as the architects of these environments. But the general public usually associates such sterile buildings with prisons and stark industrial buildings. They find them cold, impersonal, lifeless, boring, and unemotional. Studies point out that once color is added to exteriors, more positive evaluations result, while the absence of color generally brings negative reaction.

For many years, the design community in Sweden has taken an active interest in the study of people's reaction to exterior environmental color. The Department of Psychology of the University of Göteborg conducted a survey whose overall results show that most people criticized absence of exterior color and approved of its inclusion, particularly "happier" colors. As L. Sivik summarized:

> *From the interview questions common to many of our investigations carried out in relation to the urban environment, it can be concluded that* **people consider it self-evident that colour is an important factor in environmental design.** *People also think that one is made happier by "happy" environmental colours and sad by dull environmental colours. (Sivik quoted in Porter and Mikellides 1976, p. 138)*

These remarks were made almost twenty years ago, yet they ring as true now as they did then. People certainly feel more positive in a "happy" living environment than in a dull one. (See Figure C-60.) This seems to be an almost too obvious statement that one wonders why urban complexes, high-rise buildings, and the like are quite often still *not* built with this principle in mind. Even though the aesthetic values of many designers are often quite different from those of the user, surely if architecture is to serve the community, couldn't there be found a way to satisfy both the needs of the user and the architect's personal aesthetics?

One of my firm's studies provided good insight into how people react to color. In southern California, many housing complexes are being built in an imitation mission style of architecture. The predominant colors are white or off-white for walls and red or terra-cotta for roofs. We were interested in learning if the public had a great affection for this color scheme and, if so, whether public opinion could be changed by presenting alternatives to white.

We produced color renderings of several existing housing complexes. Then we interviewed people living within those complexes and asked them first how they liked the existing coloration of their buildings. It was not surprising to find that most residents had never given thought to color, having considered it an integral part of the architectural style. The repetition of white over the years had instilled the belief that it *had* to be white. Interestingly enough, residents of buildings with austere architectural form, not based on the mission style, disliked their white coloration, calling it very monotonous.

After posing the first question, we presented the color renderings and asked which they preferred: their white building, or the one in color on the rendering. Most residents were not averse to breaking with "tradition." They found the new coloration much more interesting, inviting, and pleasurable. (It should be mentioned that we did not replace white with another single color but with a variety of light wall colors and stronger chromatic accents without losing the overall architectural unity.) Most people felt especially positive about having their unit be somewhat different from that of their neighbors. This might be due to a desire for a little individuality (territorial space) among residents of high-density housing.

The Historical Misconception

Many scholars had thought that early Greek architecture used little applied color. Yet actual ancient Greek structures looked quite different from those created by Hollywood film-set designers. A white-marble ancient Greece (and imperial Rome) is a misconception. Most buildings were painted in symbolic and sometimes cosmetic colors. Some statues wore lipstick and false eyelashes! Ancient Greeks believed that the natural colors of wood, marble, bronze, and ivory were no substitute for the creation of the city as a total art form. Architecture was in fact covered with colored washes.

The Romans adopted the Greeks' use of environmental color. Their buildings were colored with bright paints, gold, bronze, marble, and mosaic. Being practical, Romans left their sculpture unpainted (unlike that of the Greeks). But excavations at Pompeii uncovered a wide range of colors that in some cases were brighter and clearer than those of the Greeks.

The influence of the Roman Empire extended over almost all of western Europe, and later, medieval architectural forms were covered with color. The coloring of medieval churches often was much brighter on the exterior than the interior. But during this period, rich color was applied to the interiors as well as exteriors of other important buildings. The cathedral of Notre-Dame in Paris had bright red, green, orange, yellow-ochre, black, and white on moldings and sculpture. There is evidence that the majority of French buildings of the 13th, 14th, and 15th centuries also were decorated in color.

During and following the Renaissance, color moved indoors. Artificial color on exteriors was abandoned in favor of natural colors. During the Reformation, color was considered sensuous, sacrilegious and vulgar.

To understand absence of color, let's return to the misconception that classical Greek architecture was unpainted. Ravages of time eroded the rich environmental colors and exposed natural surfaces of building materials. Historians and architects accepted these surface colors of ancient buildings. The classical Greek style has served as an inspiration to architects throughout the ages. Buildings in modern cities included Greek architectural elements—but without the colors that embellished the originals. The Parthenon has been considered the epitome of architectural perfection; it stands as a source of study in monochromatic excellence and purity, when in fact, it originally was painted and detailed in rich color. These established misconceptions about the past have thoroughly conditioned attitudes and design philosophies against the use of color (and in favor of form).

Modern times have seen movements and countermovements in the use of architectural color. One that had great impact was the Bauhaus, a revolutionary and functionally sound school founded in 1919 by Walter Gropius. The Bauhaus established new modes of building designs and construction, but with a definite lack of color and ornamentation. Gropius became the leading advocate of a purist and functionalist approach to architecture. White, clear, and bright meant freedom of space.

It seems odd that principles of color and color psychology were introduced into the teaching program at the Bauhaus. In the fine arts, such Bauhaus painters as Paul Klee, Josef Albers, and Johannes Itten produced some excellent work in color. Yet no allowance was made for color inclusion in architecture. The brave attack against the separation of art and architecture (a split that dates back to the Renaissance) succumbed to intrigues between art and technology factions of the Bauhaus staff. Hitler's arrival on the scene and his subsequent 1933 purge of those who opposed him resulted in the demise of the Bauhaus and subsequent attempts to reunify art and architecture. The United States welcomed Walter Gropius, Marcel Breuer, Herbert Bayer, and Mies van der Rohe; the result was a radical change in American architecture.

Architects who are graduates of Ivy League schools appear to have been educated in the Bauhaus tradition. Emphasis has been (and still is) on the linear representation of spatial dimensions. Perspective, plans, elevations, and projection drawings are the traditional method of communicating architectural perceptions. Graphics are drawn or rendered in black and white; three-dimensional cardboard models are white or gray; and the whole emphasis is on achromatic plastic qualities. The spatial effects that color can achieve and the fact that forms first reach the eye via color are often not understood, or considered.

Blend In or Stand Out?

Should architecture fit into the environment or stand out from it? Of course, there are two schools of thought on that point. Frank Lloyd Wright believed that architecture should blend into the environment, so he utilized only natural building materials. Colorful stone was as far as he would go.

Jean-Phillipe Lenclos of France also works with the natural color palette; unlike Wright, however, he makes dramatic use of natural colors. In his early work he endeavored to endow the built landscape with richly colored space that represented a painterly approach embodied in the philosophies of Fernand Léger and Victor Vasarely. Lenclos's color programs for gigantic machinery are well known.

Lenclos creates his natural palette by collecting regional color samples of earth and clay and incorporating the colors of vegetation, sky, and water. He always draws samples from specific regions and then uses them in that region, resulting in an indigenous and harmonious look. This technique is more suited to rural and suburban regions than to crowded urban areas with their lack of vegetation.

Le Corbusier used color in architecture with less regard to the natural environment. He had a great fondness for color and believed it can create a feeling of space. His geometric compositions often complemented the geometric architectural composition of a building.

Vasarely revived the idea of the polychromatic built environment of ancient civilizations, as Léger and the Dutch De Stijl movement tried to do before him. His is a new way, however, guided by the spirit of mathematics and modern science. He has broken through the limitation of the artist's traditional role and redirected his use of color and geometric patterns toward the environment. His highest goal is to transform ugly cities through the advancement of a polychromatic environment.

Blend in or stand out? It really depends on the situation. A Frank Lloyd Wright use of natural stone would stand out in an inner city composed of concrete or tinted glass, just as Vasarely's polychromy would stand out in a natural environment. Each architectural project must be evaluated as to its locale and surroundings.

Color must not be color for color's sake, nor must it be forsaken. Color is a property and the language of form, never a separate entity or

This former office building, converted into a shopping center, is a good example of a structure that stands out from its surroundings architecturally—and is further separated by its snow-white coloration. A less sterile color would have softened this effect, given more cohesion with the building sign and the products it stands for.

an intruder, unless it is applied as such. Color in the environment can lend an aesthetic quality that would otherwise be unobtainable. Color's unique contribution, if applied intelligently and sensitively, cannot be obtained through any other means. (See Figures C-56, C-57, and C-58.)

A New Role
and Challenge

In our technological advancement, humankind often is accused of despoiling land, polluting air, contaminating water, and setting itself up in conflict with nature instead of acting in harmony with it. Organizations are formed worldwide to save trees, animals, water, and everything else that is precious to us in nature or that we depend on for survival. Such concern is understandable. We must wonder where our clash with nature will end.

Who is to blame? Technology, industry, and progress, of course. Yet the average person is not likely to agree to give up the comforts that modern technology has provided. Indeed, we cannot because most of our comforts are now basic elements of our survival. It is impossible to imagine millions of today's population deciding to live in log cabins, grow and hunt their food, and travel by oxcart because their automobiles are a source of air pollution.

The solutions to environmental problems will be found not by regressing but by making use of humankind's ingenuity and technology. Already ways have been found to reduce pollution, clean up waterways, and provide purer air. Technology has even come to the rescue of nature itself, performing such tasks as turning deserts into thriving food-producing areas.

From the time when human beings first moved into caves to find shelter from the elements and built fires, we have progressively established ourselves in opposition to nature. Today we work, live, and play for the greater part of the day in artificial surroundings under our control—switching on lights, regulating temperature, and shutting out noise at will.

All innovation these days is directed toward the man-made—the architectural—environment. Rural areas are diminishing, while urban centers continue to develop at a rapid pace. The dream of one's own plot of land under God's clear blue sky and the splendor of nature as far as the eye can see is fairly removed from reality for the majority of people. Those fortunate enough to call themselves homeowners usually look out of the window not at distant fields but at someone else's backyard. Others live in apartments sandwiched between those of their neighbors.

Most people in our industrialized nations conduct their daily lives indoors or surrounded by environments of man's invention, and it is doubtful that this situation ever will reverse itself. Architects are visualizing underground communities as well as above-ground cities enveloped in domes. Perhaps colonies one day will exist on the moon, and we will live there totally independent of nature. Needless to say, more will be known by that time about our psychological and physiological functioning in relation to three major components of the architectural environment: artificial light, color, and visual pattern.

Environment is a big challenge—not just for the future, but right now. With modern technology and methods of analysis, research is uncovering heretofore-unknown evidence about light, color, and pattern. Interestingly enough, many early statements made by color pioneers—often disdained by designers as inconclusive or merely personal opinion—now have been substantiated.

As the human race is propelled increasingly into an artificial environment, we are becoming more of an indoor species, along with all the consequent psychological and physiological effects. This situation demands a new role and set of professional criteria for the designer.

Most interior architects or designers think of their profession as being more closely related to art than to science, but the time has come in which the two must walk side by side. Members of the design community, be they architects, interior designers/decorators, color consultants/designers, or lighting engineers, must consider themselves as integral to the creation of cultural, healthy environments to promote or safeguard physical and well-being.

If this is to be our goal, then we must recognize that interdisciplinary education is an absolute necessity. We often think that our aesthetic decisions, guided by innate intelligence, is sufficient for dealing with environmental problems. This just is not so. If it were, fewer design errors would be committed, well-meaning as they might be. Familiarization with the psychological and physiological aspects of man-environment research will not limit our aesthetic expression or professional aspirations. On the contrary, it will enrich them.

Küller (1981) correctly pointed out that there is a gap between research and practical application (including education). "It seems nobody is out there willing to listen," said another investigator expressing his concern. A three-year research project conducted by my firm investigating this situation also substantiates the low correlation between research and application.

But looking purely for "hard" scientific evidence that rejects all other approaches to color design is not the best solution. When working with color we must:

1. Accept sound scientific findings or indications even if they conflict with our personal inclinations;

2. Logically analyze and take into consideration empirical observations;

3. Study interdisciplinary relationships to color and environment, including psychology, human physiological functioning, and philosophy; and

4. Unite these points with aesthetic principles and our individual know-how and talent.

Only this way can we achieve true artistic freedom, the freedom to create with the knowledge that we are doing so responsibly. My personal conviction is that a designer has reached a standard of professionalism when he or she knows what *not to do* when specifying color for the environment.

The job of creating the man-made habitat has never been as important and challenging as it is today. To the aesthetic dimension of their profession designers must now add an approach that acknowledges human response to the environment. If this challenge is accepted, the man-made environment and the profession creating it are headed for a brilliant future together.

The International Association of Color Consultants/Designers

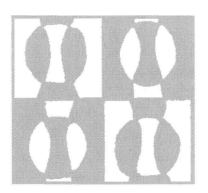

In 1957, approximately 50 architects, designers, educators, and scientists from 12 countries formed the International Association of Color Consultants (IACC) in Hilversum, Holland, known today as the International Association of Color Consultants/Designers. The motivating force was an acute shortage of professional consultants and an absence of competent training in the field.

The IACC recognized that color and light are major factors in the architectural environment. Architecture and environmental design serve human beings and must therefore be "humane." The group felt that professions connected with the creation of architecture must pay attention to human psychological and physiological response. This is where the work of the professional color consultant was to assume its responsibility. It was also the contention that "color consulting" is therefore a profession in its own right, and must be subjected to the same high standards as are found in all other professions demanding proof of competency.

IACC Seminars

The association developed the philosophy of sensible design in the architectural environment through the integration of art and science. In 1957, it also established an interdisciplinary training program under the direction of its first president, the renowned color authority, psychologist, biologist, and philosopher Dr. Heinrich Frieling. This program is not only an important prerequisite for a competent command of the laws of color; it also aims at shaping color professionals who possess comprehensive knowledge for the creation of beneficial and purposeful environments.

The educational program, known as the Salzburg Seminars for Color and Environment, is recognized for its comprehensive approach to all areas connected with color: physics, psychology, physiology, biology, color as information, visual ergonomics, light technology, color theory, art and so forth. Participants attending the complete seminar cycle may earn the IACC Color Consultant/Designer Diploma by submitting a thesis and passing an examination judged by an international board.

Through this program, the IACC has set the guidelines, criteria, and accreditation for the profession of (IACC) color consultant/ designer. An executive committee of international experts who are members of the IACC, under the chairmanship of Frank H. Mahnke, monitors the core curriculum. In 1996, the IACC seminars will also be conducted in Spanish in cooperation with the Polytechnical University of Valencia, School of Architecture, Valencia, Spain.

European Association of Color Consultants of the IACC

The IACC is represented in Europe by the European Association of Color Consultants (EACC). Besides conducting IACC seminars and representing the profession of color consultant/designer and color psychologist in Europe, the EACC also works toward promoting an understanding of the need for sensible design; advancement and recognition of the profession; and elevation of professional standards. It strives to the educational program current and of high quality through lecturers who are recognized as experts in their respective fields.

IACC Seminars in the United States

IACC seminars made their debut in the United States in 1991 as a counterpart to those conducted in Europe. The seminars are held in cooperation with the American Information Center for Color and Environment in San Diego, California.

North American Association of Color Consultants/Designers of the IACC

In 1994, the North American Association of Color Consultants/ Designers (NAACC) was founded with the participation of the first graduates from the American seminars. The association has the same general rules and goals as its European counterpart the EACC, and is the official representative of the IACC in the United States.

IACC Executive Committee

The IACC executive committee monitors the goals and function of the EACC and NAACC, conducts the examination for the IACC diploma, and also promotes the IACC philosophy on an international basis. Members of the committee come from the fields of architecture, art, the color sciences, environmental design, and psychology—representing 14 countries.

IACC Addresses

For information regarding the IACC internationally:

Frank H. Mahnke
President, IACC
11 Quai Capo d'Istria
CH-1205 Geneva, Switzerland

or
Frank H. Mahnke
c/o AICCE
3621 Alexia Place
San Diego, California 92116

For information regarding the EACC:

Prof. Gerhard Meerwein
Chairman of the Board, EACC
Augustinerstrasse 32
D-55116 Mainz, Germany

For information regarding the NAACC:

Pattie Heaton
President, NAACC
2196 East Little Cloud Cr.
Sandy, Utah 84093
or
Sherrill Mead
Vice President, IACC for the U.S.A.
2818 North 760 E.
Provo, Utah 84604

For information regarding the IACC Seminars in Europe:

Salzburger Seminare
c/o Mag. Edda Mally
Spitalgasse 25
A-1090 Vienna, Austria

For information regarding the IACC Seminars in the United States:

American Information Center for Color and Environment
3621 Alexia Place
San Diego, California 92116
or
Pattie Heaton
President, NAACC

Bibliography

Albers, Josef. *Interaction of Color*. New Haven: Yale University Press, 1963.

Ali, M. R. "Pattern of EEG Recovery Under Photic Stimulation by Light of Different Colors." *Electroencephalography Clinical Neurophysiology* 33 (1972): 332–35.

Arehart-Treichel, Joan. "School Lights and Problem Pupils." *Science News* 105 (April 1974): 258-59.

Asher, Harry. *Experiments in Seeing*. New York: Basic Books, 1961.

Barr, Danielle D. "Are Computer Screens an Office Menace?" ABA Banking Journal 76 (May 1984): 198, 202.

Beer, Ulrich. *Was Farben uns verraten (What Color Tells Us)*. Stuttgart: Kreuz Verlag, 1992.

Beral, Valerie, et al. "Malignant Melanoma and Exposure to Fluorescent Lighting at Work." *The Lancet* (August 1982): 290–93.

Berlyne, D. E., and P. McDonnell. "Effects of Stimulus Complexity and Incongruity on Duration of EEG Desynchronization." *Electroencephalography and Clinical Neurophysiology* 18 (1965): 156–61.

Birren, Faber. *Color Psychology and Color Therapy*. New Hyde Park, NY: University Books, 1961.

———. *Color for Interiors*. New York: Whitney Library of Design, 1963.

———. *Color: A Survey in Words and Pictures*. Secaucus, NJ: Citadel Press, 1963.

———. "Color It Color." *Progressive Architecture* (September 1967): 129–132.

————. "Color and Man-Made Environments: The Significance of Light." *AIA Journal* (August 1972).

————. "Color and Man-Made Environments: Reactions of Body and Eye." *AIA Journal* (September 1972).

————. "Color and Man-Made Environments: Reactions of Mind and Emotion." *AIA Journal* (October 1972).

————. "A Colorful Environment for the Mentally Disturbed." *Art Psychotherapy* 1 (1973): 255–59.

————. "Light: What May Be Good for the Body Is Not Necessarily Good for the Eye." *Lighting Design and Application* (July 1974): 41–43.

————. "The 'Off-White Epidemic': A Call for a Reconsideration of Color." *AIA Journal* (July 1977).

————. *Color and Human Response.* New York: Van Nostrand Reinhold, 1978.

————. *Color in Your World.* New York: Collier Books, 1979.

————. "Human Response to Color and Light." *Hospitals* (July 16, 1979): 93–96.

————. *Light, Color, and Environment.* rev. ed. New York: Van Nostrand Reinhold, 1982.

————. "Color and Psychotherapy." *Interior Design* (December 1983): 166–69.

————. The Symbolism of Color. Secaucus, NJ: Citadel Press, 1988.

Bond, Fred. *Color: How to See and Use It.* San Francisco: Camera Craft Publishing, 1954.

Braem, Harald. *Die Macht der Farben: Was Farben über Ihre Persönlichkeit aussagen, wie sie wirken, welche Gefühle sie auslösen (The Power of Color: What Colors Reveal About Your Personality, the Effect, and What Emotions They Trigger).* Munich: MVG—Moderne Verlagsgesellschaft, 1989.

Branley, Franklyn M. Color: *From Rainbows to Lasers.* New York: Thomas Y. Crowell, 1978.

Brody, Jane E. "Surprising Health Impact Discovered for Light." *The New York Times,* November 13, 1984.

Cheskin, Louis. *Colors: What They Can Do for You.* New York: Liveright Publishing, 1947.

————. *How to Color-Tune Your Home.* New York: Quadrangle Books.

Chevreul, M. *The Principles of Harmony and Contrast of Colors.* 1839. Reprint edited and annotated by Faber Birren. New York: Reinhold Publishing, 1967.

Clark, Linda A. *The Ancient Art of Color Therapy.* Old Greenwich, CT: Deving-Adair, 1975.

Crewdson, Frederick M. *Color in Decoration and Design.* Wilmette, IL: Frederick J. Drake, 1953.

Cushman, William H. "Lighting for Workplaces with Visual Display Terminals (VDT's)." Paper presented at the American Hygiene Association Symposium on Visual Display Terminals, Denver, March 1982.

Cytowic, Richard E. *Synesthesia: A Union of the Senses.* New York: Springer Verlag, 1989.

Dantsig, N. M., D. N. Lazarev, and M. V. Sokolov. "Ultra-Violet Installations of Beneficial Action." International Commission of Illumination, Publication CIE No. 14A, Bureau Central de la Commission (1968): 225–31.

Der Spiegel, March 1992

Düttman, Martina, Friedrich Schmuck, and Johannes Uhl. *Color Townscape.* San Francisco: W. H. Freeman, 1981.

Ellinger, Richard G. *Color Structure and Design.* New York: Van Nostrand Reinhold, 1963.

Eysenck, H. J. *Fact and Fiction in Psychology.* Harmondsworth, MD: Penguin Books, 1965.

Feller, R. P. et al. "Significant Effect of Environmental Lighting on Caries Incidence in the Cotton Rat." Proceedings of the Society for Experimental Biology and Medicine (1974): 1065–68.

Fisslinger, Johannes. *Aura Visionen: Einführung und Praxis der Aura-Fotografie (Aura Visions: Introduction and Practice of Aura-Photography).* Germering: Martin Gruber Verlag (no date).

Frieling, Heinrich. *Psychologische Raumgestaltung und Farbdynamik (Psychological Room Design and Color Dynamic).* Göttingen: Musterschmidt Verlag, 1957.

————. *Farbe im Raum: Angewandte Farbenpsychologie (Color in {The Architectural} space: Applied Color Psychology).* Munich: Callwey Verlag. 1974.

————. *"Farbgebung im OP-im Behandlungsbereich (Color Specifications in Operating Rooms)."* ZFA Zeitschrift für Allgemeinmedizin, 52 Jahrgang, Heft 11 (20 April 1976): 582–85.

————. *Farbe hilft verkaufen: Farbenlehre und Farbenpsychologie für Handel und Werbung (Color Helps Sell: Color Theory and Color Psychology for Commerce and Advertising).* Göttingen: Muster-Schmidt Verlag, 1980.

————. *Licht und Farbe am Arbeitsplatz (Light and Color at the Workplace).* Bad Wörishofen: Verlag-gemeinschaft für Wirtschaftspublizistik, 1982.

————. *Farbe am Arbeitsplatz (Color at the Workplace).* Munich: Bayerisches Staatsministerium für Arbeit und Sozialordnung, 1984.

————. *Mensch und Farbe (Human Beings and Color).* Munich: Wilhelm Heyne Verlag, 1988.

————. *Gesetz der Farbe (The Law of Color).* Göttingen: Muster-Schmidt Verlag, 1990.

————. *Bewusster mit Farben leben (Living with Color More Consciously)*. Göttingen: Muster-Schmidt Verlag, 1994.

Frieling, Ekkehardt, and Karlheinz Sonntag. *Lehrbuch Arbeits-psychologie (Textbook Industrial Psychology)*. Bern: Verlag Hans Huber, 1987.

Gebert, Frank. "Psychologische und Physiologische Wirkungen von Umgebungsfarben" (Psychological and Physiological Effects of Surrounding Color). Inaugural-Dissertation zur Erlangung des Doktorgrades der Zahnmedizin des Farchbereichs Human-medizin der Philipps-Universität, Marburg, 1977.

Gerard, R. "The Differential Effects of Lights on Physiological Functions." Ph.D. diss., University of California, Los Angeles, 1957.

Glass, Penny, et al. "Effect of Bright Light in the Hospital Nursery on the Incidence of Retinopathe of Prematurity." *The New England Journal of Medicine,* 313 (August 1985): 401–4.

Goldstein, K. "Some Experimental Observations Concerning the Influence of Colors on the Function of the Organism." *Occupational Therapy and Rehabilitation* 21 (1942): 147–51.

Grangaard, Ellen. "The Effect of Color and Light on Selected Elementary School Students." Ph.D. diss., University of Nevada, 1993.

Grolle, Johann, ed. "Aufbruch ins Labyrinth des Geistes (II): Lernen, wie Geist funktioniert" (Departure into the Labyrinth of the Mind (II): Learning How the Mind Functions). *Der Spiegel* 10/46 (2 March 1992): 238–254.

Hall, Calvin S. and Vernon J. Nordby. *A Primer of Jungian Psychology.* New York: A Mentor Book, New American Library, 1973.

Hartmann, Erwin. *Beleuchtung am Arbeitsplatz (Lighting at the Workplace)*. Munich: Bayerisches Staatsministerium für Arbeit und Sozialordnung, 1982.

Hellman, Hal. "Guiding Light." *Psychology Today* (April 1982): 22–28.

Hesselgren, Sven. *On Architecture: An Architectural Theory Based on Psychological Research.* Lund: Studentlitteratur, Bickley: Chartwell-Bratt, 1987.

Hodr, R. "Phototherapy of Hyperbilirubinemia in Premature Infants." *Ceskoslovenska Pediatrie* 26 (February 1971): 80–82.

Hollwich, Fritz. *The Influence of Ocular Light Perception on Metabolism in Man and in Animals.* New York: Springer Verlag, 1980.

Hollwich, Fritz, and B. Dieckhues. "The Effect of Natural and Artificial Light via the Eye on the Hormonal and Metabolic Balance of Animal and Man." *Ophtalmologica* 180 (1989): 188-97.

Hollwich, F., Dieckhues, B. and B. Schrameyer. "Die Wirkung des natürlichen und künstlichen Lichtes über das Auge" (The Effect of Natural and Artificial Light via the Eye). *Klin. Mbl. Augenheilk.,* 171 (1977): 98–104.

Hope, Augustine, and Margaret Walch. *The Color Compendium.* New York: Van Nostrand Reinhold, 1990.

Hughes, Philip C. *Lighting and the Work Environment.* North Bergen, NJ: Duro-Test Corporation, 1982.

————. "An Examination of the Beneficial Action of Natural Light on the Psychobiological System of Man." Paper accepted for presentation at Quadrennial Meeting of the Commission Internationale de l'Eclairage, Amsterdam, August 1983.

Hughes, Philip C., and Robert M. Neer. "Lighting for the Elderly: A Psychological Approach to Lighting." *Human Factors* 23 (1981): 65–85.

Humphrey, Nicholas, "The Colour Currency of Nature." In *Color for Architecture.* Porter, Tom, and Byron Mikellides. New York: Van Nostrand Reinhold, 1976.

————. *A History of the Mind.* New York: Simon and Schuster, 1992.

Hyman, Jane Wegscheider. *The Light Book: How Natural and Artificial Light Affect Our Health, Mood, and Behavior.* New York: Ballantine Books, 1991.

International Business Machines Corp. *Human Factors of Workstations with Visual Displays.* International Business Machines Corp., 1978, 1979, 1984.

Itten, Johannes. *The Art of Color.* New York: Reinhold Publishing Corp., 1961.

Jacobs, K. W., and F. E. Hustmyer. "Effects of Four Psychological Primary Colors on GSR, Heart Rate and Respiration Rate." *Perceptual and Motor Skills* 38 (1974): 763–66.

Jones, Tom D. *The Art of Light and Color.* New York: Van Nostrand Reinhold, 1972.

Jung, Carl G. et al. *Man and his Symbols.* New York: A Laurel Book, Dell Publishing, 1968.

Kasper, S., T. A. Wehr, and N. E. Rosenthal. "Saisonal abhängige Depressionsformen (SAD) (Seasonal Affective Disorders)" *Der Nervenarzt* 59 (1988): 200–214.

Kleeman, Walter B. Jr. *The Challenge of Interior Design.* Boston: CBI Publishing Company, 1981.

Kleiber, Douglas A., et al. "Lamps—Their Effect on Social Interaction and Fatigue." *Lighting Design and Application* 4 (1974): 51–53.

Koesters, Paul-Heinz. *Wenn Die Seele Krank Macht: Die Psychosomatische Medizin und ihre Heilungsmethoden (When the Soul Makes Us Sick: Psychosomatic Medicine and its Treatment Methods).* Hamburg: STERN-Buch im Verlag Gruner und Jahr AG & Co., 1990.

Krueger, Helmuth, and Wolf Müller-Limmroth. *Arbeiten mit dem Bildschirm—aber richtig (Working with VDTs—But Correctly).* Munich: Bayerisches Staatsministerium für Arbeit und Sozialordnung, 1983.

Küller, Rikard. "The Use of Space—Some Physiological and Philosophical Aspects." Paper presented at the Third International Architectural Psychology Conference, Université Louis Pasteur, Strasbourg, France, June 1976.

————. "Psycho-Physiological Conditions in Theatre Construction." Paper presented at the Eighth World Congress of the International Federation for Theatre Research, Munich, September 1977.

————. *Non-Visual Effects of Light and Colour.* Annotated bibliography. Document D15:81. Stockholm: Swedish Council for Building Research, 1981.

Ladau, Robert F., Brent K. Smith., and Jennifer Place. *Color in Interior Design and Architecture.* New York: Van Nostrand Reinhold, 1989.

Lawson, D. E. M., A. A. Paul, and T. J. Cole. "Relative Contributions of Diet and Sunlight to Vitamin D State in the Elderly." *British Medical Journal* 2 (1979): 303–5.

Lewis, Howard R. and Martha Lewis,. *Psychosomatics: How Your Emotions can Damage Your Health* (New York: The Viking Press, 1972, 19).

Lewy, Alfred J., et al. "Bright Artificial Light Treatment of a Manic-Depressive Patient with a Seasonal Mood Cycle." *American Journal of Psychiatry* 139 (1982): 1, 496–98.

Lewy, Alfred J., et al. "Supersensitivity to Light: Possible Trait Marker for Manic-Depressive Illness." *American Journal of Psychiatry* 142 (June 1985): 725–27.

Linton, Harold. *Color Consulting: A Survey of International Color Design.* New York: Van Nostrand Reinhold, 1991.

Loomis, W. F. "Rickets." Scientific American 223 (December 1970): 77–91.

Macaulay, Jim, and John Pliniussen. "Terminal Usage: Pro's or Con's." *Cost and Management* 8 (March/April 1984): 49–52.

Mahnke, Frank H. "Color in Medical Facilities." *Interior Design* 52 (April 1981): 256–63.

————. "Color—The Important Element in Health Care Facilities." *American Hospital Supply,* Lit. No. 8-86-05, 1986.

————. "Color, Light and Environment." *The International Organization for Color and Environment,* the quarterly communiqué IOCC 1–88.

————. "The Training of Colourists/Colour Consultants." Paper presented at the International Seminar Colour for Town, Moscow, 22–25 May 1990.

————. "Farbe und Umweltgestaltung" (Color and Environmental Design)." CRB Bulletin *Schweizerische Zentralstelle für Baurationalisierung* 90/6: 20–25

————. "Farbe und Umweltgestaltung: (Color and Environmental Design). *Applica* 13/14 (12 Juli 1991): 9-13.

————. "Mit Farben Leben: (Living with Color)." *Bauen & Wohnen Heute* (Ausgabe 94): 284-89.

Mahnke, Frank, and Rudolf Mahnke. *Color and Light in Man-Made Environments.* New York: Van Nostrand Reinhold. 1987.

————. "Industrial Environments and Color." In *The Color Compendium.* Hope, Augustine, and Margaret Walch, eds. New York: Van Nostrand Reinhold, 1990.

Mason, Peter. *The Light Fantastic.* Ringwood: Penguin Books Australia, 1981.

Mayron, L. W., et al. "Caries Reduction in School Children." *Applied Radiology/Nuclear Medicine* (July/August 1975).

————. "Light, Radiation and Academic Behavior." *Academic Therapy* 10 (Fall 1974): 33–47.

Moruzzi, G., and H. W. Magoun. "Brain Stem Reticular Formation and Activation of the EEG." *Electroencephalography and Clinical Neurophysiology.* (1949): U55–73.

Muths, Christa. *Farbtherapie: Mit Farben heilen—der sanfte Weg zur Gesundheit (Color Therapy: Healing with Color, the Soft Way to Health).* Munich: Wilhelm Heyne Verlag, 1989.

Neer, R. M., et al. "Stimulation by Artificial Lighting of Calcium Absorption in Elderly Human Subjects." *Nature* 229 (January 1971): 255–57.

New York Committee for Occupational Safety and Health. "Health Protection for Operators of VDT's–CRT's." New York Committee for Occupational Safety and Health, Inc., 1980.

Ornstein, Robert E. *The Psychology of Consciousness.* New York: Harcourt Brace Jovanovich, 1977.

Ott, John N. Health and Light: *The Effects of Natural and Artificial Light on Man and Other Living Things.* New York: Pocket Books, 1976.

————. "The Dual Function of the Eyes." The Southern Journal of Optometry (June 1979): 8–13.

————. *Light, Radiation, and You.* Old Greenwich, CT: Devin-Adair, 1982.

————. "Color and Light: Their Effects on Plants, Animals and People." *The International Journal of Biosocial Research* 7 (1985): 1–35.

Pierman, Brian C., ed. *Color in the Health Care Environment.* NBS Special Publication 516. U.S. Department of Commerce/National Bureau of Standards, 1978.

Porter, Tom, and Byron Mikellides. *Color for Architecture.* New York: Van Nostrand Reinhold, 1976.

Riedel, Ingrid. *Farben: In Religion, Gesellschaft, Kunst und Psychotherapie (Color: In Religion, Society, Art, and Psychotherapy).* Stuttgart: Kreuz Verlag, 1991.

Riedman, Sara R. *Hormones: How They Work.* New York: Abelard-Schuman, 1973.

Rood, Ogden. *Modern Chromatics.* 1879. Reprint edited and annotated by Faber Birren. New York: Van Nostrand Reinhold, 1973.

Rosenthal, Norman E., et al. "Seasonal Affective Disorder: A Description of the Syndrome and Preliminary Findings with Light Therapy." *Archives of General Psychiatry* 41 (January 1984): 72–80.

Rosenthal, Norman E., et al. "Antidepressant Effects of Light in Seasonal Affective Disorder." *American Journal of Psychiatry* 142 (February 1985): 163–70.

Sanders, Lea. *Die Farben Deiner Aura (The Colors of Your Aura)*. Goldmann Verlag, 1988.

Schaie, K. Warner. "Scaling the Association Between Colors and Mood-Tones." *American Journal of Psychology* 74 (1961): 266–73.

Scheppach, Joseph. "Wie der Mensch wirklich tickt" (How Human Beings Really Tick). *Stern* 25 (13 June 1991): 38–45.

Schiegl, Heinz. *Color-Therapie: Heilung durch die Kraft der Farben (Color Therapy: Healing Through the Power of Color)*. Munich: Droemersche Verlaganstalt Th. Knauer Nachf., 1993.

Scheurle, Hans Jürgen. *Die Gesamtsinnesorganisation: Überwindung der Subjekt-Objekt-Spaltung in der Sinneslehre (The Complete Organization of the Senses: Overcoming the Subjective-Objective-Split in the Teaching Theory of the Senses)*. Stuttgart: Georg Thieme Verlag, 1984.

————— "Pilotstudie über Farbentherapie mit Umgebungsfarben" (Pilot Study on Color Therapy with Surrounding Colors). 1993 Report on a study conducted in 1971.

Schmidsberger, Peter. "Wie gefährlich ist die Sonne wirklich?" (How Dangerous is the Sun Really?) *Bunte* 41 (10 April 1990).

Sharon, I. M., R. P. Feller, and S. W. Burney. "The Effects of Light of Different Spectra on Caries Incidence in the Golden Hamster." *Archives Oral. Biology* (1971): 1,427–32.

Sharpe, Deborah T. *The Psychology of Color and Design*. Chicago: Nelson-Hall, 1974.

Shlain, Leonard. *Art & Physics: Parallel Visions in Space, Time, and Light*. New York: William Morrow, Inc., 1991.

Sisson, Thomas R. C. "Hazards to Vision in the Nursery." *The New England Journal of Medicine* 313 (August 1985): 444–45.

Sivik, L. "Color Connotations and Perceptive Variables." *AIC Color* 1, 2 (1969): 1,064–72.

————— *Color Meaning and Perceptual Color Dimensions: A Study of Exterior Colors*. Göteborg Psychological Reports. Göteborg, 1974.

Spivack, Mayer, and Joanna Tamer. *Light and Color: A Designer's Guide*, American Institute of Architects Service Corporation, AIA Press Division, 1984.

Steiner, Rudolf. *Das Wesen der Farben (The Nature of Color)*. Dornach/Schweiz: Rudolf Steiner Verlag, 1980.

Thorington, Luke. "Light, Biology, and People, Part I." *Lighting Design and Application* 3:11 (1973): 19–23.

————— "Light, Biology and People, Part II." *Lighting Design and Application* 3:12 (1973): 31–36.

————. "Artificial Lighting—What Color Spectrum?" *Lighting Design and Application* (November 1975).

Tietze, Henry G. *Imagination und Symboldeutung: Wie innere Bilder heilen und vorbeugen helfen (Interpretation of Imagination and Symbolism: How Inner Images Heal and Prevent)*. Munich: Droemersche Verlaganstalt Th. Knauer Nachf., 1986.

Varley, Helen, ed. *Color*. Los Angeles: Knapp Press, 1980.

Watson, Robert I. *The Great Psychologists*. Philadelphia: J.B. Lippincott, 1971.

Wurtman, Richard J. "The Pineal and Endocrine Function." *Hospital Practice* 4 (January 1969): 32–37.

Wurtman, Richard J., and Robert M. Neer. "Good Light and Bad" *The New England Journal of Medicine* 282 (February 1979): 394–95.

Zamkova, M. A., and E. I. Krivitskaya. "Effect of Irradiation by Ultraviolet Erythema Lamps on the Working Ability of School Children" (translated by Duro-Test Corp.). *Gigiena i Sanitariya* 31 (April 1966): 41–44.

Index

sensory associations with, 74, 75, 173, 189
Pyramid, color experience, 10–18, 11f
Pythagorus, 30, 59

Radiation, 102
 infrared, 104–105
 ultraviolet, 104, 111–116
 visible light, 104
Recovery room, 130, 153
Red, 12, 13, 38
 associations with, 16, 55–58, 59–61
 and healing, 30, 31, 33, 36, 151, 154, 157
 in interior space, 40, 41–42, 66–67
 and mental health, 166, 168
 as safety color, 174
 sensory associations with, 74, 75, 172–173, 188, 189, 191–193
 temperature of, 73, 172
 wavelength of, 6–7
Red light, 12, 32, 33–34, 37, 39–40
Reflection. *See* Light-to-reflection ratio
Restaurants, 190–192
Restrooms, 175
Reticular formation, 21f, 22–23
Retina, 94, 96
Rickets, 114
Riedel, Ingrid, 58
Rods, of eye, 94
Romans, 198
Rorschach, Hermann, 166
Rosenthal, Norman, 110
Russian Academy of Medical Sciences, 115

Safety colors, 174–175
Salzburg Seminars for Color and Environment, 208
Saturation, 85, 91–92
Schaie, K. Warner, 80, 165
Scheurle, Hans Jurgen, 41, 73
Schizophrenia, 166–167
Schmiedsberger, Peter, 112
Schools, 180–186
 elementary, 183
 needs of, 180–181
 recommendations for, 183–186
 secondary, 184
 studies of, 181–183
Schrameyer, B., 102
Schropfl, F., 113